The
Eco Lifestyle
Handbook

THIS IS A CARLTON BOOK

Text and design copyright © Carlton Books Limited 2010

The text in this book has previously appeared in *The Little Green Book of Beauty*, *The Little Green Book of Gardening*, *The Little Green Book of Health*, *The Little Green Book of the Home*, *The Little Green Book of Nutrition* and *The Little Green Book of Shopping*, © Carlton 2008.

This edition published
by Carlton Books Limited
20 Mortimer Street
London W1T 3JW

10 9 8 7 6 5 4 3 2 1

A CIP catalogue record for this book is available from the British Library.

ISBN 978 1 84732 519 8

Printed in Dubai

Senior Executive Editor: Lisa Dyer
Managing Art Director: Lucy Coley
Design: Anna Pow
Production: Kate Pimm

The Eco Lifestyle Handbook

Sarah Callard,
Esme Floyd
& Diane Millis

CARLTON
BOOKS

Contents

introduction

We all know how important it is to think about the effect our everyday lives have on the environment, but often we feel we simply don't have time to make those all-important changes. Not any more – this book has done all the hard work for you, giving you simple tips to help reduce the damage you're doing to the planet.

For instance, did you know that simply replacing a plastic lunchbox with a metal one will help reduce greenhouse gas emissions, or that recycling rubbish bags could reduce your volume of waste by 20%? This book is packed with simple, easy-to-follow hints and helpers that will set you on the way to becoming a greener citizen.

And not only are the tips good for the environment, they're easy on your pocket too. So get reading now, and start making those little changes sooner rather than later.

Home & Office

MAKING CHANGES to your home and office is one of the best ways to reduce your carbon footprint. Whether it's a small step such as switching to energy-saving light bulbs, or a major commitment like converting to solar energy, you will be taking positive steps toward a greener future. This chapter looks at practical ways to help you "green" your living space and is packed with useful information on how to incorporate green technology into your home.

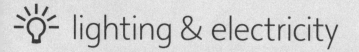

lighting & electricity

CHANGE TO ENERGY-SAVING BULBS

This is one of the easiest ways to save energy immediately. Energy-saving bulbs, also known as compact fluorescent light bulbs (CFLs), use less than five times the energy of a standard incandescent bulb. They also last up to 12 times longer than incandescent bulbs, making them a cheaper option in the long run.

REMEMBER TO SWITCH OFF

Another very simple way to save energy at home is to always switch lights off when you leave a room. Incandescent bulbs are incredibly energy-inefficient and only convert around 5% of the energy they use into light, with the remainder being lost as heat.

USE TASK LIGHTING

Rather than using a single high-watt bulb to light a whole room, try using less-powerful, energy-efficient light bulbs to light specific areas for tasks such as reading or eating.

MAKE THE MOST OF NATURAL DAYLIGHT

Arrange your living space around the natural light that is available throughout the day. In the morning in the north-western countries, for example, use rooms that face south and east, and in the afternoon and evening use those facing west. Consider fitting a skylight in dark areas such as hallways and staircases.

NO NEED TO BE IN THE SPOTLIGHT

Avoid the temptation to introduce lots of spotlights into your home. These have become particularly popular in kitchens and bathrooms and although the halogen bulbs used in spots are more energy-efficient than incandescent bulbs, the sheer number makes them a less environmentally-friendly option.

CHOOSE LED RATHER THAN HALOGEN SPOTLIGHTS

Light-emitting diodes (LEDs) are a fairly recent development in the energy-efficient lighting sector and they are the eco-alternative to halogen spotlighting. LEDs are now surpassing compact fluorescent light bulbs in efficiency. They are available in a wide range of colours and wattages so you won't have to compromise on ambience.

CHANGE YOUR MOST-USED BULBS

Start your move to low-energy lighting by switching the bulbs you use most to compact fluorescent light bulbs (CFLs). They can be applied anywhere that incandescent light bulbs are used and will generate the most savings in terms of energy and money. Any lighting left on for long periods will be much more cost-effective if the bulbs are energy-efficient.

HOW BRIGHT IS YOUR ENERGY-SAVING BULB?

Make sure you choose the right bulb for the right job: 7- to 9-watt energy-saving bulbs offer the same brightness as a 40-watt standard incandescent. The 11- to 15-watt bulbs are equivalent to 60-watt and 18- to 21-watt are the same as 100-watt bulbs.

RECYCLE YOUR LIGHT BULBS

Energy-saving bulbs contain around 5mg of mercury – a tiny amount but enough to ensure they are banned from landfill in the UK and in several US states. Make sure you take yours to a recycling centre or contact the manufacturer to find out the best way to recycle their light bulbs.

USE LESS LIGHT

Be aware of the number of lights you have on. If several light bulbs are controlled using one switch you could always take out some of the bulbs and replace when necessary. Use individual spotlights and sidelights instead of switching all the lights on.

OPEN YOUR CURTAINS DURING DAYLIGHT HOURS

Make the most of natural daylight by opening the curtains wide in the day and getting rid of light-diffusing nets or sheers. This saves the energy that you may have used in lighting the space unnecessarily and makes the most of natural solar energy.

DINE BY CANDLELIGHT

Once a week have a candlelit dinner to save energy and boost the romance in your life in one go. Make sure the candles are vegetable-oil based, however, as paraffin candles have a much greater environmental impact and have been found to emit trace amounts of toxins.

SWITCH TO A GREEN ENERGY TARIFF

Green energy can be defined as electricity derived from renewable or clean resources such as wind and solar energy, and an increasing number of suppliers are now offering green energy tariffs. This is one easy way to help reduce CO_2 emissions and invest in renewable energy. The tariffs vary considerably and the "greenest" are considered those investing in building new renewable energy sources.

heating

TURN DOWN THE THERMOSTAT

This is one of the best ways to save energy at home. The thermostat should be set at around 19°C (66°F) for a comfortable temperature. You will also save up to 10% of your heating bills simply by turning the thermostat down by 1°C (34°F).

DON'T PUT CURTAINS IN FRONT OF RADIATORS

Doing this simply funnels the heat away from the room and out of the window. Crop the curtains so they fit snugly onto the windowsill above the radiators and make sure they are lined for extra insulation.

FIT RADIATOR VALVES

Fitting radiator valves is an excellent way to control the temperature throughout the house rather than wasting energy heating rooms that don't necessarily need it all the time. Cheap to buy and easy to install, adding radiator valves could cut your energy use by around 5%.

ADD A ROOM THERMOSTAT

A room thermostat will increase the efficiency of your central heating system. If used in conjunction with other controls such as radiator valves this could reduce your energy use by as much as 15%. Just make sure you don't install a room thermostat in the same room as a radiator with valves because they will counteract each other.

KEEP BEDROOMS COOLER

Make proper use of your radiator valves and save energy. Although a temperature of 19°C (66°F) is recommended for living spaces, bedrooms can be cooler at around 15°C (59°F). Remember to set different temperatures for rooms depending on how much they are used.

INSULATE BEHIND RADIATORS

Fit a sheet of aluminium foil or insulation on the wall behind the radiator and this will help to reduce energy waste, particularly if the radiator is on an outside wall. It is also possible to buy rigid reflective radiator panels that can be used without having to take the radiator off the wall – they simply slip into the gap between the wall and the radiator.

USE NATURAL MATERIALS FOR INSULATION

Natural insulation materials (such as the kind made from fire-retarded recycled newspaper or sheep's wool) have added benefits as well as a lower environmental impact. Being natural, they are biodegradable and safe to handle. They also help to keep humidity stable because they absorb moisture when it's humid and release it when the air is drier.

FIT WOODEN SHELVES OVER RADIATORS

Putting a shelf above your radiators will force the warm air to circulate around the room instead of going straight up to the ceiling. If the radiator is under a window, the shelf will also stop the heat travelling behind the curtains.

CHOOSE A WOOD BURNER, NOT AN OPEN FIRE

If you really want a solid-fuel fire in your home, make sure it's a wood-burning stove rather than an open fire, which is very energy inefficient, losing around 85% of the heat up the chimney. Make sure you use locally sourced, sustainably managed wood that is carbon neutral.

MAKE YOUR OWN LOGS

If you have a wood burner, invest in a log maker. These practical devices turn old newspapers into "logs" that burn for around an hour. Cheap and easy to use, they provide roughly one log per newspaper. Use extra newspaper and kindling to get the fire started.

USE A CHIMNEY BALLOON

To stop draughts coming in from the chimney, invest in a chimney balloon (www.chimneyballoon.com). They sit about a foot up above the fireplace opening and you can easily fit one yourself. Chimney balloons stop draughts, heat loss, soot and debris, and have just enough ventilation to keep the chimney dry.

PUT ON AN EXTRA LAYER

Before turning up, or even turning on, your heating, wear an extra sweater and socks and save energy and money. Keep a cosy throw on the sofa, too, and cuddle up in it on really cold nights.

GET RID OF THE ELECTRIC BLANKET

As well as the health and safety concerns associated with electric blankets, they also use unnecessary energy. Instead of switching one on, fill a hot-water bottle, use thick organic cotton sheets and woollen blankets to make the bed feel warmer, and wrap up in organic cotton thermals.

WARM UP NATURALLY

Instead of turning up the heating, invest in wheat or rice packs (or make your own). These are a great way to warm up without using very much energy – just place the bags in a microwave for a couple of minutes and enjoy. They have the added benefit of easing pain, and are much more energy-friendly than heating pads.

INCREASE YOUR LOFT INSULATION

Heating is responsible for more than 75% of the energy consumption of the average household and around half of heat loss in a typical home is through the loft (attic) and walls. The recommended depth for loft insulation is a depth of 25 cm (10 in), which could save about a third of your heating costs.

ADD CAVITY WALL INSULATION

Cavity wall insulation is one of the most cost-effective energy-efficiency measures you can carry out in your home. It reduces heat loss through the external walls by around 60% and is relatively cheap to install. However, it must be carried out by an expert.

DOUBLE-GLAZE YOUR WINDOWS

Around 20% of the heat lost from an average family home occurs through single-glazed windows and badly insulated window frames. By fitting double-glazing this loss can be reduced by more than half. If you can't afford to replace all your windows, double-glaze the ones in the rooms you heat the most.

CHOOSE WOOD, NOT PVC FOR DOUBLE-GLAZING

If you decide to fit double-glazing, make sure you use wood for the frames rather than PVC or even aluminium. The energy and toxins created during the manufacture of PVC make it an environmental no-no and it's also extremely difficult to recycle.

DRAUGHT-PROOF DOORS AND WINDOWS

Around 20% of the heat in the average home is lost through ventilation and draughts. Keep the warmth in by adding draught excluders to doors and windows. Fittings are available from most DIY stores, making this an easy way to save energy.

USE HEAVY-LINED CURTAINS

Keep the heat in by drawing your curtains at dusk. Close them when it gets dark and consider adding a lining to further reduce heat loss through windows. If they are unlined, another option is to get an inexpensive second pair of curtains to act as lining material.

SHUTTER UP

Wooden shutters on windows are excellent insulators, along with the added advantage that they look elegant. Shutters could be a good option if you don't have double-glazing. If you live in an old house, check that you don't already have shutters – they may have been boarded into the wall.

PUT A JACKET ON YOUR HOT-WATER CYLINDER

Save energy by insulating your hot-water cylinder by fitting a "jacket" around it, which could cut heat loss by over 75%. If you already have a jacket on your cylinder make sure it's at least 7 cm (3 in) thick for optimum energy saving.

LAG YOUR PIPES

Insulating the pipes in your central heating system when they pass through parts of the house that you don't need to heat such as the loft is a good way to save energy. Insulation material for a standard 15-mm (½-in) pipe is cheap and effective.

LAG YOUR PIPES

Insulating – "lagging" – your hot-water pipes can help prevent burst pipes in cold weather as well as improve insulation in your home. In very cold weather, leave your heating on a low setting while you are away to prevent pipes freezing and bursting.

COVER YOUR LETTERBOX

Valuable heat and energy are lost through draughts around the home. One of the main areas where heat escapes from inside is through the letterbox (mail slot). Save valuable energy, especially if you don't have a porch area, by fitting a cover with flexible bristles or a magnetic seal that create a constant seal.

BLOCK UP DRAUGHTY FLOORBOARDS

Draughts caused by gaps in wooden floorboards waste energy and can make your home feel cold and uncomfortable. There are various ways to block up these draughts, including non-toxic sealants, underlays or hardboard, which will save you money as well as reduce energy.

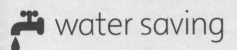 water saving

WARM UP WITH A GEOTHERMAL HEAT PUMP

Geothermal heating is one way of using a renewable energy source to provide much of your heating needs and it is becoming a more realistic option. Similar to ordinary heat pumps, they use the earth's heat from the ground instead of outside air to provide heating, air conditioning and, in most cases, hot water. It's estimated you can save 2 to 8 tonnes of carbon dioxide emissions each year via a geothermal heat pump.

TURN DOWN THE TEMPERATURE

Turn the temperature down on your water thermostat, that is. The temperature for heating water should be set at around 60°C (140°F), which is hot enough to provide a comfortable bath. If it's any hotter than that, then cold water will have to be added to cool it down.

HEAT YOUR HOT WATER WITH SOLAR ENERGY

Solar hot-water heating is now quite a practical way to create your own hot water from the sun's energy. Today's solar water heating panels may be integrated into most types of hot-water systems, including combination boilers, and can provide you with around a third of your hot-water needs.

FLUSH LESS

This may sound revolting but try flushing your toilet less often. One third of the average family's water use is flushed down the toilet – the equivalent of two baths per day.

SAVE WATER WHEN YOU FLUSH

Flushing the lavatory accounts for around 30% of total household water consumption, and an old-fashioned toilet can use as much as 9 to 12 litres (2½ to 3 gallons) of water on every flush. So, if you are replacing your toilet, choose one with a dual-flushing facility that gives you a choice of a big or small flush.

FIT SPRAY HEADS

When installing new taps (faucets) in your home, put spray heads on them as this will save water. Make sure you fix any dripping taps as soon as possible because leaks can waste up to 4 litres (1 gallon) of water a day.

HARVEST RAINWATER

Using collected rainwater could save up to 50% of household water use – the same amount used to flush the toilet, water the garden or supply the washing machine. However, rainwater harvesting systems best suit houses with large roofs and space for water storage.

GET A WATER BUTT

A water butt positioned under one of the drains is a cheap and practical way to use rainwater. It can provide all the water you need for the garden at least, which is considerable when you think that the average gardener uses 10 litres (2½ gallons) of water daily on the garden.

DON'T LET IT GO DOWN THE DRAIN

Put a container under the hot tap (faucet) while running it to save the water you waste while waiting for it to heat up. This can then be used to flush the toilet, to water plants in the garden or even as drinking water.

PUT EXCESS WATER IN THE REFRIGERATOR

Instead of letting the tap (faucet) run so that the water cools down enough to drink, fill up a jug of water and put it in the refrigerator to cool and enjoy whenever you need a drink. This has the added bonus of allowing the chlorine to evaporate from the water before drinking.

USE A WATER-SAVING DEVICE

If you are unable to replace your existing toilet, dual-flush devices can be bought separately and retrofitted to most toilets. Cistern displacement devices such as the Hippo, the Water Saver or Toilet Tummy are another way to reduce the amount of water flushed away. Insert them into the cistern and save 1 to 3 litres (2 to 6 pints) each time you flush.

YOUR TOILET ISN'T A GARBAGE BIN

Instead of throwing tissues, cotton wool balls and cotton buds (swabs) down the toilet, put them in the garbage instead. You will need to flush the toilet more often to get rid of these items, thereby wasting unnecessary water. By being flushed, cotton buds can end up polluting waterways and beaches.

MAINTAIN YOUR PLUMBING

If you have dripping taps (faucets) anywhere in the house, fix them immediately. Around 4 litres (1 gallon) of water can disappear down the drain every hour or so in this way, and up to 90 litres (24 gallons) if the drip starts to form a stream.

BOIL WHAT YOU NEED

Whenever you boil a kettle for a hot drink, make sure you only fill it with as much water as you need so that extra energy isn't wasted in heating unwanted water. The easiest way to do this is to fill the mug you are going to use with water and then add it to the kettle.

REUSE YOUR BATHWATER

In summer, recycle your bathwater by using it to water plants in the garden. It can also be used to flush the toilet during the months when the garden doesn't need it. Keep a basin by the bathtub to make this easier and save the water you would use flushing.

TURN OFF WHILE YOU BRUSH

Turning off the tap (faucet) while you brush your teeth is an easy way to use less water. This simple action can save up to 5 litres (8 pints) of water every time you brush, and if you make sure everyone in the household does the same, even more will be saved.

REDUCE YOUR SHOWER TIME

Try to lessen the amount of time you spend in the shower. An average shower uses 35 litres (9¼ gallons) of water and lasts around six minutes. Try reducing this time and don't have a complete shower simply to wash your hair, which can be done over the bathtub.

AVOID POWER SHOWERS

A power shower can use more water than it takes to fill your bathtub in less than five minutes, and three times more water than a standard shower unit in the same amount of time. Opt for a low-flow showerhead that restricts the flow of water and forces it through very small apertures.

GO WITH A LOW FLOW

Fitting an aerator to all your household taps (faucets) is a simple and inexpensive way to conserve water. These devices save water by reducing the water flow and by adding air to the water stream so that less water comes out of the tap during the time that you have it on.

WASH YOUR CAR WISELY

Use a bucket and sponge rather than a hose to wash your car, as this will save about 500 litres (132 gallons) each time. Alternatively, reserve the hose for a final rinse only. You can also buy special car wipes that don't need any water at all.

TURN OFF YOUR TAPS (FAUCETS)

If you don't have a dishwasher, avoid leaving the water running while you are washing or rinsing the dishes. This can use 9–14 litres (2½–3½ gallons) of water a minute – that's enough to run a small bath produced in just five minutes.

NO NEED TO PRE-RINSE

Even with really dirty dishes fight the urge to give them a quick rinse first before adding them to the dishwasher. Just remove any leftover food and put them straight into the machine – this could save you as much as 70 litres (18½ gallons) of water per dishwasher load.

A SHORT SHOWER SAVES WATER

A five-minute shower can use around a third as much water as a bath. In a typical household bathing accounts for around 20% of annual water use and modern bathtubs hold around 60 litres (16 gallons) of water. Fitting a water-efficient showerhead, which costs around the same as conventional ones, can reduce the amount of water you use by 30%.

RATION WATER USE FOR A CLEAN PATIO

Rather than using water flowing from a hose to rinse down the patio or driveway, fill a bucket with clean water and use that, along with a stiff brush, instead. Even better, use some of the water collected in the water butt or recycled from the bathtub for washing down outside areas.

WATCH THE WAY YOU WASH VEGETABLES

Save water when you wash your fruit and vegetables by doing this in a bowl rather than under a running tap (faucet). You can then re-use the bowl of dirty water on plants in the garden or even to flush the lavatory.

CHECK FOR LEAKS

Hidden leaks are hard to find, so it's a good idea to monitor them. If your water is metered you can check by reading your meter and then going back a couple of hours later to make sure that it reads the same when no appliances are running. If it doesn't, then you know you have a leak somewhere.

REDUCE THE USE OF APPLIANCES THAT USE WATER

Running your washing machine and dishwasher only when they are full can save you 750 litres (198 gallons) of water a week. Your garbage disposal uses lots of water too, so compost instead.

GET A METER

If your water is not already metered it's worth having one installed. Research has revealed that water meters make people more conscious about the amount of water they are using. This is also a good way to keep an eye on your consumption and to check for any leaks.

SOMETHING FISHY IN THE HOUSE PLANTS
If you have a fish tank, don't throw away the dirty water left over from cleaning it. You can use it to water your house plants – it's rich in nitrogen and phosphorus, which makes it an excellent plant fertilizer.

EGG-WATER FOR HOUSE PLANTS
Every time you boil an egg, make sure you save the leftover water for your house plants. The nutrients released from the shell of the egg during cooking are particularly beneficial for plants – just let the water cool before watering them.

air quality & conditioning

COOL OFF WITHOUT AIR-CON
While air-conditioning is great for cooling us down on stifling summer days, it also adds around 50% to the energy costs of a building, and used in cars increases fuel consumption by 10 to 14%. Don't rely solely on air-con when it's not needed – open the windows when the temperature outside is good. If you do have to use it, try to use efficient systems and do use the thermostat.

MAKE YOUR OWN HOME SCENTS
Instead of relying on synthetic air fresheners, make your own. Try adding a few drops of your favourite essential oil to filtered water in a spray container and use it to spritz areas that often need freshening up, such as the kitchen and cloakroom.

REFRESH NATURALLY
Instead of chemical plug-in air fresheners, place a few slices of citrus fruit such as lemon or orange in a saucepan, together with a few cloves. Simmer the mixture gently for an hour or so to refresh the smell of your house.

PURIFY WITH HOUSE PLANTS

Many indoor plants not only look nice but they also act as natural air conditioners. Research has shown that they can remove up to 87% of indoor pollution in 24 hours. Draecana, spider plants, peace lilies and Areca palms all act as air purifiers. Placing a yucca in the bathroom has also been found to be a good way to neutralize any bad smells from the toilet.

AVOID AIR FRESHENERS

A recent study found that many air fresheners contain phthalates, which have been linked with health scares such as cancer. Additionally, many air fresheners are "plug-ins", which use energy on a constant basis. Research indicates that a single plug-in is responsible for generating 13.5 kg (29½ lb) of CO_2 a year.

NATURAL HOME FRAGRANCE

Use bunches of herbs or flowers, ideally cut from your own garden, and essential oils to fragrance your home rather than synthetic air fresheners. Light soy candles and try making your own potpourri using dried herbs such as lavender, along with dried rose petals and camomile flowers.

KEEP YOUR HOUSE SMELL-FREE

Use baking soda to stop nasty odours in your refrigerator or garbage bin instead of chemical air fresheners. The baking soda works to neutralize nasty smells without adverse effects. You can also combine it with lemon juice and water and use it as a room spray.

CHOOSE WIND-OPERATED TO REDUCE CONDENSATION

A wind-operated extractor (exhaust) fan is the best way to resolve any condensation problems in rooms such as bathrooms and kitchens. They reduce the need to open windows and are powered simply by the difference in pressure so no energy is required at all, unlike an electric extractor.

energy-efficient appliances

KEEP IT COOL

Avoid opening the refrigerator door as much as possible and whenever you do so, make sure it's kept open for as little time as possible. Each minute the door is open takes three minutes of energy to cool it down again.

SAVE WHEN YOU COOK

If you are using the oven try not to open it unnecessarily – an open door allows heat to escape and the appliance will then use more energy getting back up to the required temperature. Also, cook bigger batches of food that can be saved and reheated later.

CHILL OUT

Defrost your freezer regularly to keep it as efficient as possible. Also, check that it is set at the correct temperature and be sure to replace any damaged door seals. Refrigerators and freezers should be positioned away from direct sunlight, cookers and boilers to maintain them at optimum efficiency.

KEEP YOUR REFRIGERATOR ON TOP FORM

Keep your refrigerator clean and well positioned. Make sure you regularly dust down the coils at the back – dusty coils can waste up to 30% extra electricity.

GREENER COFFEE MAKING

When you are brewing your morning coffee the best option is to use a cafetière – as long as you only boil the amount of water you need. The next choice is to use a stove-top coffee percolator, particularly if you have a gas cooker.

GET A HOUSEHOLD ENERGY MONITOR

These new meters allow you to keep an eye on exactly how much energy your tumble drier and washing machine need to run so that you will know how best to save energy.

TURN OFF THE EXTRACTOR FAN

Try to use the extractor (exhaust) fan as little as possible when you are cooking. When steam builds up in the kitchen the best option is just to open a window. Simple air vents fitted to windows that work by using differences in air pressure are a greener option than electric fans.

HAVE YOUR BOILER SERVICED REGULARLY

Inefficient boilers use more energy than they need so it's worth getting yours serviced on a regular basis to make sure it performs properly. If your boiler is more than 10 years old, it might be worth replacing it with a newer, more efficient model that could save energy and money on your fuel bills.

CHOOSE "A" RATED APPLIANCES

Make sure that you select the highest-rated energy appliances for your washing machine and dishwasher to save the most water. "A" rated appliances use considerably less water than other models – look out for the Energy Star and Energy Saving Recommended logos.

BUY ENERGY-EFFICIENT APPLIANCES

Around 20% of our total home energy usage is used to power electrical appliances, from kettles to computers. When any of these need to be replaced, research the most energy-efficient models you can find. In Europe, look out for the EU energy-rating label and in the US keep an eye out for Energy Star labels.

SWITCH OFF AND CUT EMISSIONS

The International Energy Agency (IEA) has launched a global initiative called the One Watt Plan to reduce standby requirements for all new appliances to below 1 watt. Research has revealed that some standby modes for televisions use two-thirds of the electricity than if they were switched on.

KEEP JUST COOL ENOUGH
The temperature of your refrigerator should be kept at an optimal functioning temperature in order to be energy efficient. This is usually 3–5°C (37–41°F) for the fridge and -17.8 – -15°C (0–5°F) for the freezer. Check the temperature controls and thermostat by placing a thermometer on the middle shelf and leaving it overnight to get a good reading.

SWITCH YOUR REFRIGERATOR OFF
If you live in an area that has cold winters and you have a garage, conservatory or outside storage, you could actually turn your refrigerator off during the coldest months and keep essentials such as milk and yogurt outside. Your refrigerator and freezer can also be switched off while you are away from your home for long weekends or vacations.

SWITCH OFF THE POWER
Kitchen appliances are some of the biggest energy consumers while on standby. Microwaves in particular often have features such as clocks that end up using more energy than the actual cooking process so switch them off at the main electrical outlet when they are not in use.

KEEP YOUR FREEZER FULL
It takes less energy to cool a full freezer than an empty one so try and keep it topped up, preferably with home-cooked meals stored in reused containers. If your freezer needs filling, add plastic bottles of water to take up the empty space.

DON'T "STANDBY" TELEVISIONS
Research has revealed that 10% of energy use in the developed world is caused by appliances, such as televisions, being left on standby. As well as wasting energy, this also costs money so make sure you switch off at the source rather than via the remote control.

SWITCH TO RECHARGEABLE BATTERIES

The average household uses around 21 batteries a year and only a very small percentage of these are recycled – less than 2% – which poses a significant waste problem. Another good reason to use rechargeables is because the power used to manufacture a battery is, on average, 50 times greater than the energy it gives out.

WAKE UP TO AN ECO CLOCK

There are several brands of water-powered clocks available. The Eco Clock incorporates a digital clock, alarm, timer and room thermometer. It is powered by a water-activated battery that just needs topping up with tap water, so you don't have to worry about plugging it in or buying new batteries.

GADGETS THAT WASTE ENERGY

Today we are surrounded by items such as electric toothbrushes, bread knives and can openers that use unnecessary energy. Traditional versions work just as well without the need for polluting batteries or mains power.

cleaning

CUT BACK ON DISPOSAL CLOTHS

Avoid wastage from disposable scourers and kitchen cloths by buying cotton cloths that can be washed and reused. Make your own scourers from the nylon mesh bags that fruit comes in. These can be stuffed inside each other and tied up to form a ball.

REDUCE THE NUMBER OF CLEANING PRODUCTS

Do you really need a separate product for each job? Streamline your cleaning cupboard to just a few items and use natural alternatives such as vinegar and lemon for household cleaning jobs rather than relying on chemical products.

USE SODA CRYSTALS FOR HOUSEHOLD CLEANING

For many years soda crystals, also known as washing soda, have been used for cleaning. They are biodegradable and don't contain phosphates, enzymes or bleach. Soda crystals are suitable for cleaning work tops, lavatories and mirrors, as well as unblocking drains and pipes.

USE ECO-FRIENDLY CLEANING PRODUCTS

Conventional cleaning products such as laundry detergents and household cleaners can leak chemical solvents and toxins into the environment. Common ingredients include petroleum-based surfactants derived from non-renewable sources, which have also been linked to health problems including cancer and hormone-disruption. A recent study also found a strong link between asthma and cleaning products.

CLEAN UP WITH BICARBONATE OF SODA

Bicarbonate of soda, also known as baking soda, makes a versatile household cleaner. Use it to get rid of smells by placing a small bowl in the kitchen or refrigerator. Shake it onto carpets before vacuuming to freshen them up and sprinkle on dishes or in the bottom of the dishwasher to absorb food odours and give crockery cleaning an extra boost.

POLISH YOUR OWN

Instead of using furniture polish in an aerosol can, create your own totally natural polish using beeswax, turpentine and a favourite essential oil to make your house smell as well as look good. Heat in a bowl over hot water until the beeswax dissolves. Add a few drops of essential oil such as lavender or pine and use a soft cloth to rub it into furniture.

SWITCH TO E-CLOTHS

Avoid using plastic scourers and sponges to clean your dishes and invest in a set of e-cloths. These are microfibre cleaning cloths that neither contain nor require chemicals. They are designed to remove the surface layer of dirt, leaving bacteria without anywhere to grow, and you only need to use water with them.

FIGHT MOULD WITH BORAX

Borax is a naturally occurring mineral that is kind to the
environment. It can irritate skin and eyes, however, so take
care when using it. Sprinkle it onto a damp cloth and wipe
down bathtubs and showers. It also inhibits mould growth, so
use it to wash down walls, or alternatively leave a thick paste
of water and Borax on the affected area overnight before
brushing off and rinsing.

SALT YOUR SILVER

Silver cleaners can be abrasive and harsh. Make your own
cleaner for sterling (not plate) silver by mixing 500 ml (1 pint)
of water with a teaspoon each of salt and baking powder and
add a strip of aluminium foil. Drop the silver into this mixture,
boil for a few minutes, then remove with tongs and polish with
a soft cloth. Add lemon juice for really grimy silver.

USE RECYCLED KITCHEN PAPER TOWELS

When buying kitchen roll make sure that you look for products
with a high-recycled content, preferably 100%. This will help to
reduce the energy used to produce kitchen roll or towels as far
less is required for recycled paper. Also, look out for unbleached
varieties to reduce the use of chlorine bleach, a pollutant.

CLEANING GOES FAIRTRADE

Certified fairtrade cleaning cloths made from a circular-knitted
natural cotton yarn are now available. They are unbleached
and can be used for cleaning, doing dishes or dry dusting.
One variety, made by Minky in the UK, uses cotton grown by
a cooperative of small-scale farmers in Mali before being spun
by accredited suppliers in Europe.

OPT OUT OF THE WASHING UP WITH A DISHWASHER

Instead of washing all your dishes by hand, you should
use a dishwasher if you have space. Research comparing
handwashing to dishwashers found that dishwashers use
just half the energy and one-sixth of the water than is
used when doing the dishes by hand.

GO LARGE

Don't buy a new plastic spray pump every time you need a refill. Instead, purchase cleaning products in the largest possible containers and refill your action pumps as and when you need to do so. There are other products you can get in bulk and decant so you won't be buying unnecessary packaging, such as food items like spices or rice or health-and-beauty products like shampoo or body wash.

GET YOURSELF A MOP

A traditional string mop lasts longer than cheaper foam versions. You can buy replacement heads for some mops but most may be washed in the washing machine – put the mop in a pillowcase first to protect your machine. Another green way to wash floors is to tie a floor-cloth to a brush. Wash the cloth afterwards and reuse.

TRY BRUSHES FOR DISHES

Rather than buying scourers with plastic handles, buy longer-lasting wooden varieties with natural fibre bristles. Look out for brushes with replaceable heads. They will no doubt cost more but they will last longer and have far less impact on the environment.

DON'T DISPOSE

Instead of disposable dishcloths that have to be thrown away and replaced every few weeks, choose cotton cloths instead. They'll stand the test of time and can be washed and reused for many months to come.

CUT DOWN YOUR PRODUCTS

Did you know that more bleach and detergent are released into the environment from household waste than during their manufacturing process? Cut down on the use of bleach and detergent whenever you can. For instance, a scrub of cold water and table salt, applied with a cloth or scourer, works just as well as bleach on cutlery and breadboards.

SAY RHUBARB TO DIRTY PANS

Degreasers designed to clean your kitchen pans are often full of harsh and toxic ingredients. You can clean the bottom of your pan without resorting to specialist chemicals by boiling up some rhubarb, which will pull the dirt off the sides (except on aluminium, where you should use vinegar).

DUST YOUR BULBS

Don't stop at dusting your mantelpieces and shelves – keeping your light bulbs dust-free could help save energy as it will increase output and so make them more efficient.

DISINFECT NATURALLY

Not only do disinfectants contain harsh chemicals that are damaging to the environment, they smell strong, too. Make your own natural disinfectant by infusing leaves of rosemary, eucalyptus, lavender, sage and thyme in water.

BE LEMON FRESH

Get rid of strong smells in the refrigerator by placing half a lemon inside to absorb the odours. Lemon also works in the microwave – just put a couple of slices in a microwave-proof bowl of cold water and switch the power on for a few minutes.

CLEAN UP WITH LEMON

Fresh or bottled, lemon juice makes a fantastic natural cleaner. Bleach wooden chopping boards by rubbing them with lemon juice and leave overnight before rinsing. Lemon juice also removes lime scale (mineral deposits) from taps (faucets) and can be used to clean worktops and surfaces.

BRING A SPARKLE TO GLASS WITH VINEGAR

Mix up equal parts of vinegar and warm water to create an ideal window-cleaning solution. Apply the mixture to the window with a piece of scrunched-up newspaper and rub. There's no need to worry – any vinegary smells will disappear once the window is dry!

GREASE IT OUT

Don't smother kitchen grease in increasingly powerful detergents, which are toxic to the environment. First, try a simple mixture of salt and bicarbonate of soda (baking soda). When mixed together, these two have powerful degreasing properties, without causing any harm to the environment.

SPRINKLE AWAY SMELLS

Instead of using room fresheners or anti-smell powders and sprays in your garbage bin to cut down on nasty odours, simply sprinkle a handful of salt inside. The salt acts by neutralizing unwanted smells.

GOODBYE FISH FINGERS

If your hands smell of fish or onions after preparing a meal, don't immediately reach for the washing-up liquid. Salt dissolved in warm water will work just as well as a handwash and will keep your run-off water detergent-free.

MAKE YOUR BATHROOM SHINE

To give your toilet a really good clean, drop a couple of denture-cleaning tablets into the bowl and leave overnight. Another cleaning tip is to add a can of cola to the bowl and leave overnight before scrubbing and flushing away.

BREW UP A CLEAN FLOOR

Tea is all you need to clean wooden floors and bring up the shine, particularly on older wooden flooring. Brew two tea bags in hot water and cool to room temperature, then apply with a mop or a cloth. The added bonus is that there's no need to rinse. Only use this on hardwood flooring to bring out the natural grain and lustre.

RINSE WINDOWS WITH VINEGAR

Instead of using window-cleaning sprays that contain ammonia, which is harmful to wildlife, wash your windows with pure soap and water and then rinse with a solution of one part vinegar to four parts water. Use washable, reusable cloth instead of paper towels.

GIVE A VINEGAR SPARKLE

Avoid harsh chemicals and use vinegar to clean your home instead. It can be added to water and used to clean floors and surfaces in place of disinfectants, removing dull, greasy films. Add ½ cup of vinegar to 2 litres (2 quarts) of water. It also gets rid of hard-water stains on glasses and gives them a real shine.

CLEAN UP WITH VINEGAR

Don't clean your toilet with limescale remover as it contains harsh chemicals that harm the environment when flushed down the lavatory into the water system. Vinegar is an excellent substitute to scrub off limescale marks.

DON'T DISINFECT

For a disinfectant that really works when you absolutely need it (for instance, when toilet-training young animals) and also gets rid of grease and even attacks rust, mix 50–100 ml (3–6 tbsp) of eucalyptus oil with 1 litre (2 pints) of water and decant into a spray bottle. Shake before use and keep in the fridge for up to a month.

CLUB STAINS AWAY

To keep fresh stains from sinking deep into clothes, immediately apply a little carbonated water or club soda. The carbonation in the water bubbles up the stain and the salts prevent the colour from sticking. Then wash as normal.

CLEAN UP WITH SALT

Salt can be used for a number of cleaning tasks around the home, avoiding the need for chemical products. Use it to remove stains from china and whiten discoloured wooden draining or bread boards.

BAKE OFF STAINS

For hard-to-beat, stubborn stains on your kitchen surfaces, dampen a sponge and apply baking powder, then wipe clean as normal. The abrasive powder will get rid of most stains, but if the mark remains, try re-soaking the stain with a solution of baking powder instead.

SOAP IS GOOD FOR YOU

For homemade liquid soap, grate a bar of pure soap (or use soap flakes) and pour into warm water. Heat until dissolved, then cool and store. Use to refill plastic hand-soap bottles in your kitchen and bathroom. The soap should last indefinitely if kept airtight and it will mean you're not continually buying more plastic.

CUT GREASE NATURALLY

If you want to avoid oven cleaners containing harsh chemicals that pollute the air and waterways, but want to remove the extra grease from your oven, add vinegar to your usual washing-up liquid or soap and wipe on with a clean cloth, rinsing thoroughly.

UNBLOCK DRAINS NATURALLY

Instead of using chemical products to clear blocked drains, try pouring down a solution of 4 tablespoons bicarbonate of soda (baking soda) and 50 ml (2 fl oz) vinegar in boiling water. If you do this regularly, it should help to prevent your drains from getting blocked again.

STARCH YOUR CARPETS

It is possible to fully clean and deodorize carpets without resorting to chemical-laden carpet cleaners or shampoo. Simply vacuum, liberally sprinkle cornstarch or baking soda, leave one hour, then vacuum again. To remove tough stains, try cold soda water or repeatedly blot with vinegar and soapy water instead of automatically reaching for the stain remover.

PLANT AWAY SMELLS

Commercial air fresheners work by masking smells and coating the nasal passages with chemicals that diminish the sense of smell by deadening the nerves. In addition, they also pollute the air. House plants act as natural air filters, so invest in a few and place them in areas like the kitchen and bathroom where they can counter unpleasant odours.

SWEEP IT AWAY

Try using a broom or a dustpan and brush as a low-energy, environmentally-friendly alternative to vacuuming floors and carpets. Some vacuum cleaners come with reusable dust bags, which you empty and reuse, but even better are those that work without bags.

IT'S A FAIR COP

Instead of chemical metal cleaners and polishes, clean copper with lemon juice or vinegar combined with salt, or try white flour to help you get the fingermarks off chrome. For brass, try equal parts of salt and flour on a dry rag, adding a little vinegar if required.

LEAVE YOUR SHOES AT THE DOOR

Cut back on the use of household cleaners by leaving your shoes at the door. This reduces dust by an estimated 60%, making your home a cleaner and healthier environment. Open windows regularly to let in fresh air and to get rid of nasty smells.

KEEP DRAINS CLEAN

Your drains can be kept open, clean and odour-free without the use of corrosive drain cleaners by simply sticking to two main rules of thumb – never pour liquid grease down a drain and always use a drain sieve to avoid any waste clogging the pipes.

DRAIN AWAY DIRT

Use a plumber's snake for clogged drains before you reach for the abrasive chemicals. Even better, opt for natural acid-alkali cleaning and sprinkle 60 ml (¼ cup) baking soda followed by 125 ml (½ cup) vinegar to fizz out accumulated gunk. Flush afterwards with boiling water.

BRUSH UP YOUR SILVER

Use a damp cloth to work white (non-gel) toothpaste into the silver you want to clean, then rinse and dry. The mild abrasive in the toothpaste will clean the silver without you having to resort to chemical cleaners.

SOME LIKE IT HOT

You don't need commercial stain remover! For grease stains on white cottons, strain boiling water through the fabric and follow with dry baking soda, or rub with washing soda in water. For other materials, blot the stain with a towel, dampen with water and rub with soap and baking soda, then wash in hot water.

WASH DRAINS THROUGH

Instead of waiting until your drains become blocked and then resorting to harsh drain cleaners, mix 30 ml (2 tbsp) each of baking soda and salt and pour into the drain, rinsing with a kettleful of boiling water and a quick cold-water rinse. Do this once a week as a maintenance measure.

BE A GOOD CLEANING EGG

To remove coffee and chocolate stains on clothes and tea towels, mix egg yolk with lukewarm water and rub onto the stain, then wash as normal.

DE-SCORCH WITH MILK

To remove iron scorches from colourfast clothing and fabrics, gently boil the scorched article in 250 ml (1 cup) soap flakes and 2 litres (4 pints) of milk for 10 minutes. Then rinse thoroughly, allow to dry and wash normally.

POLISH OFF WATERMARKS

Instead of using chemical treatments for wood, or varnishes that contain air-polluting chemicals, get rid of watermarks using a dry cloth. Rub the mark with olive or almond oil, or mix butter with cigarette ash to turn it brown, then polish.

MILK AWAY INK

A great way to remove ink stains without polluting the environment by using ammonia-based cleaners is to soak the item in milk, then wash as normal. When the milk soak gets inky, replenish with fresh milk.

laundry & clothes care

USE ECO-FRIENDLY CLOTHES DETERGENT
One of the most un-environmentally friendly aspects
of washing our clothes is the type of detergent we use.
Conventional washing powders contain chemicals such as
whitening agents and surfactants that have a detrimental
impact on the environment. Choose eco products such as
Ecover, Bio-D or Sonett.

NATURAL MOTH REPELLENTS
Conventional mothballs often contain chemicals that have
been found to be toxic and even carcinogenic. Buy or, better
still, create your own natural mothballs. Make sachets of fabric
and fill with dried lavender or herbs scented with essential oils.
Moths don't like lavender or cedarwood.

CLEAN CLOTHES WITHOUT BLEACH
If you want to get rid of blood on your clothes without using
bleach, pour salt or cold soda water onto the stain and soak
in cold water before washing. For a more stubborn stain, mix
cornstarch, talcum powder and a little water into a spreadable
paste and apply, then allow to dry and brush away.

DON'T THROW RUST AWAY
Instead of throwing away clothes which are damaged by
rust marks, saturate the rust stains with sour milk (milk mixed
with a little vinegar or lemon juice) and rub with salt. Place the
item in direct sunlight until dry, then wash it; the rust stain
should have disappeared.

ICE OFF YOUR GUM
Don't resort to expensive and highly chemical solutions for
getting rid of chewing gum stuck to clothing. Instead, rub
with ice and the gum will slowly flake off.

GREEN YOUR WASHING MACHINE NATURALLY

To give your washing machine a good clean, add a generous handful of bicarbonate of soda (baking soda) to the drum of the machine and put it on a hot wash cycle. This should get rid of any nasty smells caused by detergent build-up; done regularly it will also help to keep your machine in good condition.

WASH WITH SOAP NUTS

Soap nuts grow on trees in India and Nepal and their shells contain saponin, a natural soap. Instead of using detergent, put 6–8 soap-nut shells in a cotton bag or knotted sock and place them in the drum of your washing machine on a 40°C (104°F) cycle.

USE A MAGNETIC BALL IN YOUR WASHING MACHINE

These balls work by softening the water by as much as 70%, which helps to prevent the build-up of lime scale in your washing machine as well as the removal of existing deposits. They also reduce the minimum required temperature for cleaning clothes and the amount of detergent needed.

TURN IT DOWN

When you are doing the laundry, turn down the temperature on your washing machine to save energy. As much as 90% of the energy used is taken up with heating the water. By choosing a 40°C (104°F/warm) rather than a 60°C (140°F/hot) cycle you will use a third less electricity, and if you reduce this further to a 30°C (60°F/cold) cycle you will save even more.

A LITTLE BIT OF DIRT

It may sound obvious but washing your clothes less frequently will save a significant amount of energy. The average family uses its washing machine five times a week, which uses a staggering 26,000 litres (6,868 gallons) of water a year. Wear overalls and aprons to protect clothing while working at home.

ONLY IRON WHAT'S REALLY NECESSARY

Ironing everything from underwear to cloth nappies (diapers) really isn't necessary. Save energy (and time) by only ironing the things that need it. Is it really essential to have your underpants crease-free? Focus on the items that have to be ironed, such as shirts, and leave your bed linen alone.

CHOOSE POWDERED DETERGENT

Liquid detergents generally contain a great deal more surfactant than powders and usually they also come packaged in plastic. Surfactants (commonly used in household and bodycare products) have been found to be slow to biodegrade as well as damaging to plants and animals. Both powder and liquid compacts use less detergent per wash than the other forms.

GIVE YOUR UNDIES A NATURAL FRAGRANCE

Add small packages or envelopes of homemade herb and essential oil mixtures to your underwear drawer to give a pleasant fragrance. These sachets can also be placed in shoes and trainers to ward off bad odours. Try geranium and lavender. You can also sprinkle on cotton wool balls.

DON'T BUY ANTIBACTERIAL CLEANING PRODUCTS

Some studies have found that antibacterial products actually contribute to the increase in "superbugs" and can cause dry skin and hand eczema. Don't believe the hype: avoid products containing the antibacterial ingredient triclosan. Soap and hot water will kill germs just as effectively.

DON'T BUY INTO DRY-CLEANING

Try to avoid purchasing clothes that have to be dry-cleaned or hand-wash instead. The chemicals used in dry-cleaning carry traces of tetrachlorethylene, which has been linked to dizziness, headaches and fatigue, as well as being a potential carcinogen.

SWITCH TO ECO-BALLS

Stop using detergent in your washing machine by switching to reusable laundry balls such as Eco-balls. They last for up to 1,000 washes and work by ionizing the water via the agitation of ceramic granules within the perforated balls. And you don't need to add fabric softener because they also help to soften clothes washed in hard water.

AVOID FABRIC CONDITIONERS

Some liquid fabric softeners have been found to contain formaldehyde, which is a known carcinogen. Other chemicals found in conventional fabric conditioners have been linked to skin irritation and even cancer. Instead, add 125 ml (4 fl oz) white distilled vinegar or bicarbonate of soda (baking soda) to the rinse.

AVOID DRYING CLOTHES ON RADIATORS

Clothes drying on radiators prevents the heat reaching the rest of the room, creates damp and provides good growing conditions for mould. Instead, try to dry clothes outside whenever possible, or alternatively use a clothes airer in a room that can be well ventilated.

DRY IN THE OPEN AIR

Avoid using tumble driers if at all possible – try to think of it as a luxury. Where possible, dry clothes outside on the line – they will not only smell better, but sunlight has a natural bleaching and sterilizing effect on fabric. If you must use the dryer, avoid overdrying and use the moisture sensor control if your machine has one.

A FULL LOAD

When filling your washing machine always make sure it's full. Half-load cycles tend to use more than half the energy or water consumption than a full load so they're not as energy-efficient.

home design

GREEN YOUR ROOF

This may sound a little extreme but turf-covered roofs are becoming more popular and are now easier to put together. Planting turf on your roof creates natural insulation, thereby saving energy, improves air quality and has the added bonus of encouraging biodiversity. You will, however, need to ensure that your roof is strong enough to support the weight of the turf or plants when saturated with rainwater or snowfall.

MAKE THE MOST OF SOLAR ENERGY

If you have the option, fit large windows in south-facing walls (in the northern hemisphere) and avoid overshadowing from trees and buildings such as sheds. Cut back trees that block out daylight and keep windows clean to allow in as much light as possible. Be aware that certain trees are protected by conservationist organizations.

CREATE A CONSERVATORY

Building a conservatory or sunroom is a fantastic way to make the most of solar energy. It's also a cheaper option for insulating your house because it acts as a protective zone between the house and the outside, trapping the sun's heat and cutting heat loss.

FIT A DOMESTIC WIND TURBINE

This may seem an elaborate idea but if you live in an exposed, windy area, it could be a good way to create at least some of the energy you need for heating and lighting your home. Small domestic wind turbines are available now from many DIY outlets, and can be mounted on your roof.

PLAY ECO-HOUSE

Eco houses made from old car and tractor tyres are now available in ready-to-build kits so you can build your own totally green house to live in. They are energy- and resource-efficient, and have inventive designs. Or if you're really serious, join some like minds and build a home in one of the growing number of sustainable communities and eco-villages worldwide, such as Arcosanti in the United States.

BE A WATER REED

If you have enough land attached to your home, install a totally natural reed-bed sewerage system. It will decompose your waste and minimize the effect you have on the environment by cutting water pollution.

MAKE HAY WHILE THE SUN SHINES

Think creatively about the substances you use for insulation. Hay and straw bales are fantastic insulation and, if they are packed properly, can also help to prevent fire from spreading.

GET HIGH SPEC

For exterior windows, doors and skylights, choose the highest specification glass you can because it will help insulate your house. Or consider replacing old doors and windows with a higher spec alternative.

RAM YOUR RUBBLE

Recycle bricks by passing them on to salvage yards or donating them to local builders. If you're having building work done, use the bricks as rammed rubble to help strengthen and insulate walls.

LIVE OFF THE EARTH

Several companies now manufacture plaster made from earth, so has little cost to the environment and is biodegradable. A substitute for gypsum plaster and paint, earth plaster is a non-toxic combination of clays, aggregates and natural pigments.

ADOBE YOUR WALLS

Choose interior adobe walls for your home to increase your thermal mass and reduce heat loss, thereby cutting energy usage.

SEARCH FOR SUNLIGHT

In order to avoid relying on electric lights unnecessarily, try to arrange your space around the way light falls naturally. In the northern hemisphere, south-facing portions have the most available light (or north-facing in the southern hemisphere), so think about making these the rooms you use the most.

WOOD IS GOOD

For the sun-facing parts of your house, choose wooden floors as they make the most of the warmth they get from the sun. They hold onto the warmth for longer, meaning you're wasting less energy. But make sure you don't have gaps between floorboards that can cause draughts.

GET OUT OF THE SHADOWS

Help your house heat up naturally in the sunshine by avoiding planting trees that will overshadow it, especially on the sunny side of the house. Know the full height the tree will grow to before committing to a position. This will help reduce your heating bills and your impact on the environment.

IN THE HOT WATER

Solar hot water heaters are becoming much more common as technology makes them more efficient and less bulky. Solar power is a great way to heat water in your home, via copper pipes that transfer heat quickly.

SUNNY SIDE UP

When house-hunting or looking for a site to build your new home, remember that it should face the sunny aspect and be sheltered from the prevailing cold winds. This will make considerable savings on your heating bill.

GO SOLAR

One of the best things you can do to help save energy in your house is to have solar panels installed in your roof. Even the murkiest winter climates get enough sunshine to produce electric power at little extra cost to the environment.

GET GRAPHIC

Metal and glass structures make great additions to modern buildings because they encourage the best use of light and are very long lasting, unlike old-fashioned wood and glass structures. Choose them for conservatories and extensions.

SEE DOUBLE

Always choose double glazing for windows. The layer of air trapped inside the glass prevents heat loss into the cold outdoors and will insulate your house against heat loss in winter. Similarly it will keep you cooler in summer. The optimum space between the two panes is 1.5 cm (¾ in). A smaller one leads to greater heat loss.

SAY TIMBER

Make sure your external glazed doors have wide timber frames, reducing the glazing area that could contribute to heat loss, but retaining the perception of large openings and lots of light.

SHOOT SOME HOOPS

Use hoop pine plywood for your joinery projects – it is highly moisture resistant and reduces VOCs (volatile organic compounds, which are emitted as gases from household products and which can have adverse health effects). But always ensure your pine is from a sustainable source. Finish it in tung oil, a natural wood preservative.

THINK FOR THE FUTURE

If you're building a house or making home improvements, think about the future as well as your current needs. Try to make changes in such a way that other people can add to them in the future without having to tear the whole thing down and start again.

DO A HEADSTAND

It might sound a strange way to live, but in a double-storey house it actually makes more environmental sense to have your bedrooms downstairs and your living space at the top of the house because heat rises, and you are likely to want your living space to be warmer than your bedrooms.

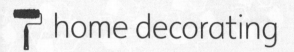

home decorating

CLEAN CARPETS

Before getting rid of a carpet simply because it is dirty, try hiring a steam cleaner. This will transform a grimy carpet and kill any clothes moths that have taken up residence. If it's really time for a change, old carpet can be used in the garden as a mulch to kill off weeds. Be aware, though, that you can't be sure what chemicals have been added to make even a natural-fibre carpet moth-proof or fire retardant.

REUSE UNWANTED BATHROOM FURNITURE

Unwanted sinks, soil pipes and even lavatories can be given a new lease of life as plant pots in the house or the garden. Use containers such as these to pot invasive plants like mint in the ground and keep them away from your other plants.

REPAIR BROKEN ITEMS

When something breaks, try getting it repaired first before you discard it and buy a replacement. In today's consumer culture we are conditioned to immediately replace items that could be fairly easily repaired. Even old furniture can be re-upholstered to give it a new lease of life.

DON'T REPLACE A SHOWER CURTAIN

If you are about to buy a new shower curtain think again before purchasing another plastic version. Plastic production has a major environmental impact so opt for a glass screen instead, with the added advantage of being easier to clean.

RECLAIMED MATERIALS FOR BUILDING PROJECTS
If you are carrying out any renovations on your home, try to buy reclaimed materials. Items such as fixtures and floors are available from salvage and reclamation yards and often you can find far more interesting and individual pieces than you would elsewhere – and for less money, too.

DECORATE WITH ECO PAINTS
Reduce your carbon footprint by up to 30 kg (66 lb) by decorating with eco-paint. Paint production is known to be extremely inefficient in terms of energy use, with the manufacture of 1 tonne of paint producing up to 10 tonnes of waste, much of it toxic.

SAND, DON'T STRIP!
The least environmentally harmful way to remove old paint is to sand it down. Paint-stripping chemicals are damaging to the environment and have been linked with health concerns. Keep the room well ventilated and throw paint shavings away in a sealed container.

FURNISH WITH FSC CERTIFIED WOOD
When buying any wooden furniture or flooring for your home, ensure that it carries the Forest Stewardship Council (FSC) stamp. This means that the wood meets the criteria for environmental, social and economic sustainability and that it is not a product of illegal logging.

ALWAYS RECYCLE UNWANTED PAINT
Never throw unwanted paint away down a drain. See if you can pass it on to any community groups or schools who may be able to use it. Otherwise it should be taken to a recycling centre, where it will almost certainly end up on landfill.

BOOST YOUR INSULATION WITH NATURAL PAINT
Natural paint manufacturers have now developed wall-insulating paint, designed to help regulate the temperature inside the house throughout the year. Ecos Organic Paints (www.ecosorganicpaints.com) claim their version will save between 10 and 30% of energy lost through walls.

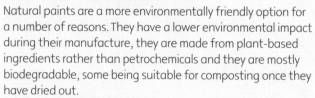

COMPOST LEFTOVER NATURAL PAINTS

Natural paints are a more environmentally friendly option for a number of reasons. They have a lower environmental impact during their manufacture, they are made from plant-based ingredients rather than petrochemicals and they are mostly biodegradable, some being suitable for composting once they have dried out.

PAINT A BETTER PICTURE

Traditional household paints aren't good for your health. In general, they are made using petrochemical-derived ingredients. These solvents contain volatile organic compounds (VOCs) that have been linked with health scares such as cancer as well as respiratory problems, headaches and eye, nose and throat irritation. Water-based paints contain less of these than oil-based.

USE NATURAL FLOORING

To avoid emissions given off by synthetic materials in conventional flooring, choose a natural option such as wood or bamboo. Wood flooring should be certified by the Forest Stewardship Council (FSC) to ensure it comes from a sustainable source. Natural fibres such as sisal, hemp and coir also make good natural floor materials.

RECLAIMED WOODEN FLOORS

If you decide to lay a wooden floor or you need to replace some of your existing floorboards, look out for wooden boards in reclamation yards and salvage stores. This is a great way to give wood a new lease of life and ensures your floor has lots of character.

GIVE YOUR HOME SOME ECO CHIC

Add colour and texture to your home with the addition of eco-friendly upholstery. Cushions made from recycled vintage shirts and ties and throws of 100% recycled wool will give your home a new look without harming the environment. For ideas visit www.ecocentric.co.uk.

LIVING WITHOUT SYNTHETICS

Carpets, paint and vinyl wallpaper can all emit volatile organic compounds (VOCs) and other pollutants that have been linked with asthma and various health concerns. Natural materials are a greener and healthier choice for decorating your home.

MAKE SURE YOUR WORKTOPS ARE RECYCLED

If you are fitting a new kitchen, look out for recycled units and fittings. Worktops made from 100% post-consumer coffee cups or recycled mobile (cell) phones are now available, as are cupboard doors created from recycled yogurt pots. Sinks made from 80% recycled steel, which is endlessly recyclable, are also available.

CHOOSE A WOODEN SLATTED BASE FOR YOUR BED

A wooden bed base not only enables air to circulate around your mattress, it is, of course, made from a sustainable material. Look out for products that carry the Forest Stewardship Council (FSC) mark certifying that the wood is from a sustainable managed source or wood that has been reclaimed.

SWITCH TO A NATURAL-FIBRE MATTRESS

We spend about a third of our lives sleeping so investing in a good-quality mattress makes sense. Cheaper mattresses are often produced from synthetic foam and can contain formaldehyde, pesticides and other chemicals. Mattresses made from natural materials are less likely to cause allergic reactions. If a new mattress has a strange smell that lasts for weeks, call the manufacturer and request an exchange.

ANIMAL DUVETS ARE GREENER
The most eco-friendly duvet fillings are made from goose feathers or down. From an ethical point of view check that the feathers have been gathered from the ground rather than plucked from a live bird. An even more animal-friendly option is to use woollen blankets and organic cotton sheets.

CHOOSE ORGANIC COTTON BEDDING
Pesticides are banned in organic cotton production so make sure you choose organic sheets and towels. The number of cotton farmers suffering acute pesticide poisoning each year is between 25 and 77 million worldwide according to a report published earlier in 2007 by the Environmental Justice Foundation (EJF) and the Pesticide Action Network (PAN).

REDISCOVER CORK TILES
Cork is a sustainable, natural material that comes from the base of the cork tree. Biodegradable and non-polluting, it is an ideal material for use on floors and walls. Cork is made up of millions of air pockets so it also makes a good insulation material, keeping warmth in and noise out.

PICK A NATURAL VARNISH FOR FLOORS
If you have a wooden floor make sure you use a natural varnish to seal it rather than a solvent-based product that may emit pollutants. Natural varnishes contain plant-derived resins and oils and allow the wood to breathe. Wooden furniture and fittings can be finished with beeswax or linseed oil.

CUT OUT CUT FLOWERS
Many cut flowers are flown thousands of miles from large-scale producers in Kenya to Europe, or in South America to North America. This creates emissions caused by "flower miles" made worse by the fact that the flowers have to be refrigerated during transit. Flower producers have also been criticised for their high use of agrochemicals.

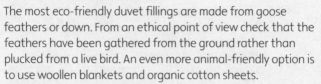

NOT SO FANTASTIC HOME PLASTICS

Whether it's food containers in the kitchen or toothbrush holders in the bathroom, plastic should be avoided whenever possible. It is a by-product of the energy-intensive, high-polluting petroleum industry. Plastics can also emit harmful vapours known as VOCs and some types are extremely difficult, if not impossible, to recycle. AFM SafeCoat in the US and Ecos Organic in the UK are both good zero-VOC paint brands.

WRAP UP IN ORGANIC TOWELS

Unbleached organic cotton towels are the most eco-friendly way to dry off in the bathroom. Cotton production uses vast amounts of pesticides and is a major global pollutant. Buying organic benefits the environment and reduces your exposure to potential pesticide residues.

USE WOOD IN THE BATHROOM

Avoid having lots of unnecessary plastic accessories in your bathroom. Choose wooden soap dishes and toothpaste holders and look for wooden body brushes and natural loofahs rather than plastic varieties. These have the advantage of being sustainable and biodegradable.

GO GREEN FOR FURNITURE

When you are looking for new furniture make sure you pick pieces made from natural, sustainable materials such as untreated wood certified by the Forest Stewardship Council (FSC). If you are renovating furniture, ensure that you use plant-based paints and finishes.

DONATE BUILDING MATERIALS

Unwanted building materials such as rubble and mortar make up a large chunk of the waste problem. If you are renovating your home and have any of these materials left over, advertise them locally or offer them to a local community project who may be able to make good use of them.

recycling & reusing

RECYCLE BY COLLECTION

Where possible, recycle your waste. Paper, plastic, glass and metal can all be recycled and most are collected by doorstep recycling schemes. Remember also to buy products that contain some recycled content, such as toilet paper, in order to close the recycling loop.

REPAIR AND REUSE

Rather than throwing out damaged clothes, make sure they can't be mended first. Even if adding a new zip or patching elbows is beyond your own capabilities, it's worth visiting a seamstress. Really damaged clothing can be ripped up to make household cleaning clothes and dust rags.

WAYS TO USE YOUR OLD PHONE DIRECTORY

There are a number of different uses for out-of-date telephone books. For example, they are good for raising the height of your computer monitor and if you have a compost heap they can be ripped up and added to it. They may also be shredded for use as pet bedding.

REDUCE YOUR JUNK MAIL

A significant amount of junk mail ends up on landfill sites each year. Once there, it biodegrades to produce methane gas, a major contributor to climate change – that's not to mention the resources used to make it, including trees and vast amounts of water. Start by switching to computerized bills.

RECYCLE UNWANTED PAPER

Recycling 1 tonne of paper is estimated to save around 15 average-sized trees. Recycle all your unwanted paper, junk mail and any printing paper you have. This saves energy because recycled paper uses 28 to 70% less energy in production than virgin paper.

FIND WAYS TO DISPOSE OF OLD APPLIANCES

If you have to get rid of an appliance such as a washing machine, make sure you recycle it. If it is still in good working order, offer it to a charity that collects white goods or a community group who may be able to use it. Otherwise, take it to your nearest household recycling centre.

REUSE OLD NEWSPAPERS

Use a log-maker or a plant pot-maker to recycle old newspapers. The main reason to recycle paper is not to save trees – because they are a sustainable crop – it's to reduce the loss of wildlife habitats as old forests are replaced with managed plantations.

BUY RECYCLED TOILET PAPER

Around 270,000 trees are flushed down the drain or end up as rubbish all over the world every day, according to the World Wildlife Fund (WWF). Buying recycled toilet roll will help to reduce illegal logging and boost the market for recycled products.

JOIN A TOY LIBRARY

If your home is gradually filling up with your children's toys, why not investigate the nearest toy library? A toy library will help to reduce waste and save you money in the process. It's also a good way to meet other parents.

REDUCE, REUSE AND RECYCLE

These are the three main rules to keep in mind. Try to reduce the amount of household waste you create by avoiding packaging, over-buying food and recycling as much as you can. Reuse items when possible: for example, yogurt pots make good containers for seedlings.

GIVE YOUR MOBILE (CELL) PHONE TO CHARITY

If you change your handset, be sure to recycle the old one. Millions of phones end up on landfill every year. Many conservationist groups and organizations operate recycling schemes that raise money for specific charities, while phone companies and electronic-goods stores often have recycling bins where you can simply drop off your old phone.

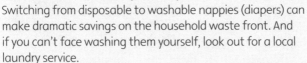

USE WASHABLE NAPPIES (DIAPERS)

Switching from disposable to washable nappies (diapers) can make dramatic savings on the household waste front. And if you can't face washing them yourself, look out for a local laundry service.

BE NEIGHBOURLY

Sharing your tools and DIY equipment with neighbours, friends and family is a good way to cut back on unnecessary "stuff" and the waste it causes. There's no reason why everyone on your street needs to have their own workbench or lawnmower. This is also a good way to boost community spirit.

CREATE YOUR OWN RECYCLING SYSTEM

Make recycling in your home easier by creating your own recycling system. Use boxes that can be carried and emptied easily. Have different containers for materials such as paper, plastic, glass and metal and use stackable bins that take up less space.

PASS ON YOUR READING GLASSES

Thousands of pairs of reading glasses could be used by someone else but they end up on landfill sites instead. Recycle your glasses to help some of the estimated 200 million people around the world who need glasses but can't afford them. Visit Vision Aid Overseas (www.vao.org.uk) or the Lions Club International (www.lionsclubs.org) for more information.

PUT CARDBOARD TO GOOD USE

If your regular recycling scheme doesn't accept cardboard, it's usually possible to find a good home for it elsewhere. It can be broken up and used to prevent weeds in the garden or simply ripped up and added to your compost bin.

REUSE UNWANTED CARPETS

Carpets have a big environmental impact so try to get as much use as possible out of them, even when they're no longer good enough for your home. Use old bits of carpet to line the bottom of cupboards or the boot (trunk) of your car.

JOIN A RECYCLING NETWORK
Stop unwanted items such as furniture and electrical equipment from going to landfill by joining an online recycling forum such as Freecycle. This is a great way to get rid of your "rubbish" as well as to obtain things you really need, thereby reducing waste and saving you money. Visit www.freecycle.com for more information.

rubbish & home waste

USE BIODEGRADABLE BAGS IF YOU CAN
Make sure you buy biodegradable versions of rubbish bags and freezer bags (although ideally you should use a reusable container to store food in the freezer). The same goes for nappy (diaper) sacks, if you are also using them. This means that they will decompose rather than just sit in landfill.

BUY RECYCLED RUBBISH BAGS
Make sure you buy garbage bags and garden sacks made from 100% recycled materials. This will help to close the recycling loop and reduce the plastic waste in landfill. It also saves energy because it's much less intensive to recycle plastic than to make plastic bags from oil.

KEEP DESIGNATED RECYCLING BINS
Separate your waste according to type: paper waste, cans and/or aluminium, plastic and glass. There are now handy receptacles that have three-drawer options and can-crushers too.

DISPOSE OF BATTERIES CAREFULLY
Think twice about disposing of batteries. They are a serious source of toxic waste and should not be thrown in domestic waste receptacles. If they end up on landfill sites they can enter the water system. Find out if your local authority has a facility for toxic-waste disposal, or even better, invest in a battery recharger rather than throwing out batteries.

KNOW WHAT CAN BE RECYCLED

Many items can be recycled, including: clothing and shoes, paper, aluminium cans, plastic carrier bags, cardboard, plastic bottles, glass, household appliances, steel cans and kitchen waste. Use a special disposal service for hazardous materials such as batteries, oil, transmission fluid, paint and paint thinner, and other materials. In the USA, earth911.com has a recycling search guide that allows you to find a place in your area that recycles your item.

indoor pests

NO MORE ANTS

To get rid of ants without resorting to chemicals, locate the entrance to the nest, squeeze a lemon onto it and leave the peel. Ants will also retreat from lines of talcum powder, chalk, bone meal, charcoal dust and cayenne pepper.

SUGAR AWAY INSECTS

Don't use poisonous insecticide powders to kill cockroaches and ants – these might enter the food chain and poison other wildlife, too. Borax mixed with icing (confectioner's) sugar will kill them, but is harmless to other animals.

ANTS IN YOUR PANTS

Common household pesticides can easily find their way into local water sources, sometimes at levels that can harm aquatic life. Don't sprinkle toxic ant powder in your cupboards – hang sage and pennyroyal instead to deter ants – they hate the smell and will leave your food alone.

PLUG AWAY COCKROACHES

To get rid of cockroaches without poison, plug all small cracks along skirting boards (baseboards), wall shelves, cupboards and around pipes, sinks and bathtub fixtures. For a trap, you can try lightly greasing the inner neck of a milk bottle and putting a little stale beer or a raw potato in it.

LEARN TO LIVE WITH SPIDERS

Spiders are great for pest control because of the large number of insects they prey on, including a number of pest species. If you can leave them alone to peacefully co-exist with you in your home, they will help you by catching insects that infest house plants as well as flies. If they live by windows they will prevent pests from entering.

CLOSE YOUR WINDOWS

A sunny window is the most common entrance for flies, so close open windows before the sun hits them during the day. If you stop flies from entering your home in the first place, you won't be tempted to use aerosol insecticides to get rid of them.

POT YOUR MINT

The potent chemical compounds in pesticides are far more harmful to the environment and to you than the insects themselves. For a natural deterrent, if you want your windows open but don't want them to be an invitation to flying pests, grow mint in pots around windows. As mint is a natural insect repellent, this will keep them from entering.

TRAP FRUIT FLIES

For a natural way to trap annoying fruit flies, pour a small amount of beer into a wide-mouthed jar to attract them. Use a rubber band to secure a plastic bag across the mouth of the jar and poke a small hole in the bag. Flies will enter through the hole and not be able to find their way out again.

MAKE SOME FLYPAPER

Use regular sticky flypaper to catch unwelcome flying guests, or better still, make your own by dipping yellow paper into honey. Hang up with a saucer below to catch the excess drip. It may seem a bit messy but it's very effective and all-natural.

TRAP SILVERFISH

To trap silverfish, mix up one part treacle to two parts vinegar. Place the mixture near cracks and holes where pests live. Silverfish can also be repelled by treating table legs and cracks in cupboards with a mixture of borax and honey.

REPEL MOTHS NATURALLY

Moth-proof your clothes using a mixture of lavender oil and cedarwood oil, which are natural moth repellents. Commercial moth repellents usually contain para-dichlorobenzene, a carcinogenic toxic. Very high usage of p-DCB products in the home can result in dizziness, headaches and liver problems.

DON'T SHUT YOUR TRAP

If you leave rodent poison in your kitchen or roof space, you can't control the amount of poison they ingest. You will also run the risk of harm to domestic pets or family members who may encounter the poison. Traps are a much greener way to get rid of them. Alternatively, choose a pest removal company that employs humane, non-toxic methods.

NO MORE MOTHS

To trap moths, mix one part sugar syrup with two parts vinegar and place it in a margarine or yogurt container. Clean it regularly. Cedar chips or black pepper also works well as all-natural moth deterrents – use them in cloth bags placed in drawers or hang them up.

GET HOT WITH PESTS

Instead of using pesticides for house plants, blend two or three very hot chilli peppers, half an onion and a clove of garlic in water. Boil, then allow to cool and transfer to a sealed container. Steep for two days and strain. Used as a spray, this liquid is good for indoor and outdoor plants and can be frozen for future use.

GET RID OF FLIES
Instead of using poisonous aerosol fly spray, make a package of cloves, eucalyptus and peppermint to hang in kitchen cupboards and drawers as a deterrent.

BAY AWAY WEEVILS
Steer clear of insecticides that can leak poisons into the food chain. As a harmless way to keep weevils out of your flour, rice and pulses, simply add dried bay leaves to the containers in which you store them.

WASH AWAY FLEAS
If your pets are infested with ticks or fleas, prepare a herbal rinse by steeping rosemary in boiling water and allowing it to cool. Wash the pet well with soap and warm water, dry thoroughly, then apply the rinse. Do not towel down your pet, as this will remove the residue, but make sure your pet is dry before letting him out.

BURN AWAY MOZZIES
Instead of smothering yourself in chemical mosquito repellents or worse using electric mosquito repellent, burn citronella candles or use citronella oil to stop mosquitos in their tracks. The oils from the citronella plant are used to make topical lotions and sprays but choose a brand without further additives.

PEPPER YOUR WEEVILS
Beans and grains are weevil favourites. To keep the pests away, hang small cloth sacks containing black pepper in your food containers or in your storage cupboards. Alternatively, add soapberries to cupboards because weevils hate the smell.

KEEP CLOTHES CLEAN
Moths are attracted to body oils on clothing, so keep vulnerable clothes clean, dry and well aired to avoid attack. Camphor can be used as it is the major non-toxic ingredient in mothballs.

GET MINTED
Peppermint oil is an excellent deterrent of rats and mice. Sprinkle your roof space and cupboards regularly with peppermint to keep them away.

home entertainment

DOWNLOAD MUSIC
With modern technology it's easier to download pretty much any kind of music you want to listen to rather than to buy the actual CD, or at least, download every other album you purchase. This helps to cut down on waste, as well as the energy used during production and transportation of hard copies.

GREEN MULTIMEDIA
In these days of the iPod you can still be green and wired for sound – and audio too, for that matter. Invest in a wind-up Eco Media Player, designed by Trevor Baylis, the originator of the Freeplay technology (available from www.ecotopia.co.uk). You can watch movies or music videos, look at photo albums and listen to your choice of music or radio via this technology.

REUSE YOUR OLD CDS
Each year billions of unwanted CDs are produced – a substantial portion being sent to the landfill. If you can't locate a recycling scheme, use them as coasters for cups and glasses, underneath plant pots or as reflectors in your driveway.

GET WOUND-UP
Avoid the need for mains power or even batteries by investing in some wind-up technology. Wind-up radios, torches and lights are widely available having been introduced by the Freeplay Foundation, which developed the technology to improve communication in the world's poorest communities.

HAVE AN EARLY NIGHT
Rather than sitting up with the heating, TV and lighting on, why not revitalize with an early night once or twice a week and save some energy in the process? Reading with the aid of task lighting rather than watching TV under a bright light also saves energy.

SWITCH OFF YOUR PHONE CHARGER
Make sure you switch your phone charger off at the wall when your phone isn't plugged into it, otherwise you are simply powering thin air. Around 95% of the energy used by mobile (cell) phone chargers is wasted with only 5% being used to charge the phone itself.

DONATE YOUR OLD MAGAZINES
If your household gets through a lot of magazines, why not pass them on to your local doctor, dentist or hospital? Otherwise they may be recycled via most collection schemes or at recycling centres. Magazines can also be used as alternative wrapping paper and are sometimes appreciated by nurseries and schools who use them in creative projects.

REDISCOVER YOUR LIBRARY
We live in a consumer culture but do you really need shelves and shelves of books and DVDs that you rarely watch again? Libraries lend CDs and DVDs and are a great way to cut back on your conspicuous consumption without missing out on the latest releases.

TRY BORROWING INSTEAD OF BUYING
Ask around to see if you can borrow books, magazines, video games, newspapers, CDs or DVDs from friends or neighbours before buying. There are also exchange shops where you can swap your DVD or book for another, such as www.swaptree.com and bookmooch.com.

the work commute

RACK IT UP
Petition your boss to put up a well-lit bike rack close to your office building, if not inside. Having a safe place to store bikes might encourage more people to cycle to and from work, and so help reduce pollution.

BE A TELECOMMUTER
To cut down on pollution caused by your daily commute to work, investigate the possibility of telecommuting one or two days a week by working from home or a local office. Email and video-conferencing from a home webcam makes this more viable than ever before.

JUMP IN THE POOL
Some people manage to cut the energy they use to commute to work by car-pooling. When four or five people go in one car rather than separate vehicles, it cuts down on air pollution. In addition, all the cars in the pool will benefit from lower mileage and petrol (gasoline) expenses.

JOIN A FRIEND
Commuting is a major cause of traffic pollution. If every person in the UK who regularly drives to work on their own were to get a lift with someone else just once a week, it would reduce traffic by 12% to 15% during rush hour, meaning less greenhouse gas emissions.

COMMUTE THE GREEN WAY
Walk or ride your bicycle to work instead of taking the car. If you have a long way to travel, trains and buses are better than cars because they cut down your pollution impact.

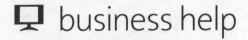 # business help

MAKE SOME SENSE
Ask your company to swap their water-wasting taps (faucets)
for sensor varieties, which release water only when you put your
hands in front of them. If your company has shower facilities or
is installing them, timed sensors can also be used there, which
automatically turn off after a few minutes. People will soon adjust
to taking shorter showers and conserving water in the process.

GLOVE UP SAFELY
If latex gloves are being used in your place of work, make
it plain, non-PVC versions. Avoid powdered gloves or those
containing vinyl – they can release poisons when incinerated.

OUTSOURCE CAREFULLY
Many offices outsource their cleaning and maintenance. Make
sure the contractor your company chooses is taking steps to
protect the environment by minimizing their use of chemicals in
the products they use. If not, ask them to consider swapping to
a contractor who does.

CLEAN GREEN
Encourage your office to implement green cleaning materials
and practices. For instance, alternating the use of an electric
vacuum cleaner with that of a mechanical carpet sweeper will
help cut electricity by half.

GET A MICRO MINI
Microfibre mops are a new invention. They have washable
cloths, minimizing waste and detergent use, so are great for
public areas. Make sure your cleaners at work are using them,
or encourage them to change.

TIME OUT
Install a timer programme for lights, computers, printers and
other electrical items to shut down for the night and weekend.
The system can be overridden if individuals are still working,
but it ensures that CO_2 emissions and energy costs are cut.

CHOOSE A GREEN COURIER

If your office sends packages by courier, try to use a bicycle courier rather than cars or motorbikes in an attempt to reduce environmental pollution.

AUDIT YOUR ENERGY

Get your employer to do an energy audit or bring in a specialist carbon footprinter to advise managers on where they can make changes that will help the environment. An audit will show you problems that may, when corrected, save money.

FIX IT

Use reusable fixers like staples, string, paper clips or non-toxic adhesive instead of clear sticky tape, which produces toxins when it's manufactured, can only be used once and doesn't biodegrade.

BE AN OFFICE ANGEL

Don't complain about those fluorescent office lights – in fact, they're extremely energy efficient. But often they are too heavily used – try to use some portions only, or take out every other strip.

DON'T LEAVE IT ON

Make a sign for your office door that says "Last one out, turn off the lights" – often office lights burn right through the night. This will remind cleaners who work in the evening to turn out lights, too.

SHUT DOWN

Encourage your colleagues to shut down their computers when they're not in use unless they've got a low-energy sleep option. This should be done before lunchtime breaks and in particular before going home at the end of the day.

TAP THE PROBLEM

Water tap (faucet) aerators reduce the amount of water used by creating an illusion of more water flow. This is particularly important in a large building with public toilets, as these are often hotbeds of water wastage.

FAN YOURSELF COOL

A ceiling fan in an office is a better choice than air conditioning because it uses far less electricity. It moves the air around the room to produce draughts that are cooling – a healthier choice than artificial cooling.

DON'T DISPOSE OF FILTERS

Instead of disposable paper filters in your office coffee machine, use mesh or permanent cloth. Otherwise it means throwing a filter away every time you've made a cup of coffee.

DRY THE SENSOR WAY

Make sure your office toilets don't have throw-away paper towels. Request sensor dryers that automatically release air if you put your hands in front of the sensor, but don't waste energy at other times.

DON'T PICK YOUR SPOTS

Instead of energy-guzzling spotlights, offices should choose smaller power-saving spotlight bulbs that use only 11 watts. This simple change could mean that the office uses a tenth of the energy it used to for lighting

SAY NO TO SOLVENTS

Instead of solvent-based markers, use crayons, china markers or coloured pencils. They will help the air in the office stay free of chemicals.

USE LEAD REFILLS

Disposable pencils waste wood as you are never able to use every last bit of them. Opt for a metal refillable pencil instead. It's always sharp and you won't waste any lead because you can use it all.

SHARE A PAPER

Instead of everyone in the office buying their own newspaper, leave one copy in the staff room or reception area so that staff can share the news during lunch and coffee breaks.

SORT YOUR ENVELOPES

One of the major turn-offs to reusing envelopes is that you can never lay your hands on one of the right size. Create an envelope sorting system for your used envelopes so you can choose the size you need with little fuss.

A MUG'S GAME

Instead of relying on disposable polystyrene or plastic cups at work, take in your own ceramic or china mug so you can sip with a free conscience!

USE A GLASS

Instead of a water dispenser with throw-away paper or plastic cups, keep a supply of glasses nearby and encourage people to use them instead. Alternatively, fill up with your own reusable water bottle.

TAKE A LUNCH BOX

Take your packed lunch to work in a reusable container instead of clingfilm (plastic wrap). A plastic container is useful but metal is a better choice in terms of reducing toxins.

DON'T GO FOR THE BURN

If your office has waste that is usually incinerated, remember that this process releases poisonous dioxins. Encourage your bosses to explore alternatives to incineration.

USE YOUR WASTE CAREFULLY

Some energy manufacturers now use modern techniques like pyrolysis to produce energy from commercial waste like shredded rubber, sewage sludge, wood wastes and chicken litter. Make sure your company makes the most of its waste.

TICK THE BOX

Do an office inventory with a column titled "throwing away" and one titled "recycling". Every time you throw something away or recycle it, put a tick in the appropriate column. Your aim should be to have more recycling ticks.

TAKE STOCK
Why not run an office competition to get everyone to make a list of everything they throw away during the course of a day? The idea is to go through this list to see if they could be recycling any of the items.

TALK ABOUT IT
Help educate your colleagues about the environment by making a point of telling them when you're making a decision based on green issues. They may start taking your point of view on board.

POST A NOTICE
Why not set up an environmental bulletin board where you can post notices about local environmental meetings, news and green tips? It will encourage your co-workers to think about their impact on the environment.

INVEST ETHICALLY
Encourage your company pension plan to invest ethically – in other words, investments made with companies who make it their business not to harm the environment.

MAKE GREEN BUSINESS DECISIONS
Take a closer look at the companies you do business with – are they making any effort to be environmentally friendly? Don't make business decisions based on cost and customer service alone – take green issues into account as well.

TALK TO THE BOARD
Lobby your company's directors to set up a committee or bring in a specialist to monitor its environmental performance and take steps to minimize the effect on the environment.

JOIN A CLUB
Why not encourage your company to join the World Wildlife Fund's international network for reducing one's carbon footprint? They help businesses across the globe to become more environmentally friendly.

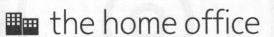 

the home office

USE NATURAL LIGHT
Natural light is known to increase productivity. Place your computer near a window so you can illuminate your monitor by natural rather than artificial light, and you'll save on your electricity bill, too. If the glare is too harsh to see the screen, simply turn your desk so you are facing the window.

IONIZE YOUR OFFICE SPACE
Make sure you keep house plants in your office as they will help counteract the negative radiation effects of electrical equipment in a small space. Or invest in an ionizer that does the same job (preferably a solar-powered one).

GET GEEKY WITH YOUR MUSIC
Don't use a separate radio or CD player in your home office. These require batteries and are energy inefficient. Most PCs are now geared up for you to listen to radio, CD or download music as you work, meaning you're only using one source of power.

LIMIT CD BURNING
Instead of buying CDs to transfer data from home to business offices, download your files onto a USB thumb drive or MP3 player (many can act as mini hard drives). You'll save on CD wastage and reduce the environmental pollutants released in their manufacture.

DON'T BE A LASER HEAD
Ozone damages the natural balance of the atmosphere's top layers and takes many years to break down. Because laser printers release ozone into the environment, they're best avoided. If you already have one, use it only when really necessary.

FAN YOUR WORKSPACE
If you can't open a window to increase air circulation and reduce radiation effects, install a ceiling fan or use a desk fan to help create gentle air turbulence.

WORK ASPECTS

Try to position your home office in the sun-facing portion of
your house where it will get as much natural light as possible
during the day. (This means south-facing in the northern
hemisphere, or north-facing in the southern hemisphere.)
Open windows to encourage fresh air and good ventilation
around the electrical machinery.

GET FRESH IN THE OFFICE

When you're thinking about planning your home office,
remember that synthetic carpets, petroleum-based paint and
poor ventilation can all contribute to tiredness and nausea – try
to maximize on fresh air and natural fibres.

WARM YOUR WATER

Use natural materials and water in your office to maintain
humidity. Water droplets in the air will help you to reduce ion
depletion caused by electrical equipment. A fresh bowl of warm
water on the floor or desk is a good way to do this.

HAVE A CUPPA

Drink a cup of tea or coffee by your computer! Steam from your
hot drink is absorbed into the air around you and reduces the
effects of radiation, restoring the natural balance.

BUY RECONDITIONED

Instead of buying a new PC when yours needs replacing,
consider investing in a reconditioned machine. Nowadays, many
reconditioned computers are just as powerful but you won't be
wasting all that plastic and metal casing, and you'll save money.

USE A DESK LIGHT

In your home office, try to use desk lights instead of overhead
lights. The latter use larger bulbs and therefore take up more
energy. Remember that it's better for your eyes not to have too
much glare on the screen, too.

REDUCE YOUR ELECTRICS

All electrical equipment releases electromagnetic radiation, thought to be damaging to health if it permeates your home. Use it as little as possible, and reduce the effects by sitting in front of your screen rather than to the side of it. Also, sit well back, away from the screen.

FLATTEN OUT YOUR VISION

Flat screens use less energy and emit less radiation than standard monitors, so replace your TV and PC screens with flat screens if you can. A smaller screen is usually a better choice as it uses less power to do the same job.

SEND APPLIANCES TO SLEEP

While computers are not being used they can "sleep" rather than employ an active desktop or screensaver. The sleep mode allows your monitor go to sleep when not in use, and to re-launch very quickly. The sleep function can reduce energy wastage by 65%.

SEND A MESSAGE

Send emails instead of relying on the postal service, particularly when you are writing to people in other countries where planes are being used to transport the post, thereby hiking up the environmental cost.

UNPLUG YOUR EQUIPMENT

If your electrical equipment doesn't have a sleep function (note that this is not the same as standby, which uses energy), make sure you turn it off and unplug it when it's not in use.

SLEEP ELECTRICITY-FREE

It's not known how harmful electromagnetic radiation from equipment in your home can be, but it's worth keeping machines away from sleeping areas to reduce possible effects while you sleep.

KEEP IT REAL

Wood effect finishes can give off compounds (called VOCs) that release toxins and so pollute the environment. Choose natural solid wood, metal or glass for your desk at home.

BULK IT UP

Order supplies for your home office in bulk rather than ordering single items when you run out. That way, your transportation costs will be kept to a minimum because of reduced delivery runs.

DO SOME SOLAR SUMS

Choose a solar-powered calculator rather than one that relies on chemical batteries. Calculators require very little power to keep working and most now have solar panels.

BE A CLEAN FREAK

Clean and dust your computer regularly to ensure optimal functioning. Don't forget the area behind the screen and where the wires join the base at the back as dirt and dust can easily accumulate here.

RECYCLE YOUR INK

Choose a company that recycles printer cartridges – most now run recycling schemes by which you can send back your printer cartridges to a central base to be reused and resold. This is essential to cut down on the amount of plastic thrown away.

DON'T CHOOSE COMPOSITE

Don't buy a desk made with composite materials that may use PVC in their manufacture, but choose solid wood acquired from a sustainable source.

CORRECT THE GREEN WAY
Aim to use correction tape that covers errors or lifts them off without the use of solvents. When you must use fluid, the water-based type made for photocopiers is better than solvent based, as both the manufacture and disposal of the latter have detrimental effects on the environment. Water-based varieties are better for your health as well.

HIRE A CARPENTER
Instead of spending lots of money on a new desk for your office, do your bit for the recycling movement by investing in some salvaged wood and paying a carpenter to make you one to measure – it will have the added advantage of fitting the space exactly.

TRAY A BIT HARDER
When you're choosing trays to organize your paperwork, select those made from metal or wood rather than plastic. Not only does this help limit our reliance on plastic products but it looks more attractive, too.

INVEST IN A PEN
Instead of disposable pens that are thrown away after only a short period of use, buy refillable ones. Although they cost more, you can choose a design of pen you really like, knowing that you'll enjoy using it for longer.

FILE DOWN YOUR METAL
To do your filing without a guilty conscience, buy metal filing cabinets with recycled paper suspension files. They last for many years – and it is quite easy to purchase them second hand.

SET UP A SYSTEM

Organize a paper recycling system for your home office, separating card and paper into specific piles to make sure you aren't being tempted to throw it away with your office rubbish. Or invest in a separate recycling bin so you can set aside anything that can be recycled.

STICK IT NATURALLY

Choose natural glue made from animal or vegetable products rather than glue created from chemicals. In general, those in sticks or pots are better than those in tubes.

STICK ON SOME LABELS

Use stickers to label files and folders instead of plastic tags. A better choice than ready-glued would be gummed versions that you wet on the back (like you do envelopes). Or better still, use a paper clip to attach loose paper as a label.

KEY IN YOUR DATA

Use a USB key for your PC instead of a CD-Rom or DVD-Rom, which is larger and therefore requires more packaging and transportation costs.

DON'T TRASH YOUR DISKS

Computer disks take an average of 450 years to degrade, and while they do so they can leach damaging oxides into water supplies and so threaten wildlife. Electronic waste includes toxins such as mercury, lead and cadmium – all which can have a hazardous effect on the environment and health. Reuse or send to a recycling programme. Some recycling centres supply the disks as materials to be re-made into useful objects. Remember to clear your computer drive before recycling.

CHOOSE A SCHEME

Wherever you can, make sure you choose recyclable items and subscribe to schemes – usually it will save you money as well. Many companies now have "take back" recycling schemes for plastic pen casings, floppy discs, rewritable CDs and other office materials. The amount of bulk material a company produces makes recycling even more important.

RECYCLE YOUR MAT

Many companies offer mouse mats made from recycled plastic. If you have an infra-red mouse, you don't need a mat at all. Some "print your own" companies now also offer mats from recycled materials, so choose one if it's available.

PASS IT ON LOCALLY

Before you throw out your computer, check out any local IT recycling schemes in your area. If you want to donate your machine to be reconditioned for re-sale, your local computer technician or repair shop should be able to point you in the right direction.

DONATE YOUR PC

When you've finished with your computer, instead of throwing it on the scrap heap, why not donate it to a school, charity or children's group? That way, others benefit from your trash and you won't feel guilty about wastage.

SEND BACK YOUR PHONE

Make sure you recycle your mobile (cell) phone when you've finished with it. Although the metal isn't toxic, LCD screens and batteries will release toxins into the environment as they break down. Your phone operator should be able to help.

paper & stationery supplies

GET AGRO FOR AGRIFIBRES

Try to buy non-wood (wood-free) paper whenever you can. Alternative materials include hemp, kenaf, agricultural residues and even denim scraps. Many agrifibres yield more pulp per acre than forests or tree farms, and they require fewer pesticides and herbicides.

SUPPORT TREES

Buy paper with at least 30% post-consumer recycled content, and encourage your school or workplace to do the same. This way you will support the paper recycling industry and save trees.

SORT OUT YOUR LEAVES

Did you know there are nine different grades of paper? Most of the time recycling centres will do the sorting for you but it helps them if, in advance, you can loosely sort your paper into different types like white, newspapers and glossy magazines and flyers. At the very least divide your paper into black printed and colour printed.

THIN OUT YOUR PAPER

Always buy the thinnest variety of recycled paper for your printer. The thinner the paper, the less paper is used per sheet and so wastage is reduced. Save thick versions for printing important documents.

COPY LESS

Wherever you can, reduce the number of copies of documents you make to the absolute minimum. In your next meeting, could one copy be shared between two people? Can you present a report in a digital form, such as a power point presentation or an email, rather than as a hard copy?

KEEP A BIN
Make sure your office has a paper recycling bin that's emptied regularly. If the bin starts to overflow, colleagues will stop using it.

REMEMBER THE SCRAPS
It takes 28% less energy to recycle than to produce paper from scratch, so do recycle all office paper, including envelopes, packaging, magazines and newspapers.

PAPER CUT
Paper comprises over 40% of solid waste in the USA (about 72 million tons annually). With little discernable difference in quality, there's no excuse not to buy recycled whenever you can.

BACK-UP LISTS
Don't put used envelopes in the recycling bin straight away – make the best use of them by using the blank back for to-do lists or shopping lists.

USE EVERY INCH
Use paper as many times as you can. For example, if you're throwing away a letter that only takes up half a page, cut off the blank piece and use it for lists and scrap paper before you recycle.

DROP A FONT SIZE
Dropping a font size when printing your documents – and going for less space between the lines – means you save both ink and paper. This is a good option for documents you are reviewing or using as back-up hard copy rather than sending out. Choosing a font with thin letters rather than thick, rounded ones will help you save paper because more words will fit onto a page. Next time you're producing a document, experiment with fonts to see which takes up least space.

THINK OUTSIDE THE ENVELOPE
Envelopes can be reused many times by pasting labels over the address, then adding your own postage. Open them with an envelope opener rather than tearing to keep them in good condition for longer. Envelope reuse labels are available from Friends of the Earth at www.foe.org and www. ecotopia.co.uk.

MAKE BEST USE OF PAPER

Paper can only be recycled four to six times before it's useless, so make sure you use as much of it as you can. Make it a rule of thumb never to throw away a blank piece of paper.

THINK LESS INK

Most modern printers have a draft output option that uses less ink than regular printing. Unless you need to use the extra ink for photos or presentations, click the draft option for everyday printing.

PRINT DOUBLE-SIDED

Make sure you print on both sides of paper. Most printers have double-sided printing functions, or you can do it yourself by printing alternate pages and running the paper through twice.

LOOK ONLINE FOR NEWS

Instead of buying a paper-heavy newspaper, read your news online, watch it on television or subscribe to a telephone text or email messaging service to keep you updated on current issues.

GO DIGITAL

Take digital photographs and store them on your PC or in albums online. You can share them with your friends and family without wasting film and paper. If you must have paper albums, keep waste to a minimum and print only those that you really want to keep.

INVEST IN A SHREDDER

It may be worth investing in a paper shredder if you keep small pets such as rabbits or guinea pigs. You can use the shredded paper as pet bedding and the soiled bedding may then be composted in the garden.

USE BOTH SIDES

Think carefully before you print – do you really need a hard copy of that email? If you do have to print out documents make sure you use both sides of the paper if possible and always buy recycled printing paper. Have a recycling bin handy to make it easier to do the right thing.

computers & hardware

GO NATURAL IN THE OFFICE

Green PCs are made using low-energy components and use up to 75% less energy than a typical PC. For a green office, team your PC with a bamboo keyboard and monitor plus a recycled car tyre mouse mat. Visit greenpc.org for a range of new, refurbished and second-user computer equipment.

LOOK OUT FOR THE ENERGY STAR

When you are buying equipment such as a PC, make sure it has the Energy Star mark (see also www.energystar.gov). Products that carry this international mark, which was developed by the Environmental Protection Agency (EPA) in the US, are proven to be more energy-efficient than others.

USE THE 15-MINUTE RULE

Appliances such as computers, printers and scanners all use energy so it's vital that you turn them off when they're not in use. The general rule is that if you're not going to use something for 15 minutes or more, switch it off rather than leaving it on standby, and save energy.

MULTITASK

If possible, have your home computer in a room that is used for other activities such as watching TV or eating. This means you won't have to waste extra energy heating and lighting a separate space just so you can use the computer.

CHOOSE A GREEN ISP

If you have a home computer look for a green service provider for your Internet access and email. Find one that uses energy-saving business practices such as encouraging staff to use public transport and carbon offsetting. Visit www.greenisp.net for more information.

EXTEND THE LIFE OF YOUR COMPUTER

When choosing IT equipment, always look for items that can be upgraded. You should be able to add extra memory or a larger hard drive to your computer. If you can't upgrade it satisfactorily, donate it to a community group or school.

GET A BUS TIMETABLE

Leave your car at home for meetings, and pin up your local bus timetable somewhere that you can easily see it. Short journeys are often easier by public transport, especially if you know when exactly the next bus or train is due.

USE REFILLED PRINTER CARTRIDGES

Where possible, buy refilled printer cartridges for your home computer. This will help to reduce waste and often they have the advantage of being cheaper than brand new cartridges. It's also important to send off your old cartridges to be refilled. Visit www.cartridgeworld.org for more information.

CHOOSE A LAPTOP

A laptop consumes fives times less energy than a desktop PC; though not quite as powerful, they make up for that in versatility. Or consider a small-form-factor (SFF) desktop computer (such as the Apple Mac Mini), which relies on energy-efficient notebook components.

AVOID HAZARDOUS MATERIALS

In Europe, Restriction of Hazardous Substances (RoHS)-approved products exclude such harmful substances as lead, mercury and cadmium, and must use 65 % or more reusable or recyclable components. In the USA look for models selected by the EPA's Electronic Product Environmental Assessment Tool (EPEAT), which is based on RoHS standards.

Gardening

ARE YOU UP TO DATE on insecticide-free pest control? Do you know the secrets of good composting? Are you working with nature and ecosystems? If you want to garden in an environmentally conscious, organic and sustainable way, then this section contains a wealth of practical tips that will set you on the path to becoming a truly "green" gardener. Not only does responsible gardening enable you to grow food free from chemicals and pesticides, reduce pollution, recycle your food scraps and garden cuttings into crops that will grow more food and create a haven for wildlife, but it will also put you in touch with nature and its cycles, and allow you to contribute to a cleaner global environment.

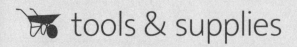 tools & supplies

BE CAREFUL HOW YOU BAG IT
A lot of lugging things round goes on in a garden – prunings to the compost, harvested veg to the kitchen, leaves to your leafmould container. Instead of using plastic sacks to carry these items, look for eco-friendly alternatives such as long-lasting trugs created from recycled plastic or tyres, woven bags made of recycled plastic and biodegradable jute leaf and hessian sacks.

GET TOOLED UP
Choose garden tools made from sustainable wood or recycled plastic and rubber, not PVC, especially for water-containing items like rain buckets and hoses, as well as compost bins.

SAVE ON PLASTIC LABELS
Instead of buying plastic plant labels to mark where you have planted your seeds, consider investing in labels that you can re-use, such as hand-carved green oak labels. Or make your own by cutting strips from old margarine or ice-cream tubs. Children's wooden ice-lolly (popsicle) sticks are also worth saving for this purpose and they will biodegrade.

CUT BACK ON YOUR KIT
Try to avoid using electrical tools such as leaf blowers and vacuums, hedge trimmers, shredders, brush cutters and pressure washers in the garden. There will always be an alternative way to get the same job done without using electrical power.

INVEST IN PAPER BAGS
You can buy brown paper (grocery) bags cheaply online and they are invaluable in the garden. Store saved seeds in them over the winter, for example, or use them to bag up fruit from your own trees to give to visitors or neighbours. Once used, they can then be added to your compost.

 soil care

PROTECT YOUR SOIL
In nature, it can take around 1,000 years to produce 2.5 cm (1 in) of topsoil so protect your soil with an organic mulch like straw, bark or leaves. This will keep it from being eroded by wind and drying out in the sun. Also, be sure to stockpile and reuse topsoil if you are having work done in the garden.

DON'T OVERDIG
While turning the soil, breaking up any large clods and digging in compost can help improve soil structure, there is some evidence that digging too often will have the opposite effect, so give your spade a rest. Instead, spread manure or compost over the surface of the bed and allow the worms to transport the manure deep down into the soil.

AVOID PEAT
In the UK and Ireland, over 94% of peatbogs have been damaged or destroyed in order to keep gardeners supplied with peat, which is used as a soil improver, mulch and growing medium. But these bogs are important sites for wildlife and also help absorb carbon dioxide from the atmosphere. It can take from 7,000 to 10,000 years to produce a layer of peat 7–10 m (23–33 ft) thick. In the US, most of the peat comes from Canada, where it is strictly regulated, but it still takes many years for a bog to recover. The message is, don't use peat in your garden.

FORK YOUR SOIL
Forking compost and other organic material into your garden soil will help because it breaks up clumps of hard earth to encourage better drainage, and it boosts circulation and humidity levels, meaning you'll have to water less. Adding compost can overcome some typical soil problems as it can help improve clay soils by making them lighter and by helping sandy soils retain water. Composting supplies nutrients to plants and encourages strong healthy growth.

EXPLORE PEAT-FREE ALTERNATIVES

For improving soil and planting, look for peat-free "multipurpose composts", which include coir-based mixtures, or use your own compost of leaf mould. For mulching, try bark products, cocoa shells, pebbles or cardboard. To increase soil acidity, try pine needles or composted heather or bracken.

DIG YOURSELF GREEN

Digging is perhaps the single most important thing you can do to condition your soil. Use a shovel or hoe to turn over and break up soil. This will add air pockets, which help to repel root-dwelling insects and oxygenate soil, which in turn encourages plants to set down healthy roots.

mulches, feeds & fertilizers

GET MULCHING

Stop weeds in their tracks, reduce water evaporation from your soil and prevent soil erosion by using a mulch on top of your beds and borders. Organic mulches gradually biodegrade and help soil structure – they include compost, leaves, bark chippings, straw, manure and recycled woodchip. Other mulches include landscape fabric and products made from recycled rubber tyres.

MAKE LEAF MOULD

Let your autumn leaves rot down to make leaf mould – a good soil improver, lawn conditioner and mulch. You can use all sorts of leaves but avoid evergreen leaves such as holly, laurel or Leyland cypress and other conifers as they take much longer to decay. Keep them in tied black plastic sacks (with a few holes in the side) or a wire mesh leaf mould bin, or buy a loose-weave jute sack that will biodegrade. Leaves are slower to rot than other compost items, taking a year or two, so they are best recycled separately.

CARPET DANGERS

Using carpets as mulch on your vegetable patch, especially if allowed to decompose over time, is not such a good idea. Many carpets, including those made of natural fibres, are treated with toxic moth repellents and fire retardants. Safer alternatives include cardboard over newspaper, weed-control fabrics and permeable mulch matting that can be reused.

DON'T USE FERTILIZERS

The manufacture and distribution of artificial nitrogen fertilizers requires large amounts of energy, but some studies estimate that only half the amount of fertilizer is actually used by the plants. The rest can be washed away into rivers and streams, causing pollution. An organic garden should get all its nutrient needs from recycled organic materials such as compost and manure. However, you can buy organic fertilizers to correct major deficiencies.

A COMFREY TEA FEED

The herb comfrey can make a valuable liquid feed. Take a tub, fill it with 3 kg (6½ lb) comfrey leaves and 45 litres (95 pints) of water, then leave for three to five weeks – it won't smell too good, so keep a lid on it! Strain or use a ladle to remove the resulting liquid, which can be used as a feed for tomatoes, runner or dwarf beans and potatoes.

NETTLE METTLE

Nettles make a good liquid feed as well, especially young nettles cut in spring as this is when they have the highest levels of major nutrients. Leave 1 kg (2 lb) to steep in 10 litres (21 pints) of water. Cover with a lid and use after two weeks. But don't forget to dilute it first – one part nettle liquid to ten parts water.

FEED PLANTS WORM TEA

The liquid that comes out of a wormery can be diluted (one part to ten parts water) to feed your plants. Remove the rich, crumbly compost every six months or so from the wormery. Just make sure you pick out the worms and then put them back in with layers of cardboard, a bit of soil and some kitchen leftovers.

RAISE YOUR PH WITH EGGS

The ground limestone used by organic gardeners to add lime to their soil requires large amounts of fossil fuel to quarry, grind and transport. Instead, add egg shells (local organic, of course) to your compost heap and spread the compost over your soil.

ASK FOR LEAVES

As well as collecting fallen leaves from your garden and pavements to make leaf mould, try asking your local authority for leaves that have been collected from parks and cemeteries. Or why not arrange a leaf-gathering event at your local school or community woodland? Avoid those collected from roads, which may contain unwanted contaminants.

KNOW YOUR MANURE

While animal manure can be a great way to improve your soil, it is essential that you check where it's coming from. Manure from a non-organic farm is likely to be polluted with residues of veterinary products, such as antibiotics that are fed to most intensively reared farm animals on a daily basis, or the remains of toxic worming products. Get your manure from an organic farm or a local source that can provide guarantees regarding its purity.

HEAP IT HIGH

To get the best out of your manure you should compost or stack it so that the nutrients in it are stabilized. This also helps break down any harmful residues that it may contain. To stack it, mix the manure with bedding material such as straw and leave, covered, for six months. You may need to leave it for at least a year if wood shavings are the bedding material as they are slow to break down.

GROW GREEN MANURES

Rather than leaving your bed empty over winter, grow a green manure. These are plants grown specifically to improve the soil, and are dug back into the soil in early spring. Benefits include: adding nitrogen to the soil by absorbing it from the air and "fixing" it in their roots, improving soil structure, smothering weeds, protecting soil from heavy rain and preventing nutrients leaching out of the soil into streams and rivers; also providing a home to wildlife. Try clover, alfalfa, mustard, buckwheat and tares.

composting

MAKE FRIENDS WITH WORMS

Worms can do the composting for you – 500 g (1 lb) of composting worms will eat about 1–1.5 kg (2–3 lb) of waste a week. You can buy wormeries (worm bins) or make your own (but don't use garden worms as they won't survive). Either way they require constant warmth, moisture and darkness. A wormery doesn't need much outdoor space either – it will fit on a balcony or even sit indoors.

DON'T WASTE YOUR WASTE

If you're not going to compost your garden waste, don't just dump it in with your other trash. Take it to your nearest municipal tip where they will have facilities for it to be collected and composted. Or find out if there's a community composting project in your area that would be happy to take the waste.

BONFIRES ARE BAD

Burning your garden waste is not only a waste of good composting material, it also produces smoke-containing pollutants such as carbon monoxide. And by producing carbon dioxide and heat, it does little to reduce global warming.

MAKE COMPOST

Making your own compost is the easiest and best way to give your plants the greatest possible soil. Around 45% of most household rubbish could actually go straight into a compost bin, which saves the energy needed to collect and process what would otherwise be destined to clog up landfill space.

MAKE YOUR OWN COMPOST

Instead of buying peaty compost, make your own compost using garden cuttings and kitchen peelings which would otherwise be thrown away. Yard trimmings, leaves and selected food scraps can all be composted, including fruit scraps, vegetable scraps, coffee grounds, stale bread and eggshells. Do not include meat, bones or fat. Compost makes an excellent growing medium for seeds and plants and acts as a soil enricher.

HEAP O' COMPOST

If you throw away your kitchen waste (vegetable and fruit peelings and cereals) or flush it down the drain with a masher system, it will only add to landfill and pollute waterways. Composting the waste is the most environmentally friendly option. Refrain from adding cooked food as it attracts vermin. Materials that should only be composted in limited amounts include wood ashes, which is a source of lime, sawdust, which requires extra nitrogen, plants treated with herbicides (the chemicals need time for thorough decomposition) and shredded non-recyclable paper.

HEAP UP YOUR LEAVES

Don't burn your leaves in the autumn as this contributes to air pollution. Instead, add them to a compost heap where they can biodegrade and so enhance your soil in years to come. Fallen leaves carry 50 to 80% of the nutrients a tree extracts from the soil and air, including carbon, potassium, and phosphorus. A mulch of leaves spread over a garden limits weed growth, adds organic matter and protects the soil.

PAPER CHASE

If you have a compost heap, don't forget to add dry items like newspaper. The best way to get the right balance is to collect kitchen waste in sheets of newspaper, fold them up and then add to the heap. Shredded paper will break down much easier. It is common to add too much newspaper, so recycle it instead if you have a lot you need to dispose of. Don't add glossy, laminated, treated or coloured pages, such as comics, to your compost.

INSTALL A FOOD DIGESTER

You can recycle all your food, including fish, cooked meat and bones, in a food digester. Digesters, which should be rodent-proof, need to have their base below ground level since over 90% of the waste will be absorbed by the soil as water. Once the digester is full – roughly every two years – the residue can be removed and then dug into the ground.

WHAT BELONGS IN A COMPOST BIN

You can toss in all your uncooked fruit and vegetables, lawn clippings and most other garden waste, egg shells, tea bags and coffee filters; also newspaper and cardboard and old cut flowers. Don't add cooked foods, dairy, meat and fish products, cat litter and pet waste, perennial garden weeds or weeds in seed, plastic, glass or aluminium.

COMPOSTING KNOW-HOW

Getting to grips with just a few composting "rules" will give you the best results and lessen the likelihood of bad odours. Make sure you keep your compost moist. Turn the mix occasionally and aim for a combination of 50% greens (wet materials like grass cuttings and fruit and vegetables) and 50% browns (dry items such as cardboard, egg boxes and leaves). If your compost tends to be wet and sludgy, add more browns, but if it's too dry bring in more greens.

JOIN A LOCAL PLAN

If you don't want a compost bin or heap in your own garden or you haven't got space, consider joining a local composting scheme. In many areas you can choose to either deliver waste or have it collected from your doorstep. It's then made into compost used in local parks and allotments. Some organizations, such as Starbucks Coffee, will hand out their organic waste if you ask them; it usually comes in large amounts so if you are an urban composter, you will need to have someone to share it with.

RECYCLE YOUR COMPOST BAGS

Save empty bags of compost or growing media and use them again as grow bags. Fill with homemade compost and flatten them to force air out, then tape or wire the open end shut. Lay flat and make x-shaped holes approximately 45 cm (18 in) apart and water well before planting out tomatoes, lettuces or other seedlings. You can also plant potatoes in them (pierce some drainage holes in the bottom) or use to line hanging baskets.

SPEED UP THE ROT

If it seems as though nothing much is happening in your compost heap, it might need a little help. You can buy organic compost activators and accelerators which contain microorganisms especially cultured for composting. Or you can do it yourself by adding fresh urine to the mix – it is high in nitrogen and acts as a good activator. But you can have too much of a good thing so don't start thinking of your compost as an outdoor lavatory!

BIN THE COMPOST

If you live in an urban area and want to start your own composting system, invest in a sturdy compost bin with a sealable lid to keep rodents out. Rats, seagulls and other vermin can ruin the composition of compost. Place it on a balcony or a deck outdoors and put an extra lid or tray underneath the container as a drip tray. Don't use compost as a replacement for potting soil as it is too heavy; mix about one part compost with three parts potting or topsoil.

SOME LIKE IT HOT

A hot compost is the quickest method – it can take just 12 weeks to break down. It can also be beneficial for killing off any weed seeds that might end up in there. For a hot compost fill the compost up in one go, turn the heap every few weeks and chop up tough and bulky material. You can also buy a hot composter that includes an insulating jacket.

HELP YOUR HEAP

Protect your compost heap from the rain with a rain cover. If it gets too wet, the compost composition is ruined. Or purchase a composting bin with a lid to keep your compost protected from the elements.

PLAN YOUR KITCHEN FOR COMPOSTING

You'll be much more likely to keep your vegetable peelings and fruit skins for composting if you have a small container on hand to store them in. If you are installing a new kitchen, make sure you plan for composting and create space for a bin beneath your main work surface.

BURY THE GOODS

If you are worried about flies being attracted to your compost heap, make a hole in the centre and bury your kitchen waste in the middle of it to hinder flies and other pests.

PEEL AWAY PESTS

To ensure your compost heap stays fresh and keeps insects at bay, try adding lemon peel and basil, both of which are smells that flies and other insects find repelling. It will make the heap smell sweeter to your nose as well!

FORK OUT FOR QUALITY COMPOST

Turn your compost with a fork every six to eight weeks and leave in a warm place for best results. Or invest in a compost bin with a turning system to keep everything moving around regularly. Temperatures of about 50°C (122°F) are best.

SPENT MUSHROOM COMPOST

This is a waste product from the mushroom-growing industry and it is usually quite inexpensive (to find some, try "mushroom growers" in your phone directory or online). Being slightly alkaline, it's useful if you need to correct the pH level of the soil and it can also be used as a mulch to help keep down weeds. But you do need to check with the source whether any pesticide residues might be present, particularly organochlorides, which are used against the fungus gnat, or any chemicals.

buying plants & seeds

PICK YOUR PLANTS WISELY

To maximize your chances of having healthy, beautiful plants that don't need treatment for pests and disease, make sure you pick the plants to suit the condition of your garden. Find out what type of soil you have – clay, sandy, silt, peat or chalk. Study the path of the sun around your garden and investigate the average rainfall for your area. It's usually easy to check what grows well by taking a look at your neighbours' gardens.

START WITH SEEDS

Buying established plants from a garden centre might give you quick results, but transporting these plants to and from the shop will increase your carbon footprint. Ordering via the internet will reduce it or, even better, try growing your own from seed and discover just how satisfying it is.

ADOPT A VEGETABLE

Help save a rare vegetable variety under threat of extinction. Britain's organic growing charity, Garden Organic, looks after over 800 varieties of rare and heirloom vegetables in its heritage seed library (HSL) and offers the chance to adopt one of these vulnerable varieties through its "Adopt a Veg" scheme. Diversity of varieties means crops are less likely to fall foul of pests and diseases on a massive scale.

BUY ORGANIC SEEDS

Conventional seeds may well have been harvested from chemically grown plants and many are also treated with insecticides or fungicides prior to sale. Opt for organically certified seeds where available.

SAVE NATIVE PLANTS

Wild plants are under threat from introduced invasive species, habitat loss and climate change. Do your bit by planting native wild plants in your garden. They will be better adapted to the local environment and repay you by requiring less maintenance. In the UK you can find native plants for your area using the Postcode Plants Database (www.nhm.ac.uk/fff). In the US, visit www.michbotclub.org/links/native_plant_society.htm to locate the native plant society for your state.

LOOK FOR TRADITIONAL PLANT VARIETIES

The best seeds to choose are open pollinated, locally adapted, traditional seeds – preferably organic. Avoid the first-generation hybrids (F1 hybrids) available from mainstream suppliers as these reduce genetic diversity and often require fertilizers and pesticides to see the best results. There are 10,000 heritage apple varieties compared to just a few F1 hybrid apple types.

AVOID GM WHENEVER POSSIBLE
Genetically modified seeds – where the DNA of the plant has been changed – threaten the purity of seeds everywhere through cross-contamination. In some countries, such as the US, there is no legal requirement to label GM seeds, so the best way to avoid them is to buy organically certified seeds.

KEEP IT SIMPLE
Begin with the easier vegetable seeds: beans, lettuce, peas and peppers give the best chances of success because they produce seed the same season as they are planted. They are also mostly self-pollinating, which minimizes the need to be mindful of preventing cross-pollination.

SOW THE SEEDS OF SUCCESS
Make sure seeds are thoroughly dry before storing them. Keep them in paper envelopes or packets (not in plastic) in a cool, dry room – and never in a greenhouse. And don't forget to label them!

GET SWAPPING
Look out for local seed-swapping events – often held by allotment or gardening groups. Or search online for seed-saving or heritage seed organizations in your area that also provide advice on seed-saving techniques.

PROPAGATE ALL YOU CAN
Another way to avoid expensive, energy-guzzling trips to the garden centre is to propagate plants from existing plants – either yours or your friends' (but not annuals and biennials, which are always grown from seed). This will require some research on the best technique for the plant in question: division, stem cutting or layering.

BECOME A SAVVY CONSUMER
When buying plants, purchase them in the smallest possible container as they are usually not much further behind in growing terms than those sold in larger, more expensive sizes. You can keep the pots for potting your own seedlings. Check also that the growing media in the pots does not contain peat (see page 83).

WHERE DOES IT COME FROM?

Knowing the origins of a plant is especially important for native, wild plants and bulbs since many, such as bluebells and snowdrops in the UK and the small whorled pogonia and white lady's slipper in the US, are stolen from the wild.

GO NATIVE

Native plants are better suited to meet the needs of local wildlife, and some wildlife species are entirely dependent on the availability of certain native plants. The Karner Blue butterfly in the US, for example, is endangered because of the disappearance of its larval host plant, wild lupine. In the UK, all native butterfly species are suffering from loss of habitat and in the past 200 years, five species have become extinct.

DON'T PLANT SOUVENIRS

In many countries it is illegal to bring plants or seeds from other countries back home with you, but if you do, don't plant them in your garden. They are non-native species that might introduce unwanted pests or diseases.

CHECK ON CACTI

There's a flourishing illegal trade in cacti that is wiping out native populations, particularly from Mexico. Some species are totally banned from international trade and some require an import permit, too. The majority of cacti for sale have been artificially grown in nurseries and are legal, but cacti that are imported into a country do require a permit. If in doubt, check the documentation.

BE A HERO

The only time it is acceptable to take plants from the wild is when they are about to be destroyed by development. If you pass a building site with wild plants that need saving, ask the land owner if you can take them.

TAKE THE PLASTIC BACK

If you can't avoid transporting plants home from a nursery in plastic or polystyrene trays or pots, ask your retailer if you can return them so that they can be reused.

 growing plants

GROW YOUR OWN
Reduce your carbon footprint, save money, amaze your children and experience the true meaning of pride by growing your own fruit, vegetables and herbs. You don't need a huge amount of space, a greenhouse or lots of special equipment to be eating a "house" salad in summer and homemade soup in winter.

ROTATE YOUR CROPS
To help control pests and diseases and improve the fertility of your soil, make sure you don't grow the same vegetables in the same place each year. The four plant groups to rotate are: roots, cereals, brassicas and legumes – check which group yours belong in and move them round each year.

TRY NATURALISTIC PLANTING
Pioneered in Germany and Holland, this style of planting steers clear of formal borders and plants according to habitat, with the emphasis being on plants developing as they would naturally. This kind of planting requires less regular maintenance and plants are cut back just once a year. See *Planting the Natural Garden* by Piet Oudolf and Henk Gerritsen (Timber Press, 2003).

START SIMPLE
Be sure to keep your enthusiasm high by starting with some easy vegetables and fruits. For a big harvest with minimal effort try tomatoes and courgettes (zucchini). Strawberries are a firm favourite and some herbs and lettuces should thrive on your windowsill, where you hopefully won't forget to water them!

PLAN AHEAD FOR HALLOWEEN
Grow your own Halloween lanterns as well as enjoying great-tasting soup, pies and cakes. Pumpkins suit warm, sunny conditions with well-drained soil. Sow seed in spring and keep the pumpkins from rotting by placing them on a bed of straw while growing. Once ripe, cut them off with a knife to leave a length of stalk and put outside for ten days in full sun to harden fully.

ROOT OUT MORE WATER

Avoid water loss from your soil by planting long-rooted species that draw water from the deeper layers of the soil instead of a lot of short-rooted varieties that will compete for water.

AVOID THE CROWDS

Don't overcrowd plants in your garden – naturally, plants leave one another a bit of space to avoid passing on pests and disease. Help your garden to be healthier by respecting their space and you'll need less chemical intervention.

STOP THE SPREAD

The minute you notice one of your plants is diseased, get rid of it to avoid it passing on the disease. Make sure you dispose of it away from the garden – adding it to your compost could encourage the disease to spread.

PRIVATE PATCH

If you want to grow your own vegetables but don't have the space, contact your local community office to see if there are gardening projects or allotments in your area where you could start up your own vegetable patch. There may also be urban gardening schemes operating in your neighbourhood, where you can spend time growing vegetables and take some of the fruits of your labour away.

DIG UP A DWARF

Don't give up on the idea of growing your own vegetables because you haven't got enough space for a vegetable patch or herb garden – dwarf varieties of most vegetables can be grown in containers and will withstand pretty much any weather condition, except for extreme wind. Even roof-top gardens or container-grown plants can provide extra fresh food during the summer months.

KEEP POTATOES HEALTHY

Potatoes hold onto toxins if pesticides are used. Buy organic or, if you want to protect your home-grown potatoes from flea beetles, try interplanting with collard greens. Never add lime before planting potatoes, as this can encourage scab.

KEEP FAMILIES APART

To ensure that your vegetable patch grows naturally and you
get the best from your crops, avoid planting similar species (like
broccoli and cabbage) together as they compete for nutrients.
Instead, go for an even spread of different plant varieties.

SQUASH IN THE VEG

If you don't want to create a whole separate vegetable patch
in your garden, or if you haven't got space, simply plant them in
among your border plants to make the most of your garden space.

BEYOND YOUR BACKYARD

There are many opportunities to practise your gardening skills
away from the home – contact your local authority to find
out about volunteer groups linked to a local park or green
space, how to start a school gardening club, or ways to begin
fundraising to create a public garden.

GET SPROUTING

You can grow sprouts in a tray or spare jar but without proper
drainage fungi and bacteria may grow, so it might be worth
investing in a sprouter that has multiple layers and trays with
drainage holes. Make sure you buy organic, non-GM sprout seeds
(try your local health food store), which you soak. Mung and radish
beans take 12 hours, alfalfa and quinoa 4 hours. Rinse and then
grow, remembering to rinse each day. They could be ready to eat
in as little as 12 hours for quinoa and 5–6 days for most others.

USE NATURAL TIES

When tying up climbing plants choose ties made of natural fibre
or buy a roll of jute string that will eventually rot, rather than
plastic-coated wires. The latter might also cut into your plants.

BOOST YOUR CULINARY OPTIONS

As well as fruit and vegetables, be sure to grow some herbs,
if only on a windowsill. Start with those you use regularly and
experience the thrill of snipping minutes before eating. This will
also save you buying costly vacuum-packed, pesticide-laden
herbs that have been flown in to a supermarket near you. Try
chives, mint, basil and parsley.

RECYCLE PLASTIC INTO POTS

There are plenty of containers in which you can grow seedlings rather than throwing them away. Try yogurt and sour cream pots or polystyrene drinking cups, for example – just make sure water can drain out the bottom by piercing a few small holes in them first.

MAKE YOUR OWN

You can create seed pots out of egg boxes, toilet paper tubes – good for sweet peas that need room for long roots – and newspaper (search the internet for various sites that give folding instructions). Pots made from recycled paper and cardboard can be put straight into the ground without disturbing the seedlings' roots, as the pots will naturally biodegrade.

MUSHROOM MAKER

You can purchase hardwood logs that are already colonized with mushrooms to grow in your garden or even buy mushroom spawn which can be grown on toilet paper rolls. Always buy logs from a sustainable source.

CREATE A MULTI-STOREY

Borrow this idea from Africa, where water and fertile land are scarce, particularly in crowded urban areas. Line some old tyres with used plastic bags, fit loose wooden slats along the bottom, allowing room for drainage, and then fill with soil. Use wooden stakes to arrange the tyres in layers – like a wedding cake – and plant crops on each tier. Water from the top down – the loose slats will allow the water to trickle through to each level. Mulch on top of the soil also helps to retain moisture.

AFTER THE FIZZ HAS GONE

Build your own planters from old drink cans. You will need around 500 to make a 1.5 m (5 ft) diameter planter. Make a cardboard circle template to the above measurement. Fill each can with soil and plug with newspaper. Line up in a single layer along the outer edge of the circle, with bottoms facing out; glue together with waterproof glue. Add another layer on top. Once you have reached about six layers high, slide out the template. Fill the inside space with soil and plant with flowers.

# water & irrigation

PLAN AHEAD WITH NEW GARDENS
If you are creating a new garden, you can incorporate water-saving ideas into your plan. For example, if you are on an exposed site consider putting up windbreaks or planting shrubs or hedges to achieve shelter and shade. Use large plants and garden structures, too, to create areas of light shade in exposed, sunny spots.

SET UP A TRICKLE
Make your own trickle irrigation system using a hose with pinholes in it set on low flow. This is much healthier for the soil than soaking it once a day or week, as it more closely mimics natural weather systems and will reduce disease.

WATER AT NIGHT
Instead of watering plants in the heat of the day when lots of water is lost through evaporation, mimic their natural state by watering in the early morning or evening, when dew would naturally form. The plants will be able to take up more water because the sun won't encourage evaporation and you'll waste less.

LESS IS MORE
Instead of watering plants a little bit every day, give them more water less often – 2.5 cm (1 in) a week is better than a little every day as it mimics natural rainfall conditions and encourages efficient water use by plants.

TAKE THE LEAD
If you're following the green code and collecting rainwater, make sure you don't collect it from lead roofs or guttering because it may contain compounds that could be harmful if they get into the ecosystem.

DRIP COLLECTION
Take care never to waste water. When watering hanging baskets, put your plant pots or containers below to collect the excess water, which can then be re-routed to other plants or the lawn itself.

CONSERVE WATER

Hosepipes can suck up 1,000 litres (264 gallons) of water an hour and a sprinkler may take up as much water in an hour as a family of four uses in a day. If you must have a hosepipe, then fit a trigger nozzle to control the flow. An aerating nozzle allows you to water roots without washing away the soil or having to use the less-efficient spray pattern.

SAVE THE RAIN

Divert water from your gutters into a water butt, or several if your roof area is large. Even in dry areas 24,000 litres (6,340 gallons) can be collected from the average roof. Make sure the butt is made from recycled plastic, position it close to your garden and look out for inexpensive butts offered by water companies.

GO GREY

Grey water is water that you've used, such as bathwater and washing-up water. It can be recycled to water your garden – either save it yourself or install a special system of outlet pipes. Never store grey water, and don't use water that contains strong cleaning agents or chemicals. Don't use it on edible plants either.

FILTER YOUR WATER

Grey water from baths, showers and so on can be filtered through a bucket of straw – fill a well-perforated bucket with straw and allow the water to flow through it. Or, for the more ambitious, you can have a reed-bed system installed, where bacteria on the roots of reeds breaks down waste in the water.

INVEST IN DRIP IRRIGATION

A drip irrigation system uses a network of plastic pipes to carry a slow, even flow of low-pressure water to plants. It delivers water to the roots of plants and reduces water use by half. You can buy kits online or pay for expert installation.

BEAR DROUGHTS IN MIND

There are many plants that will do well despite the summer heat – herbs of Mediterranean origin, for example. As a general rule, most plants with small, leathery and grasslike or succulent leaves will fare well in droughts, as will those with grey or hairy leaves.

PROVIDE SHELTER

Shade and shelter will stop the sun and wind drying out your garden. Use trees and shrubs to provide shade for other plants. Remember also that features like large trees and house walls can shelter the soil from rain.

WEATHER-WISE

How many times have you watered the garden only to watch the rain come down an hour or two later? Make sure you don't waste water by checking the weather forecast before you start.

YOUR TRUE WATER NEEDS

Your garden probably doesn't need as much water as you might think it does. A good soak every couple of weeks is better for plant growth than regular light watering, where the water never reaches the plant roots. Dig a hole of a spade's depth in your soil to test – only water if the soil feels dry to the touch.

CLEVER WATERING

Create a saucer-shaped dip in the soil around your plants to collect water and do your watering when it is cool – early morning or evening – to prevent the water evaporating.

BACK TO YOUR ROOTS

For an easy, effective way to water, take the cap off an old plastic bottle and cut off its base. Bury it in the ground next to your plant and water through the bottle so the water goes straight to the roots, right where it's needed.

HELP OUT YOUR SOIL

Add compost to free-draining soils to improve water retention. For heavy soils, add compost and sharp sand or grit to open up the structure, improve water retention and reduce the chances of clay soils cracking during a dry summer.

ADJUST YOUR EXPECTATIONS

You may need to put your idea of lush, verdant lawn to the back of your mind and get used to some browning during the summer. Your grass will recover in the autumn but you can help it by reducing the number of mowings and raising the cutting level of your mower.

 # weeds & pests

AVOID PESTICIDES AND HERBICIDES

The British public spends around £50 million annually on pesticides such as slug pellets and weed killers, and each year American homeowners apply at least 90 million pounds (40,000 tonnes) of pesticides to their lawns and gardens. These chemicals endanger wildlife and could be putting you and your family's health at risk. A recent study, for example, has found a clear link between two commonly used weed killers and birth defects in children.

DISPOSE SAFELY

Don't throw your unwanted pesticides down the drain. A survey has shown that 20 to 30% of people are doing just that, leading to the contamination of water supplies and the endangering of wildlife in rivers, lakes and groundwater. Just leaving them in the shed isn't a safe solution either because children might be able to reach them. Contact your local authority for advice on where to take your hazardous waste.

GET YOUR HANDS DIRTY

You can get rid of many pests with your bare hands. Pick aphids (greenfly) off leaves and drop into soapy water or vegetable oil, or go out at night for a slug or snail blitz. You can make a slug tea with your night-time pickings by leaving the slugs in a bucket of rainwater for a few weeks. The liquid can then be poured over popular slug patches, where it is said to deter them.

USE A WATER CANNON

A strong blast of water from a hose will blow many insects off your foliage without having to resort to a single chemical. But try other less water-wasteful methods first.

MAKE A HOME FOR THEM

For an earth-friendly approach to controlling slugs, recycle the black packs in which your seedlings or annuals arrive. Place the empty containers upside down near the base of plants. As the plants mature, hide the containers under the leaves. Each morning, check for pests. If you find any, simply empty the container.

MAKE YOUR OWN INSECTICIDE

Boiling rhubarb leaves releases oxalic acid, which can kill leaf-eating insects such as cabbage caterpillars and aphids. Boil about 1.5 kg (3 lb) of rhubarb leaves in about 1.8 litres (3 pints) of water for about 15 to 20 minutes. Cool, strain, and mix with soap flakes before spraying on plants. Take care as rhubarb leaves are poisonous to humans if ingested; they are fine on the ground however as the poison breaks down when the leaves are decomposed.

PREPARE THE GROUND

Make sure you reduce the number of hiding places for common pests like slugs and snails. Keep on top of weeding and prune the branches of shrubs lying on the ground. Dig over the soil to bring slugs to the surface and do keep lawn edges trimmed as slugs like to hide under the long grass.

BUG THE SLUGS

Spread the following around your plants to deter or kill slugs: cedar bark or gravel chips, crushed eggshells, herbs (rosemary, lemon balm, wormwood, mint), needles from conifers, seaweed, wood ash, soot and coffee grounds (collect them from your local café or workplace). A sprinkling of bran may also prove effective – although slugs eat the stuff, it swells inside and so kills them.

ENCOURAGE NATURAL PREDATORS

Consider introducing ducks, geese and chickens into your garden, and encourage toads to stay by installing a pond and plenty of shady damp areas. Not only will they all enjoy dining on your slugs, but ducks and bantams tend not to damage your plants at the same time.

HERBAL PEST CONTROL

Instead of sprinkling poisons around your home to kill pest invasions, you can use herbs from your garden. Try hanging sprigs of fresh sage, pennyroyal, rue or tansy in your kitchen cupboards to deter ants. Both ants and flies are repelled by the smell of mint, so plant some by your kitchen door and windows. Dried bay leaves placed in flour, rice and pulses helps to keep weevils away, too.

BEER DRINKERS

Bury a bowl and fill it with stale beer – it attracts slugs and they will die a boozy death. You can also use grape juice or a tea made from yeast, honey and water. Be sure to keep the lip just above the surface to stop beetles falling in. Slugs, however, will happily climb over.

ENLIST LITTLE HELPERS

Children can be surprisingly eager to round up the slugs and snails in a garden. Offer an incentive such as a prize for the biggest creature and your pest-control problems could be over. Should any little ones get the slimy stuff on their fingers, you can remove it with a mixture of warm water and vinegar.

LURE THEM IN

Buttered leaves or scooped-out grapefruit halves can be placed around vulnerable crops as a lure for slugs. Remove them by hand when enough have gathered there. You can also clear a bed before planting by placing a heap of cut comfrey leaves on it – clear the leaves and the feeding slugs a few days later at night.

THE BARRIER METHOD

You can buy copper tape, rings and mats, which act as a natural repellent to slugs due to the tiny electrical charge from the metal. Eco-friendly recycled boards that give individual protection to each plant for three weeks are also worth a try. They are impregnated with salt and sulphate, so a slug- and snail-repelling ring forms around the top of the "wall".

BRING IN THE LADIES

Ladybirds (ladybugs) – both adults and larvae – eat most types of aphids and you can now buy them in. One pack of 250 larvae can cover approximately 40 sq m (48 sq yds) and is a particularly good way of introducing ladybirds, especially in existing aphid colony infestations in greenhouses, and also in outdoor areas as they will remain local until they become adults. Adult ladybirds can lay many eggs, so helping to continue the colony of pest control.

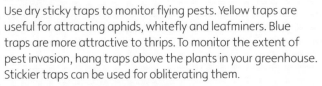

STICK IT UP

Use dry sticky traps to monitor flying pests. Yellow traps are useful for attracting aphids, whitefly and leafminers. Blue traps are more attractive to thrips. To monitor the extent of pest invasion, hang traps above the plants in your greenhouse. Stickier traps can be used for obliterating them.

GO EASY WITH ORGANIC PESTICIDES

As a last resort, there is a small range of pesticides and fungicides available to organic gardeners, such as pyrethrum and insecticidal soap, but these should be avoided if possible. They are still poisonous and can harm wildlife beyond the intended target.

SEND FOR THE NEMATODES

You can buy nematodes from mail order catalogues or the internet. They are microscopic worms that enjoy nothing more than eating some of the worst enemies in your garden – slugs, vine weevils, chafer grubs and leatherjackets. Sachets of them can be sent through the post and refrigerated, then applied to the soil provided it is at least 5°C (41°F).

WISE UP ON PESTS

Get to know your adversary's habits and you are on the way to beating them. Carrot fly, for example, are attracted to the scent of the carrot. Thin out your seedlings in the evenings when the carrot fly is not about and ensure that any soil disturbed is firmed back down with your hand – carrot fly lay their eggs in loose soil around the seedlings.

HELP THROUGH THE WINTER

Create overwintering homes for ladybirds (ladybugs) and lacewings, which are particularly voracious aphid-eaters but sensitive to cold winters. Bundle short sections of hollow bamboo canes together and place in a sheltered spot.

TRY COMPANION PLANTING
Get to know which plants can help others by being grown close together in beds and borders. For example, plant marigolds with tomatoes to deter aphids, sow mustard seeds around brassicas to prevent flea beetle damage, while garlic planted around roses can also deter aphids. You can interplant rows of carrots with onions or leeks to disguise the smell that attracts carrot fly.

MIX WHAT YOU GROW
Mixing flowering plants with your vegetable and fruit plants encourages pest predators such as parasitic wasps, hoverflies and lacewings, the adults of which feed on the nectar from the flowers.

MAKE YOUR OWN CLOCHES
Use old plastic water bottles to make cloches to protect young seedlings and plants from attack. Cut off the bottom, or cut in half, and remove the cap to allow air and water in. Place over your seedling and bury it in the soil for support.

DETER THE NIBBLERS
If rabbits and deer are a problem then try planting some of the following: azaleas, bamboos, buddleia, box, choisya, clematis, pampas grass, daphnes, euphorbias, gaultherias, hydrangeas, hypericums, peonies, rhododendrons, yew or vinca. In tough winters, though, even these may come under attack.

SCARY SCARECROW
Stuff some old clothes with newspaper, or for a longer-lasting solution, sew some hessian together. Fill with straw and use a broom handle for support. Old clothes, a hat and scarf provide the finishing touches to your scarecrow, and children will love creating his face. Hammer the broom handle into the ground and the birds will keep their distance.

BE A CHIVE BUNNY
Aphids hate chives, so they're a great choice to plant alongside your roses to help keep the pests away. (If your roses are already suffering from aphids, pick them off by hand instead of using pesticide. Remember to wear gloves to protect your fingers from the thorns.)

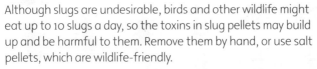

PELT WITH SALT
Although slugs are undesirable, birds and other wildlife might eat up to 10 slugs a day, so the toxins in slug pellets may build up and be harmful to them. Remove them by hand, or use salt pellets, which are wildlife-friendly.

USE YOUR OLD CDS
Put those unwanted CDs to good use by hanging them over your plants or newly laid lawn to scare away the birds. String them up on a length of twine supported by bamboo canes, or along a clothesline.

ROOT OFF THE PROBLEM
Don't use weed killer in your garden. It might appear to be the quick-and-easy option but could make your weeds grow back stronger. Weeding by hand is very effective as it weakens the weed at the root. Pull up weeds before they go to seed and self-spread and make sure you get the whole weed including the root.

MAT YOUR WEEDS
Instead of weedkiller, use mulch between flowers to prevent weeds getting a hold in the first place; for really hardy weeds that grow through the mulch, use flax matting, cardboard or weed-reducing matting.

BUILD A HOTEL
Try to leave an area of dead wood in your garden as an insect "hotel", where natural insect life is encouraged to develop. It doesn't have to be large – a few broken-up logs will do and you'll soon reap the wildlife benefits.

DUST TO DUST
Pyrethrum dust, which is made from chrysanthemums, will kill your unwanted aphids but it can also damage some susceptible plants and cause harm to other, beneficial insects. Use it with care.

KEEP SPIDERS HAPPY
Don't kill spiders – they are important pest killers. Try and co-exist with them in your garden, remembering that they're doing you a favour by keeping your space pest-free.

CHOOSE NON-TOXIC DUST
Diatomaceous earth (also known as DE, diatomite or diahydro) is a highly porous dust made from a naturally occurring, chalk-like sedimentary rock. It consists of fossilized remains of diatoms, a type of hard-shelled algae. DE controls pests by causing dehydration and death. It is a dangerous dust and should be used with care, and not inhaled. Make sure it's not the crystalline or chemically manufactured variety you're buying.

DEVILISH DETERRENT
According to garden mythology, the best way to remove the pests from your garden is to collect slugs and create a liquid of their dead remains, allowing it to decompose in natural rainwater for a few weeks. Then use the liquid around plants to protect them.

SQUIRT WITH SOAP
Use a squirt of mild soapy water to kill aphids and greenfly on roses and other garden plants – it prevents them from flying and subsequently suffocates them.

CATERPILLAR CULL
If you have a major caterpillar or slug problem and need to use chemicals, the least toxic and therefore most environmentally friendly option is pyrethrum dust because it kills the lower species but isn't passed up the food chain.

MAKE THE DUST FLY
Stop slugs and snails from munching their way through your plants with sawdust. It dries them out, effectively paralyzing them by preventing them from creating their slimy trail.

JUMP ON THE DERRIS WHEEL
If your garden is really overrun with pests and you need to use a pesticide, choose Derris. This is a natural pesticide made from tropical plants (but be aware that it will kill all insects, not just the ones you don't want around). Its active ingredient is rotenone, a naturally occurring chemical with insecticidal, mite- and spider-killing and fish-killing properties. It is used for insect control and for lice and ticks on pets.

MAKE ORGANIC PESTICIDE

For a totally organic pesticide, stand a large handful of tobacco leaves in about 4 litres (8 pints) of warm water for 24 hours, then use as a spray on leaves to repel insects. But beware – this water is poisonous to humans and pets as well.

DUST CAREFULLY

Sulphur (in dust or liquid form) controls mildew on roses and other flowers and vegetables, and although it's safe for animals, it can be fatally poisonous to fish, so be very careful when using it around water.

WARD OFF PESTS WITH ONION

To stop harmful insects taking hold in your pesticide-free garden, plant onion plants, which will repel the larvae of insects and stop them reproducing.

NET A GOOD CROP

Fine netting such as muslin (cheesecloth) placed over flower and vegetable beds will protect seedlings from chewing insects, keep cats and birds away and prevent flying insects from laying eggs.

GROW SOME GARLIC

Growing garlic near your roses is a great way to protect them from greenfly, who can't bear the smell and won't come anywhere near. Alternatively, an infusion of garlic in water can be sprayed onto plants.

COLLAR YOUR PLANTS

Stop hatching larvae from burrowing into the soil surrounding your plants by using "collars" made of stiff paper. Cut a piece 30 x 30 cm (1 x 1 ft) and fit it snugly around the base of the plant on top of the soil. Use a paper clip to hold it in place.

THE EARLY BIRD CATCHES THE WORM

Birds are much more efficient than people at killing bugs, so for pest control, encourage birds into your garden with a bird cone or nut hanger. Flickers, warblers, finches, jays, robins, grackles, sparrows, cedar waxwings, starlings and many other birds will consume thousands of insects every day.

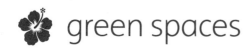# green spaces

KEEP IT GREEN
A green garden can help reduce the impact of climate change on your property. With rainfall and temperatures both predicted to rise, it can soak up sudden downpours and maintain surface temperatures better than paved areas. Researchers have found that adding just 10% to the existing green cover of high-density urban areas can keep maximum surface temperatures below today's levels up until the 2080s.

BE PROACTIVE
Your support counts! Ask local garden centres and nurseries to stock more native plants, and to stop selling peat and toxic pesticides. Find out how your green spaces are managed and lobby to prevent local authorities from using weed killer and other toxic chemicals. You could also join an environmental, organic gardening or wildlife organization.

THE BIGGER PICTURE
Green gardening practices also form part of systems or philosophies including permaculture and biodynamic agriculture. Exploring these areas will give you fresh ideas for your garden, and perhaps stimulate an interest in other areas of sustainable living.

IT ADDS UP
Your one garden may seem insignificant but a whole nation's gardens make up a significant amount of vital green space. In the UK alone, an estimated 15 million domestic gardens cover an area greater than all of the designated National Nature Reserves combined.

BE STREET TREE WISE
Don't support tree removal in order to make it easier to park your car. Trees absorb pollution, cool and humidify the air and provide a valuable home for wildlife. On top of all that, in some areas a tree-lined street can add up to 15% to the value of a property.

KEEP YOUR FRONT
Don't be tempted to pave over your front yard. Research has
shown that even tiny front gardens or green verges are vital
for urban wildlife, and they can house more than 700 different
species of insect.

OPT FOR A GREEN DRIVE
If you move your car fairly regularly, then there are plants that
will tolerate being parked over. They need to be low-growing and
tough enough to withstand occasionally being driven over. Try
creeping jenny, bugle and various thymes. Leave planting pockets
in paving or gravel to ensure there is soil for them to grow in.

MAKE GOOD USE OF YOUR ROOF
Installing a green roof on top of your garden shed will help
provide a home for wildlife and reduce the potential for flooding
as a green roof lowers water run-off from a roof by at least
50%. It will also protect your roof from the effects of the
weather and ultra-violet light, and will help keep a potting shed
cool during the hot summer months.

NO NEED TO HEAT
To be really productive many gardeners heat their greenhouses in
the winter months but you may be able to keep yours warm enough
if you do the following: install your greenhouse below ground level
to reduce the chance of frost, insulate it, and site it against a wall
which will give off the heat absorbed during sunny days.

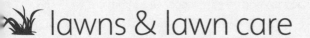 lawns & lawn care

DON'T CREATE A CHEMICAL LAWN
The Pesticide Action Network North America claims that of the
30 commonly used lawn pesticides in the US, 19 are carcinogens,
13 linked with birth defects, 21 with reproductive effects,
15 with neurotoxicity, and 26 with liver or kidney damage.
Also, 27 are irritants and 11 can disrupt the hormone system.
Do you want your kids to play in this kind of environment?

LEAVE THE LEAVES
Use your lawn mower to mow over leaves on the lawn with the grass box off – the shredded leaves will soon disappear into the lawn. Or keep the grass box on and add the chopped-up mown leaves and grass to a leaf-mould heap. They will rot more quickly than whole leaves.

DITCH THE PETROL (GAS) MOWER
The average lawnmower contributes about 1.2 kg (2 lb 10 oz) of CO_2 emissions a week and petrol mowers produce more CO_2 than electric versions. In fact, with 54 million Americans mowing their lawns each weekend with petrol-powered mowers, the mowers are said to account for at least 5% of America's air pollution.

USE YOUR OWN POWER
Other than ultra low-emission lawnmowers that can cut emissions by up to 80% over traditional models and improve fuel consumption, the best environmental option is to use manpower – so buy a push mower.

HARNESS THE SUN'S POWER
If your lawn – and budget – are big, consider a Swedish-built solar-powered "auto mower", which has collision sensors to prevent it from clattering into your wall or patio.

REDUCE YOUR LAWN
If the size of your lawn means a push mower is impractical, then consider reducing the area you have to cut by creating wildflower meadows and areas of longer grass. Both are great for wildlife.

HARDY GRASS
For a lawn that needs less watering, choose well-adapted, hardy and disease-resistant varieties of grass such as ryegrass or bluegrass, or zoysia or bermuda grass. This will help you save water without a noticeable difference in the appearance of your lawn. Watering in the morning when there is less chance of evaporation will help you conserve water.

CUT BACK ON CUTTING
Reduce the number of times you cut the grass. This will save energy and benefit the lawn in dry climates, as longer grass shades the soil and also traps dew.

PLANT A HERB OR FRAGRANT LAWN
Add to the biodiversity of your garden by planting low-growing aromatic herbs and flowers in your lawn. A camomile lawn can be very drought-resistant and is fragrant when walked on or cut. Other plants to try include wild thyme, yarrow, Corsican mint and white clover.

TURF REINFORCEMENT
Rubber crumb, which is made from recycled car tyres, can be sprinkled over your lawn and brushed in. It will eventually be drawn down, where it will create a more open soil structure and improve the root structure of your lawn.

USE A MULCHING MOWER
A mulching mower recycles grass clippings by chopping them into fine particles before pushing the particles down into the turf, where they provide moisture and nutrients for your lawn. This, in turn, reduces the need for any fertilizers. A season's worth of mulching is said to provide 25% of a lawn's fertilizer requirements.

KEEP YOUR CUTTINGS
Either let your grass cuttings stay on the grass to slowly release nutrients back into the soil or use them as a mulch for other plants in the garden – mix with leaves and spread them around shrubs in the autumn.

GIVE BULBS A GO
Break up the monotony of a lawn and attract insects to your garden with drifts of spring flowers such as crocus, snowdrops, snake's head fritillaries and dwarf narcissus. These bulbs can be planted under the turf and will grow well if the lawn is given a trim in late autumn.

MOLE CONTROL

If moles are making a mess of your lawn, try using a solar-powered mole deterrent. This is a plastic stake that emits a sonic pulse into the ground to discourage moles from tunnelling under your lawn.

STAY ON TOP OF YOUR LAWN

Rather than relying on a battery of synthetic fertilizers that can contaminate ground water, ensure your lawn is in top condition in the first place. Top-dress it with leaf mould and compost in autumn and apply an organically certified fertilizer if absolutely necessary.

TEA-BAG LAWN

Fill gaps in your lawn by reusing your tea bags. Simply place moist, used tea bags on a bare spot, then sprinkle with grass seed. The tea bags will provide moisture as they gradually decompose.

BE A SHARP OPERATOR

Keep your mower blades sharpened; blunt blades will tear grass rather than cut it, making cutting the grass more time- and energy-consuming. Damaged grass also needs more water than healthy grass.

DON'T OVERWATER

Be careful not to overwater your lawn. If you do, you run the risk of shallowing the roots, leading to a vicious circle whereby your grass needs more and more water but gets weaker and weaker at water uptake. Err on the dry side when watering your lawn and ensure your sprinklers or water system treat the whole area uniformly; underground sprinkler systems ensure the lawn is evenly treated and waste is minimal.

EMBRACE IMPERFECTIONS

Instead of weeding out your lawn to remove all the dandelions and buttercups, see if you can live with an imperfect lawn for a while. It's unnatural to have one species dominant, so if you can live with some extra lawn guests, you'll be doing the local wildlife a favour.

DON'T MOW SO LOW

If you want your lawn to stay weed-free, keep the grass long rather than cutting it short. This way, the taller stems will shade the roots and prevent weed growth. Aim for at least 7 cm (3 in) for natural weed prevention.

GROW YOUR GRASS

Allow your grass to grow high, to at least 4 cm (1.5 in) before you cut it, or the grass will be weakened because the roots won't get a chance to deepen into the soil if the top of the grass is continually being cut.

LET CLIPPINGS LIE

Leave your clippings to lie after mowing the lawn rather than collecting it with a mower bag or raking it away as this will help feed and replenish soil. But don't do this if it's very cold or damp, or if the clippings are very long, as they might suffocate the grass.

TINKLE YOUR SPRINKLE

Sprinkler systems use as much water in an hour as a family of four do in a whole day – make it a rule of thumb not to use them. Instead, use the hose for short periods or even a watering can.

MAGIC MIX

Fine-blade fescue requires even less fertilizer and water than bluegrass or ryegrass. It's a good idea to have a mix of two or three different grass species for your lawn.

trees & hedges

KEEP YOUR TREES

Trees are good for you, the climate and wildlife. Patients have been shown to recover from surgery more quickly when their hospital room had a view of trees. Trees provide a safe home for many species of birds and insects; they also filter the air, allow shade and absorb carbon dioxide.

THE RIGHT TREE IN THE RIGHT PLACE

When choosing a tree, be sure you will still be happy with the position once it has reached maturity. You don't necessarily have to keep it far from your house. Tree roots do not have the capacity to break up the large concrete foundation block of a modern building, but houses built on shrinkable clay soil may be affected indirectly because roots can dry the soil – and lead to subsidence – but this can become worse if a tree is suddenly removed.

A TREE ISN'T JUST FOR CHRISTMAS

Buy a rooted Christmas tree and you will be able to plant it outdoors at the end of the festive season and (if you keep it in a container) re-use it the following year. Be sure to acclimatize the tree to being outdoors again for a month before planting, and start it off in a sheltered area with some natural light. Gradually move it down the garden to a more exposed area. But beware – Norway spruce grows to 30 m (98 ft).

WILDLIFE-FRIENDLY SPECIES

Willow, birch and beech are favoured by many native insects. Ermine moth larvae feed on the leaves of the bird cherry tree. Yew and holly, with their dense foliage and branches, are good for greenfinches and treecreepers often nest behind the loose bark of larger mature trees. Bats feed on caterpillars that live on willow trees.

USE YOUR TRIMMINGS

Don't just throw out the twigs and branches cut from your tree or hedge. Some will make stakes to support climbing plants – coppiced hazel is particularly good for supporting peas, while others can be used to create a trellis, edging for beds, or woven baskets and screens.

BEING SMALL IS NO EXCUSE

There is a tree for every garden! Even in a small garden there is usually room to plant at least one tree. Smaller species include acers, Tibetan cherry, crab apple, pussy willow and hazel.

PLANT A HEDGE

Hedges are living fences which are great for wildlife –
hedgerows have been recorded as providing shelter or food
for 600 plant species, 1,500 insects, 65 birds and 20 mammals.
They also make better windbreaks than fences since they
absorb the wind and can be a stronger barrier against intruders,
particularly those comprised of prickly hawthorn, blackthorn
and holly. You'll also be helping to replace the many hedges lost
to intensive farming – it is estimated that 5% of UK hedgerows
are lost each year due to neglect or removal.

MAKE YOUR HEDGEROW MIXED

Hedges provide a natural habitat for many insects, birds and
mammals, as well as security, privacy and shelter. The best
hedges for wildlife contain several species that come into leaf,
flower and fruit at different times. Try hawthorn, blackthorn,
guelder rose, field maple (hedge maple), yew, beech, native
privet, berberis and holly. You can also include small trees, such
as crab apple and elder.

TRIM BY HAND

There's no need for power-consuming electric hedge trimmers.
Use long-handled secateurs or get out your ladder and use
pruning shears.

AVOID LEYLANDII

A Leylandii cypress hedge may grow quickly – 1 m (3 ft) per year
up to a height of 45 m (148 ft) – and does provide nesting
opportunities for birds, but the trees suck up large amounts
of water and nutrients from the soil, cast deep shade and are
of less benefit for wildlife than traditional hedges grown with
native species.

GO EASY ON THE PRUNING

If you're pruning a tree, do so in the autumn when there aren't
any nesting birds. Try to leave some hollow tree branches (as
long as they're not threatening to fall off), since these provide
good nesting places for tawny owls and other birds.

screens & fences

WAYS WITH WILLOW
Willow (*Salix*) is very tough and fast-growing. It can be woven into a living screen to make domes, arbours and screens that will then shoot and grow into a larger growing structures. Or you can create a soil-filled framework of dry willow in which ground cover plants are grown. Willow screens make good windbreaks and attract insects and birds.

NEW-STONE ALTERNATIVES
New stone comes at a high environmental cost due to the energy used in quarrying and transporting it. Alternatives include using reclaimed stone or building cob walls – local mud mixed with straw or heather, rammed earth walls, wattle and daub or a hazel lattice covered in mud and straw.

A GREEN SCREEN
There are a few green-screening products on the market. One consists of a welded wire trellising system available as a standalone fence; it is filled with earth and plants grow over it. The other is made from recycled plastic tubing covered in coir fibre, a natural waste product, which is designed to be covered with climbing plants.

A SUNFLOWER SCREEN
Sunflowers can make an unusual summer screen. Choose several varieties that grow to different heights. Sow seeds outdoors in April and by mid-summer you will have a flowering screen and an abundant source of cut flowers.

BUILD YOUR OWN TRELLIS
Help your climbers on their way up by building a trellis from hazel poles. Cut two poles to about 2 m (6½ ft) long and drill a hole at each end approximately 50 cm (20 in) from the mid-point. Attach two lengths of sisal rope to the wall or fence, 1.5 m (5 ft) apart, and thread the hazel poles onto the rope, tying a knot in both lengths of rope after each one. To finish off, make a knot under the final rod and trim away the excess.

GROW YOUR OWN BAMBOO

Instead of using bamboo that has been flown across the globe, grow your own for use as plant supports or screens. It takes three years to grow sufficiently to make 2–3 m (6½–10 ft) long canes. Cut above a joint, dry them slowly for up to six months and lash together to form a screen.

HEAD UPWARDS

Train climbing plants up fences and walls. They provide sheltering sites for insects and spiders, nesting and roosting spots for birds, and beautiful flowers as a bonus. Climbers that are best for wildlife include honeysuckle, ivy, wild clematis, wisteria and Virginia creeper.

BRING YOUR WALLS ALIVE

Seek expert advice on turning the walls around your garden or your home into "living walls" – vertical gardens where plants are rooted in a fibrous material that is then anchored to a wall. They can provide the same insulating benefits as green roofs, give a home to wildlife and reduce the possibility of flooding.

USE NATURAL RESISTANCE

Some woods are better able to resist decay. For example, oak and sweet chestnut will last 20 years when in contact with the soil and 40 years above ground, while larch lasts 10 years in soil and 20 years above it.

PRESERVE YOUR POSTS

Wood preserver contains some harsh and potent chemicals. So instead of treating your posts with it, rather set them in metal shoes that will protect them from decomposing, or set them in concrete for a permanent solution.

BUILD ALTERNATIVE RAISED BEDS

There are plenty of eco-friendly raised bed options. Use old bits of wood or concrete available from salvage yards or local refuse centres; create them from old tyres stacked together. Or use railway sleepers, but check they are untreated if you are growing edibles. You can also buy raised bed kits made from recycled milk jugs and plastic scrap.

DON'T USE CREOSOTE
Never use creosote wood preservative for your garden wood
because it can leach into the soil and give off vapours. This can
continue for up to seven years after the application. Instead,
choose preservers based on boron, zinc and copper.

WHERE DOES YOUR FENCING COME FROM?
The wood used in your fencing could well have come from forests
that are not managed sustainably – Illegal logging is rife in Russia,
for example, where the larch for many timber fences is sourced. It
is also likely to have been treated with toxic chemical preservatives.
Instead, always use untreated wood from a sustainably managed
forest that carries the Forest Stewardship Council (FSC) label.

EXPLORE SYNTHETIC WOOD OPTIONS
There are a range of synthetic wood products now available
made from recycled plastic and polystyrene, such as waste
packaging for electronic goods and waste drinking cups. They
generate no waste during manufacture and are completely
recyclable. What's more, they are maintenance-free and can be
used in fencing or elsewhere in your garden. Just double check
the amount of recycled material used before you buy.

USE AN ORGANIC PRESERVATIVE
There is an alternative to toxic, synthetic preservatives. For
fence panels that are not in contact with the soil, apply linseed
oil or similar products that allow the wood to breathe. Boron-
based timber preservatives are also acceptable in organic
gardening since they are safe for people and the environment.

BEWARE RAILWAY SLEEPERS
Popular though they may be for edging raised borders, old
railway sleepers have often been treated with coal tar creosote,
which the Environmental Protection Agency (EPA) in the US has
determined is a probable human carcinogen and which is banned
from use in the European Union. It doesn't mean you have to give
up these recycled products altogether but do make sure they
are not used where they will come into contact with children and
food, and don't use them where there is a risk of frequent skin
contact. Better still, track down untreated sleepers.

paving & drives

KEEP PATIOS SMALLER

Paved areas absorb more heat than green spaces and release
this heat back into the atmosphere in the cool of the night.
This can significantly contribute to temperatures rising in heavily
paved urban areas – called the "heat island effect" – which in
turn leads to greater use of energy-hungry air conditioners.
Keep as much of your garden as green as you can.

ADOPT SUDS

A Sustainable Urban Drainage System (SUDS) will prevent
flash flooding that is likely with more intense periods of rain
expected as a result of climate change. Paving, tarmac and
concrete increase the amount of rainwater that runs off by
as much as 5%, so avoid creating heavily paved areas – set
paving in sand, rather than mortar, use resin-bonded gravel
and aggregates held in cells made from recycled plastic, or
use permeable paving with gaps that allow water to drain
into the soil or to be stored.

NOTHING IS CONCRETE

After water, concrete is the second most-used product
on the planet, but a key ingredient of it is cement, the
manufacture of which produces more than 5% of global
carbon dioxide emissions. If you must use concrete, source
a mixture that uses recycled aggregates and which replaces
Portland cement with materials that would otherwise be
landfilled, such as PFA (pulverized fuel ash) or GGBS (ground
granulated blastfurnace slag).

WHAT LIES BENEATH

Paving is often laid on concrete, sand and crushed rock, but
these elements are all non-renewable, so ensure you use only
the minimum depth necessary. Where safe, lay stone without
mortar or concrete to allow for future reuse; re-source old
gravels and sand from beneath paving you have demolished;
and always use recycled brick or concrete instead of new
quarried material.

REDUCE PAVING

With rainfall predicted to get heavier, paved areas will increase the risk of flash flooding in your area. Plus, water runs off paved areas, picking up pollutants on the way, which often end up in rivers and waterways via storm drains.

BREAK UP THE SEA OF PAVING

A terrace doesn't have to consist of a big strip of paving. Plant low-growing herbs in cracks between paving slabs – fill with compost and sow seed in spring. Keep watered and avoid treading on them until established. Varieties to try include lady's mantle, Corsican mint and creeping thymes.

REUSE AN OLD PATIO

If you are getting rid of a paved area in your garden, be sure to reuse as much of it as possible. Broken paving may be placed at the bottom of pots to assist with drainage. It can also be crushed and used in drainage systems, and unwanted rubble may be used to build a stone-and-earth mound – great for hibernating newts, frogs and lizards.

USE RE-USE

If you do choose conventional concrete block and slab paving, bricks or cobbles, then try re-use. Ask at salvage yards, municipal waste recovery centres and check out freecycle sites online. When laying paving, slope it so that the water runs onto the garden.

LIMIT YOUR LIMESTONE

Demand for limestone pavement stone for use in garden rockeries is leading to the devastation of naturally occurring limestone pavements and the special plants that live in them. There is no way of telling whether water-worn limestone is from a legal or illegal source, and large amounts of illegally obtained pavement stone are being sold. Wherever possible, use reclaimed stone or buy moulded resin rocks cast to look like pieces of limestone pavement.

STONE AT A PRICE

Imports of natural stone account for around 10% of the UK market for home paving, but sandstone from India is being mined often by very young children, working long hours in inhumane conditions. Many stone quarries in China are no better. Seek a supplier who can prove their stone is ethically sourced or find your stone at a reclamation yard.

STEPPING STONES

Ask yourself whether you really need to have a whole path – it would be far better to use just a few stepping stones or set old logs into the grass than to add to the amount of concrete or stone already in your garden. You could also create paths from chipped wood or bark, recycled glass chips, crushed brick or recycled aggregates.

WALK WITH RUBBER

Try walking on rubber when outdoors by laying floor tiles made of 100% recycled rubber designed for use outside the home. They're anti-slip and weatherproof, and even come in a variety of colours!

GO WITH GRASS PAVERS

You don't have to pave over an area of your lawn to make a pathway or drive; instead install a grass paver, a grass-reinforcement system which consists of a hollow grid (ideally made from recycled plastic) that is filled with topsoil and seeded with grass. These prevent erosion of the soil and absorb storm water, preventing it from flowing straight into the drains.

NOT-SO-FRIENDLY GRAVEL

Gravel is often recommended as an environmentally friendly material because it allows water to drain freely into the soil and consumes no energy in manufacture, but it might have been strip-mined off the seabed, destroying marine life, or removed from existing river systems. Ask your supplier to confirm that habitats at source are not threatened by the removal of the gravel.

 decking

BEWARE TOXIC DECKS

A lot of decking is treated with toxic preservatives and in the not-too-distant past is likely to have been pressure-treated with chromated copper arsenate (CCA), which is 22% pure arsenic. CCA-treated wood for residential use is being phased out, but supplies might still exist in stores, so ask before you buy.

GO TO THE RECLAMATION YARD

Salvaged timber is a great option for decking, provided it has not been treated with preservatives. Look for a durable hardwood, such as oak, which does not need a preservative. If you can't find used timber then make sure the timber you buy carries the Forest Stewardship Council (FSC) label, which means it will have come from a sustainably managed forest.

TRY ALTERNATIVE DECKS

There are a variety of eco-friendly decking options out there, such as tiles which snap together made from the durable Bolivian Ipe hardwood. This is naturally resistant to rot, decay, insects and mould without chemical treatment.

GREEN CLEAN YOUR DECK

Decks are notorious for getting slippery and slimy after a year or so in a damp climate, but rather than use harsh chemicals to clean them, look instead for green alternatives that are non-toxic and biodegradable.

USE RECYCLED PLASTIC DECKING

Look out for decking made from recycled plastic – it already accounts for around 10% of the US decking market. It looks good, is low-maintenance and contains no toxic chemicals.

USE A BRUSH

Instead of powerwashing your decking with a hose, save water by giving it a good brush with a firm-bristled broom.

outdoor furniture & accessories

BE LOW-ENERGY

Resist the urge to put energy-hungry accessories in your garden, such as patio heaters, hot tubs and under-tree lighting. Where once gardens were places for quiet contemplation of the natural world, they have now become extensions to our houses, where we expect all the same comforts. Remember that these come at a cost to our climate.

TOO HOT TO HANDLE

Over 600,000 gas-powered heaters adorn the patios and decking areas of UK households alone, adding in excess of 350,000 tonnes of additional carbon emissions to the atmosphere every year. Their use has also exploded in hotels and bars since the smoking ban came into effect. Our advice? Just put on another sweater!

WHEEL YOUR BINS

Wheelie bins, rollout carts and recycling containers aren't the prettiest sight, so give some thought to where they're going to be placed on your property. One solution is to build a simple slatted screen or shelter out of reclaimed timber (also a great material for building fences).

NO NEED FOR NEW

With eBay and various other websites offering the opportunity to buy or swap unwanted items, you should be able to find garden furniture to your liking at a fraction of the cost of buying new. Try to avoid driving miles to pick it up, though.

GET A GRASS SEAT

The greenest garden seat of all is one made of – you guessed it – grass! Create a turf table and chairs using chicken wire and rest assured you've got the greenest furniture in town!

OIL YOUR OUTDOOR WOOD

Linseed oil is an excellent wood preserver for garden furniture. Not only is it totally rainproof but it is also nourishing – so you can be sure your wood will be kept in tip-top condition, whatever the weather outside. Linseed oil is completely natural so you don't have to worry about chemicals either.

CHOOSE PAINT CAREFULLY

Be careful about the paint you use on garden furniture, fences and sheds. Some paints contain chemicals that can leach into the soil, causing damage to the very plants and animals you're trying to encourage.

CAST YOUR NET NEARBY

Cast-iron garden furniture is a good green choice because of its durability – you won't need to replace it soon. But make sure you check how far it has travelled from the manufacturer and buy local, if possible.

SAY NO TO TROPICAL HARDWOODS

Avoid garden furniture made from tropical hardwoods which comes from uncertified sources – the UK is the main importer of tropical hardwood furniture in Europe. Instead, look out for alternatives, such as furniture made from recycled aluminium, a garden bench created from reclaimed scaffold boards, tables made from cable drums and recycled timber, or loungers constructed from reclaimed teak and recycled-tyre stools.

LOOK FOR CERTIFICATION

When buying wood products for your garden, check they carry either the Forest Stewardship Council (FSC) label or the "SmartWood Rediscovered" label from the SmartWood's Rediscovered Wood Program, which certifies wood that might otherwise rot, get chipped up or be dumped in a landfill. Sources include dilapidated buildings, "nuisance" or fallen trees on urban or suburban land and unproductive trees in orchards.

MAKE YOUR OWN FURNITURE

If you live in the country then it shouldn't be too hard to find tree stumps to make into tables or seats, or you could go to a local sawmill and ask for off-cuts. Ensure the stump is set into the ground and then shape using a chainsaw. Temporary furniture can also be made by roping together straw bales.

SWING INTO ACTION

You don't have to buy special play equipment for the kids to keep them active. If you have a tree with a strong branch, make your own swing by tying a recycled tyre to the branch or drill a hole through the centre of a disc of wood (an old chopping board would do). Insert some strong rope through the hole and knot it. Secure it really well to the tree by looping over the branch and knotting firmly. Test it before letting the kids play on it.

FIT SENSORS

Make sure all your external lights use infra-red sensors (ask your electrician to fit them on existing lights) that are adjusted to come on when you pass in front of them. This will ensure lights operate for the least amount of time necessary.

USE THE SUN'S POWER

There is a huge range of solar-powered outdoor lighting available now, so there's no excuse for running electric cables round your garden. Use just a few lights where you need them most, such as along paths or near terraces, but be sure to keep some areas of your garden as dark as possible for the sake of wildlife.

LEADING LIGHTS

Make sure you choose garden lights that are photovoltaic, meaning they run from solar power rather than using up electricity. There are many different types on the market, from plant level lighting to security spotlights.

ORGANIC FAIR-TRADE HAMMOCKS

A hammock is one of the simplest and best seating options out there but look out for hammocks made from organic cotton that carry a fair-trade mark to guarantee good pay and working conditions for those making them. Make sure also that you use trees to support the hammock rather than buying a metal or wood stand. If forced to purchase a stand, buy a wooden one and check it carries the Forest Stewardship Council (FSC) mark.

BEWARE OLD PLAY EQUIPMENT

Until relatively recently most wood for outdoor use, including play equipment, was pressure treated with chromated copper arsenate (CCA). Since 2004, in the US, and later in the EU, CCA has not been allowed for use in woods destined for residential uses due to health concerns over the arsenic used, which is a known carcinogen. But if you buy second-hand play equipment it might have been treated with CCA – check whether the wood has a greenish tint.

LEARN TO LOVE THE DARK

Light pollution is a growing problem around the world. Not only is it a waste of energy, it also has a detrimental effect on birds and animals. Stray night-time light can confuse their natural patterns and affect breeding cycles. While the problem is mostly due to badly designed street and road lighting, security lights and floodlights, you can do your bit for the planet either by letting your garden get dark at night or using low-intensity lights that are directed downwards.

LANTERN LIGHT

For a soft evening glow, you can buy lanterns made from recycled glass or make your own from old jam jars, empty baby food jars, and so on. Use tapers to light the tea lights and save your fingers.

NATURAL INSECT REPELLENTS

An evening eating out under the stars on your patio can be ruined by mosquitoes. Try citronella oil – in candles or in a candle-lit vaporizer – to deter the little critters. Keep some tea tree oil handy to soothe any bites, too.

barbecues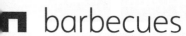

BE WARY OF BARBECUES
Just as with patio heaters which can release 7 kg (15 lb) of CO_2 in just a couple of hours, some of the latest top-of-the-range barbecue grills are among the least eco-friendly, relying on gas or electricity to power them. You might as well stay in the kitchen! Keep it simple with a homemade barbecue, or buy a small one with a plain design that uses materials from a sustainable source.

MAKE YOUR OWN BRICK BBQ
You can build your own brick barbecue grill – a great way to use leftover or salvaged bricks – or use a roasting tin instead. It should be about 7 cm (3 in) deep and you can use a metal cake rack or some chicken wire as the grill. Stand it on some bricks, but be absolutely certain it has cooled down before touching the tin. You'll find lots of ideas for brick barbecues on the internet.

AVOID BRIQUETTES
Half of all UK barbecues use wood charcoal, but up to 90% of the 40,000 tonnes of charcoal burnt in the UK each year is sourced from abroad, often from vulnerable tropical forests and mangrove swamps. There's enough woodland near most of us to be able to supply local charcoal, which also reduces transport pollution. Look for local, sustainable suppliers that carry the Forest Stewardship Council (FSC) logo.

MAKE USE OF THE ASH
Charcoal ash (but not briquette ash) can be used as a fertilizer and will raise the pH of acidic soils, but it's very alkaline and should be applied sparingly. You can also sprinkle a little of the ash around your plants to keep slugs at bay.

DITCH THE DISPOSABLE
Disposable barbecues are a waste of resources – they cannot be recycled or composted. For a longer-lasting alternative, try a bucket barbecue, which consists of a galvanized bucket with air holes in the sides and bottom, a wooden handle and removable grill top. Stand on paving or sand and use sustainably sourced charcoal.

CHARCOAL DANGERS

In the US, 63% of barbecues are fired with briquettes, which consist of waste timber and sawdust mixed with cornflour (cornstarch) to bind, and a hydrocarbon solvent, similar to lighter fluid, to help them start easily. But according to the US Environmental Protection Agency, charcoal briquettes release 105 times more carbon monoxide per unit of energy than propane and a lot of toxic volatile organic compounds. However, propane or liquid petroleum gas is not the answer either, as it's a fossil fuel and a net contributor to atmospheric CO_2 levels.

USE A CHIMNEY STARTER

Lighter fluid or self-lighting briquettes will give off volatile organic compounds (VOCs) when burnt, which in some people can cause irritation to the eyes, nose and throat, and sometimes more severe reactions. If you are using charcoal, try a chimney starter instead. This consists of a metal cylinder with a grate near the bottom – unlit charcoal is put inside the cylinder and newspaper placed under the grate and lit. The charcoal at the bottom of the cylinder lights first and the "chimney effect" ignites the remaining charcoal above.

MAKE IT A RARE TREAT

You should be aware of the health risks associated with barbecues. Smoke from both charcoal and wood produces not only hydrocarbons but also tiny soot particles that pollute the air and can aggravate heart and lung problems. Also, meat cooked on a barbecue can form potentially cancer-causing compounds – the hotter the temperature and the longer the meat cooks, the more compounds produced.

SWEDISH HELPER

You'll wonder how you managed without Swedish FireSteels. Developed by the Swedish Defence Department, they produce a spark up to 3,000°C (5,432°F) in the wet or cold by moving a striker across the steel. Ideal for starting barbecues, provided you have some kindling to hand.

ALL-NATURAL FIRELIGHTERS

It is now possible to buy natural firelighters online. Fair-trade fire sticks from Guatemala are handmade from the stump of the ocote tree. They are 80% resin but dry to the touch and make good natural firelighters.

 # water features

SOLAR-POWERED WATER FEATURES

Imagine sitting on your patio, sipping your drink, while listening to the sound of water splashing. This tranquil moment is quite easy to recreate with the purchase of a solar-powered water feature – you can even buy a bird bath complete with detachable solar-powered fountain.

PUT A BALL IN IT

Instead of installing a pond heater, just leave a tennis ball floating on the surface of your pond in winter. You can remove it on frosty mornings to ensure the pond does not freeze over entirely. Avoid breaking the ice or pouring salt or hot water into the pond as this could be damaging to fish and anything else living in there.

ADD A "GREEN" FOUNTAIN

Reduce the amount of electricity used in your garden by installing a solar-powered fountain in your pond, which can be lit with floating solar lights. As well as looking good, a fountain will also oxygenate the water and can circulate up to 380 litres (100 gallons) per hour. You can also purchase solar-powered pond oxygenators for this purpose.

REDUCE THE NEED FOR MAINTENANCE

Site your pond where it receives maximum sunlight and minimum leaf litter. If leaves still blow into it, put a net across the pond in autumn and add the collected leaves to your leaf mould pile. The better the quality of the water, the better it will be for wildlife.

CREATE A MINI-POND

You can use virtually any water-tight container to make a pond – old enamel sinks or stone troughs, for example. Whichever you choose, fill it with rainwater (if using tap water, allow to stand for a few days to allow the chlorine to evaporate) and plant with native plants.

FEATURE YOUR WATER

Check water features regularly for leaks and damage. Also make sure they recirculate water rather than it running off.

MAKE THE MOST OF YOUR POND

Avoid non-native water plants and build your pond near longer grass or a border to give any wildlife that come to drink and bathe there cover. Position it near a wood pile or rockery for extra cover for hibernating newts and amphibians, or simply leave some loose stones and wood close to the edges of the pond.

WEED WITH CARE

Don't use chemicals to kill weeds such as blanket weed in your pond. Clear weeds by hand and leave for a while on the edge to allow any insects it contains to find their way back to the water. Then compost the remains. The best time to clear a pond is in the early autumn when it's least disruptive to wildlife.

CREATE A NATURAL SWIMMING POND

For the ultimate in getting back to nature, build a swimming pond in your garden. More than 1,000 natural swimming ponds have been built in Austria, Germany and Switzerland alone. They are a chemical-free combination of swimming area and aquatic plant garden, which are self-cleaning due to the natural cleaning properties of plants.

COVER YOUR POOL

If you do have a swimming pool in your back garden, at least make sure you cover it when not in use. This will reduce water loss, prevent heat escaping and ensure it stays as clean as possible, minimizing the need for chemical cleaners and filtration.

organic gardening

GET OUT AND ABOUT

Organic gardening and farming are increasingly popular so there should be plenty of opportunities for you to visit farms to get inspiration and tips. Contact an organic certifying body such as the Soil Association in the UK or the CSA (Community Supported Agriculture) in the US, or an organic gardening organization, to find them. They may also know of a network of like-minded organic gardeners for you to join.

GARDEN ORGANIC

It's not just about rejecting the usual array of pesticides. Organic gardening means buying locally, rejecting genetically modified products, reusing and recycling as much as possible (including water), feeding the soil, nurturing wildlife, avoiding artificial fertilizers and preserving heritage seeds.

BEWARE THE WORD "ORGANIC"

Not because organic is bad, but because the use of the word can be. Gardening items that are labelled as "organic" need only be of living origin – so your organic manure might be from battery chickens. Only those products that are certified as organic by an official certifying body are guaranteed to have been produced under strict organic standards.

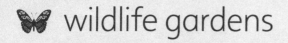 # wildlife gardens

FEED THE BIRDS
Plant food for birds in your garden. Grow sunflowers and leave
the seed heads on or string them up for birds to feed on. Allow
rosehips on the roses to go to seed over winter – again, the
birds will make good use of them.

SHARE YOUR FRUIT WITH THE BIRDS
If you leave some fruit on your bushes, trees and vines you
will be helping birds and other wildlife. Not only does the fruit
provide a valuable source of food but the trees also allow
shelter for insects, birds and small mammals.

KEEP IT MESSY
The more quiet, undisturbed places in your garden the better
it is for wildlife. Leave drifts of autumn leaves under hedges
– you might find a hibernating hedgehog below them. Don't
remove woody stems from pampas grass in the winter as they
make excellent nest sites for solitary bees, while slow worms
will thank you for rough grass, rocks and logs, and ladybirds
(ladybugs) enjoy sheltering in hollow-stemmed plants left
through winter.

GET YEAR-ROUND COLOUR
When selecting plants, choose those that flower and bear
fruit at different times of the year to make your garden space
attractive to wildlife all year round. A great idea is to plant
a winter and summer climber over your trellis so you'll have
colour whatever the season.

UP CLOSE AND PERSONAL
Encourage children to engage with the wildlife in your garden
by investing in a solar insect theatre. This consists of an insect
viewing chamber made from timber and a solar light that
automatically comes on at dusk, attracting moths, lacewings,
butterflies and other interesting flying insects into the chamber.
The lower shelf also has solitary bee nesting holes.

LEARN TO LOVE BATS

A tiny common pipistrelle can eat around 3,000 midges, mosquitoes and other small flies in a single night. Moths, beetles and crane flies (daddy long legs) are popular with other species. Encourage bats into your garden by planting a mixture of flowering plants, trees and shrubs to attract a diversity of insects, especially night-blossoming versions. Bats are a protected species in many countries.

MAKE A LACEWING MOTEL

Cut the base off a 2-litre (2-quart) empty soft drink bottle. Slide a roll of corrugated cardboard inside the bottle and string some fine wire across the bottom to keep it from falling out. Tie string around the top of the bottle, with the cap left on, and hang in a sheltered position by the end of summer. The lacewing larvae will thank you by eating your aphids.

COMPOST WITH CARE

Compost heaps can shelter slow worms and toads, and grass snakes that may also lay their eggs there. Take extra care when turning your heap or digging out the compost.

LEAVE OLD TREE STUMPS

Aged tree stumps are an important habitat for many insects, especially the endangered stag beetle, and a rotten log by a pond provides a great site for egg-laying dragonflies.

FEATHER A NEST

Keep fur that you have groomed from your cat or dog (and any hair from home haircuts) and put it out on a bird table or high on a twiggy bush in spring – it could be just what a nesting bird is looking for.

MAKE YOUR OWN BIRD FEEDER

Stick two twigs through the bottom third of a small plastic water bottle so that they cross over each other and leave enough of the twigs sticking out for the birds to stand on. Half-fill with bird food – nuts and seeds – and hang it on a nearby tree using string pushed through the top third.

KEEP CATS AWAY

You don't want to fatten the birds up only to find you're making a tasty meal for the local cats! Make sure you put your bird table at least 2 m (6½ ft) from undergrowth that might provide sneaky hiding spaces for cats, and keep nesting boxes well out of their way. Also, add a bell to your cat's collar as a warning to birds.

LURE IN INSECTS

If you have a variety of insects in your garden you are likely to attract plenty of wildlife, such as bats, to feast on them, so tempt them in with a mix of flowers. Try flowers with long narrow petal tubes, such as evening primrose and honeysuckle for moths, pale flowers that can be seen in poor light to attract insects at dusk, and single flowers, which tend to produce more nectar than double varieties; also flowers with insect-friendly landing platforms and short florets, such as those in the daisy or carrot families.

A FEW HOLES WON'T HURT

Don't fill in holes in walls and fencing, especially screw holes, as these can be used by leafcutter and red mason bees – both are docile and won't cause additional damage. They are two of the best pollinators.

BUILD A POND

A pond is an absolute essential for any self-respecting wildlife gardener, but check that it has gently sloping edges to make it easy for hedgehogs and frogs to get out – it's not uncommon to find hedgehogs drowned in garden ponds.

LEAVE SOME GAPS

Small animals like hedgehogs need gaps under fences and sheds to get through as they like to roam and will have set "runs". A gap under a shed could provide the perfect place for them to nest. A beneficial garden guest, a hedgehog will clear your garden of slugs, snails and insects.

FATTEN THEM UP

Birds benefit from fat as a valuable food source, especially during the winter, so make sure you provide fat feeders in your garden. You can make your own by mixing solid fat such as lard or dripping with seed, nuts, raisins and bird peanuts. Push into drilled holes in small logs or branches, or try an upside-down coconut or yogurt pot.

OFFER SHELTER TO BEES

Bees, especially orchard mason bees, will make their homes in drilled blocks of wood (drill holes into a piece of soft wood). You can also use paper drinking straws stacked on their sides in a waterproof box. Search the internet for ways to make bee homes or try: www.fs.fed.us/wildflowers/pollinators/beebox.

DON'T FEED WILD ANIMALS

As a general rule, apart from birds, wild animals should not be fed. The food you give them could affect their health and becoming reliant on humans for food might limit an animal's survival skills. Remember to properly dispose of food remains and packaging.

CREATE A WILDFLOWER MEADOW

To make your own meadow, you can leave an area of grass uncut and see what grows (although you should cut it at some point to stop shrubby plants taking over). Or sow wildflowers in an area of cleared ground – ideally of poor-quality soil to keep the weeds at bay. Wildflower seed mixes are readily available.

PLANT CLIMBERS

Climbing plants, such as ivy and wild honeysuckle, will provide cover for nesting birds, hibernation sites for butterflies and food for insects. So get busy putting up that trellis!

MORE FISH, LESS FROGS

Fish eat frogspawn and tadpoles so if you want frogs to keep your insect levels down, limit the number of fish in your pond.

 # preserving wildlife

GIVE BACK A DAY
Volunteer for a day's work at your local nature reserve. Nature reserves need to be managed by humans to stay in the best condition. Often, this can be done through local organizations and even one day of your time can make a huge difference to accomplishing something for local plant and animal welfare.

DOWN ON THE FARM
Many farmers would like to help habitats develop but are under too much financial pressure. Lobby your government for measures, such as grants and one-off incentives, to encourage farmers to save natural habitats.

FOXGLOVE FUN
Bees like white, blue and yellow flowering plants with deep flowers and lots of nectar. Foxgloves and hollyhocks are great bee favourites, so try and plant some in your garden. Encouraging natural habitats helps support the ecosystem.

BUILD A BEE BOLTHOLE
Drill holes in a block of untreated wood and hang it under the eaves of your house or garden shed to provide a bee shelter where solitary bees can rest and make their home. But make sure it's protected from wind, sun and rain.

CAP YOUR FLUES
Place caps over all chimneys and vents on your roof to prevent birds, ducks and mammals like squirrels and raccoons from taking up residence and becoming a nuisance or getting trapped.

BASK IN THE SUNLIGHT
Attract butterflies to your summer garden by adding a light-coloured rock or garden sculpture. This provides a surface for basking in the early-morning sun. Make it a few feet high for protection against predators.

BOX YOUR BATS

If you have a bit of room in your garden, help the local wildlife by putting up a bat box. Bats are natural predators of night-flying insects like moths and flies, and will help keep your patio insect-free on summer evenings.

HOME MOVIE

To really make the most of wildlife in your garden, invest in a bird box with a pinhole camera inside. They transmit images to your own TV set so the whole family can watch them day and night and see the chicks grow up.

BOX UP A BIRD HOME

Why not add a few nestboxes to your garden to provide a nesting site and shelter for birds. Choose a tree or a high wall, but avoid sunny spots or anywhere accessible to cats or foxes. Be patient – it may take a season before the nestbox is settled and the birds make it their home.

DRIVE CAREFULLY

Be alert when driving in rural areas or near wildlife refuges to avoid hitting or running over wild creatures. Animals do not recognize the danger from an oncoming vehicle so it's important you allow them time to move out of the way.

LEAVE IT TO THE EXPERTS

Do not attempt to raise or keep wild animals yourself. Not only is it illegal, but wild creatures do not make good pets – captivity poses a constant stress, stopping them from developing normally. They are usually unable to be returned to the wild. Contact a wildlife organization, such as the RSPCA in the UK or the ASPCA in the US, for advice.

DON'T MOW

Before mowing your lawn, walk through the area first to make sure no rabbits or ground-nesting birds are in harm's way. It only takes a couple of weeks for these babies to grow and leave the nest, so leave the mowing until then.

DON'T TOUCH
As a general rule, leave infant wildlife alone. A parent may be nearby or will return soon, but may not do so if you have interfered with their young. The only exception is baby birds that have fallen from the nest, in which case you can gently return them using a towel or cloth. The best chance for their survival is for their parents to look after them.

CHOOSE LIFE
Before you fell a tree in your garden, check carefully that no wildlife species are using it as a home or nesting in it, especially around springtime, when many birds are building nests and laying eggs. As long as your trees aren't diseased, leave them standing rather than cutting them down.

TEACH THEM WELL
Educating children to respect and care for all wild creatures and their habitats is important. They'll understand why nests, burrows and other wildlife homes should never be destroyed and that wild animals and birds should not be trapped or touched.

SEEING IS BELIEVING
Binoculars are a great choice for wildlife watchers who respect wild animals. They enable you to see close up what's happening without invading the animal's territory or scaring it away. Zoom lenses are also good for this. Make sure you do not make any loud noises, are wearing suitable clothing and are respectful of the wildlife.

DON'T FLY THE NEST
Leave bird nests alone – birds are highly sensitive to smells and if they can scent a stranger's aroma on or near their nest, they're likely to abandon it and might not re-breed.

ADOPT SOME SPACE
If you haven't got room for a wildlife sanctuary in your own garden, why not adopt an area of local habitat nearby? Several conservation organizations have schemes whereby you can directly help protect an area of local wild habitat.

BUTTERFLY BUSH

Adult butterflies need plants like buddleia in the garden to provide nectar. What many people don't know is that they also need water, so attract them to your garden by filling a shallow dish, or a rock or tree hollow with water.

BE A RAINFOREST ANGEL

You can become a guardian of the Amazon by donating money to the World Wildlife Fund. It will go toward setting aside land in the Amazon for protection and teaching the local people how to watch over it. Visit the World Wildlife Fund website to find out about more ways you can help: www.wwf.org.

STEP IT UP

If you have areas of open water on your property, such as a pond or water feature, make sure you have steps or a structure that is easy to climb up. Many different wild animals die each year after getting stuck in ponds and artificial water features. Rocks are a natural solution to ensure they have a way out.

LEAVE THEM ALONE

Prevent your pet cats and dogs from attacking or playing with wildlife. Don't allow them to run without supervision and raise your cats as indoor pets. Many wild animals are injured each year by domestic dogs and cats.

RAISE A GLASS

To stop collisions, alert birds to large expanses of glass in your home, such as patio doors or picture windows, and cut down on reflection by hanging streamers, putting bird silhouettes on the glass surface or allowing the glass to get a little dirty.

GIVE WILDLIFE A BREAK

One of the biggest problems for wildlife is habitat loss, so why not create some habitat in your own garden? Create a bird or butterfly sanctuary in your garden. Put up bird feeders for seed-eating birds like finches, jays and sparrows. If you grow the right flowering plants you'll also provide nourishment for nectar-eating birds such as hummingbirds and orioles.

DON'T DROP PACKETS
Crisp (potato chip) packets are a potential suffocation hazard to wild mammals. They lick the packet to get the high levels of salt, but when the packets get stuck on their noses they can't breathe.

DON'T BE FISHY
Do not leave fishing line or fish hooks unattended or lying about outdoors because it may be harmful to animals and plants. Similarly, try to retrieve any kite string left on the ground or entangled in trees.

DON'T OIL YOUR PANS
Never leave motor oil unattended and uncovered. Birds can easily fall into containers and, because the oil destroys their natural feather oils, few survive such an ordeal.

CLEAN UP WILD HABITATS
When you visit picnic or camping areas, clean up any rubbish, especially if it's been around food. The scent may fool animals into thinking that aluminium foil, plastic bags and other food containers are food. When eaten, these may cause them serious harm.

CUT UP YOUR RINGS
Always cut up the plastic that holds your four-or six-pack of beer before you throw it away. The rings can cause severe damage to wild birds through strangulation and may also get caught on dolphins' noses, leading to suffocation.

RUN A REPORT
If you come across an abandoned car, report it to the police immediately as it could be a potential hazard to wildlife, especially if it catches fire.

KEEP YOUR DOG ON A LEAD
If you're walking your dog in an area that contains wildlife, keep it under control or on a lead. Dogs can disturb ground-nesting birds even to the point of abandoning their nests. The same applies on beaches, where they can disturb seashore animals.

KEEP IT QUIET

Did you know noise travels farther at night because of the colder layer of air near the earth? Turn the volume down a notch to ensure you're not scaring wild animals.

MAKE SOME MONEY

Organize a sponsored event or sale at your school or club to raise money to help preserve wildlife habitats, either locally or across the globe, through a charitable organization.

BE A LITTER PICKER

Pick up refuse that could harm wildlife and take special care with items that pose a tangling or suffocation risk like bits of string, rope, clingfilm (plastic wrap) or plastic bags.

 # container gardening

CONTAIN YOUR GARDEN

A great range of plants can be grown in containers on your windowsill, balcony or patio. There's almost nothing that won't grow in a container so try some of these: tumbler tomatoes, strawberries, trailing cucumber, oriental greens, chard and herbs such as chives, parsley and mint.

USE WATER-RETAINING GRANULES

These will help to reduce the amount of water needed in your containers, many of which dry out far more quickly than in beds and borders. Manufacturers claim that an increase in soil water-holding capacity of 300 to 800% is possible in some soils.

NO NEED FOR MOSS

Sphagnum moss is commonly used as a liner for hanging baskets as it keeps plants moist, while allowing oxygen to reach them. However, this moss comes from peat bogs and its use threatens the already depleted precious environment. Use alternatives such as recycled wool (cut an old woolly sweater to fit), coir or hemp fibre.

MAKE YOUR OWN

There are plenty of objects that can be turned into plant pots – try old tyres, a chimney pot, ceramic bowls, an old wheelbarrow or even larger tin cans. Just make sure you drill some holes in the bottom to allow water to drain. If you want to age the ceramic containers, paint yogurt on the outside and keep in a shady spot to promote the growth of lichen.

GROW HERBS ON YOUR WINDOW

Space is no excuse! You can now buy a mini plant-propagator, called the BeanPod, which attaches to windows with a sucker. Inside each bean-shaped pod is a disc of compressed coco-fibre peat that, when watered, expands into enough soil to fill the bottom half of the pod. Sow the seeds provided – basil, chives or parsley – and keep watering. You can even have a herb garden next to your desk at work!

COVER THE TOP

Containers are notorious for needing a lot of water because the growing media dries out quickly. To prevent some of this moisture loss, cover the surface of the soil with mulch, such as wood chippings or pebbles.

LINE YOUR POT

Terracotta pots in particular tend to lose water quickly. When planting up a new pot, line it with a plastic carrier bag. Pierce drainage holes in the bottom to prevent water loss from the sides.

STAYING ALIVE

To keep your plants alive while you are on holiday (and spare the neighbours from having to constantly come round and water them for you), put a small plastic bottle filled with water (with one minute pinhole in its base which sweats rather than drips) on top of the soil in the pot. This will slowly drip water into the pot.

POTS CAN BE MOVED!

Instead of constantly watering your container-grown plants, consider moving them to a shadier spot during a long hot, dry spell to prevent evaporation. Equally, move your hanging baskets to a cooler location if you are going to be away for more than a day or so.

USE A GUTTER

A piece of leftover plastic guttering can be used to grow salad leaves. Take 1 m (3 ft) lengths of guttering, fill with compost, sprinkle with a pinch of salad seeds and cover with a thin layer of compost. Keep on a windowsill and the salad should be ready to plant out into a bigger container or in your garden after three weeks or so, at which point you can start off your next lot of seedlings.

 # home & garden

PLANT-BASED CLEANING

Simmer the leaves and flowering stems of rosemary, eucalyptus, juniper, lavender, sage or thyme in water for 30 minutes. Strain the water and use as a disinfectant around the home. Refrigerated, it will last for up to a week.

HAVE A PLANT DETOX

Studies have shown that the air quality in our homes could be worse than outdoors due to the prevalence of pollutants such as volatile organic compounds (VOCs) released from upholstery, curtains, plywood, stains and varnishes, paints and carpets. But many common house plants can remove these chemicals from the air. Among 50 house plants tested for their ecological benefits, the areca palm, lady palm, bamboo palm, rubber plant, *Dracaena deremensis* "Janet Craig", Boston fern and peace lily ranked highly.

CUT BACK ON CUT FLOWERS

In the UK, 80% of bought cut flowers are imported, usually by air, and in the US imports make up about two-thirds of the cut-flower market. Reduce your carbon footprint by growing your own supply. You'll need a sunny spot with well-drained, fertile soil and some shelter from strong winds. Varieties to try include: dahlias, chrysanthemums, zinnias, snapdragons, cosmos and sweet william. Be sure to pick regularly to encourage more blooms and to prevent flowers from trying to set seed.

A PLANT-BASED MEDICINE CHEST

Grow herbs that are known for their medicinal properties and create your own remedies. Among those worth trying are: coriander (chewing the leaves or infusing as a tea is said to relieve an upset stomach); calendula (steep the flowers in hot water and use the drained liquid as a healing mouthwash for gums); lavender (for sleep sachets) and thyme (as a tea sweetened with honey it can help relieve sore throats and coughs).

GROW AN INDOOR HERB GARDEN

Growing organic herbs on a sunny windowsill throughout the winter provides some much-needed green colour and adding them to your cooking will give you a nutritional boost. The best ones for small containers are parsley, mint, chives, rosemary, oregano and thyme.

PICK GREEN FOR YOUR PICNIC

Make the most of your lawn or the shade of a tree by spreading out a picnic rug and eating al fresco. You can buy picnic blankets made from "shoddy" wool, which is the wool left over from the production of virgin wool blankets, and biodegradable picnic sets made from sustainable bamboo husk, which can be composted.

EAT YOUR WEEDS

Perhaps this will help encourage you to get on your knees and start pulling them up – some weeds make tasty additions to salads. Try eating varieties such as dandelion, purslane and lamb's quarters when young and tender, but don't pick them at the roadside, where they may be affected by dirt and pollution.

DON'T CHOP WOOD FOR FUEL

Invest in a logmaker (look out for those made from recycled plastic). They convert newspapers, junk mail, shredded paper, wrapping paper, cardboard, card packaging, dry leaves, wood chips, twigs and sticks, even dried tea bags into fuel logs by compressing and encasing them in newspaper.

EXPERIENCE NATURAL FRAGRANCE

Instead of relying on toxic synthetic fragrances, grow fragrant flowers and herbs which, fresh or dried, will fill your home with natural scents. To make a simple pot-pourri, mix together dried rose petals, lavender flowers and leaves, lemon balm leaves and marigold petals in equal amounts. A few drops of essential oil will revive the scent when it starts to fade.

Food &
Nutrition

WHETHER YOU'RE INTERESTED in avoiding pesticides in food or want to get the optimum nutrition from your diet, this chapter will help you make the healthiest and most eco-friendly choices. Learn which foods require the greatest energy resources, the impact of artificial ingredients on the nutritional quality of your food and all about issues such as animal welfare and environmental pollutants. Global food and agricultural systems account for up to 30% of all human-induced global warming – and food is responsible for 31% of the average European household's impact on climate change, so the foods you choose matter for the environment.

shopping for food

MAKE A LIST BEFORE YOU GO SHOPPING
Get into the habit of planning the week's meals and writing
a shopping list before you go out. This helps to reduce the
amount of waste food you have and also saves you money,
as long as you stick to it and don't get lured into impulse
purchases. It's best not to shop when you're feeling hungry!

DON'T START THE CAR
The weekly food shop is something many of us do in the car – in
fact, shopping accounts for 20% of car journeys in the UK, and
12% of the distance covered. But driving just 10.5 km (6½ miles)
to the supermarket emits more carbon than flying a pack of
Kenyan green beans to the UK. Buying more local food should
allow you to walk and/or cycle to the shops and this exercise
will help your health, too.

GROUP SHOPPING
Join forces with friends and buy in bulk to cut down on
packaging. Certain groceries, such as cereals, rice and pasta,
can be bought in bulk from wholesalers, as long as you meet
their minimum order – then it's just up to you to divide it up.
This is a great way to reduce packaging and save money.

SHOP FROM HOME
Do your food shopping online to cut down on carbon emissions
caused by driving to the supermarket. Recent research has
revealed that getting your groceries delivered by an online
delivery service is around 30% more energy efficient than
travelling to the store itself to shop.

PICK THE BEST

If you must shop in a multiple, and 72% of UK grocery sales takes place in supermarkets, then at least ensure you are supporting the best green performer. Find out how UK supermarkets are doing against a list of green indicators in the National Consumer Council report "Green grocers: how supermarkets can help make greener shopping easier", which is updated every few years – www.ncc.org.uk.

ONLINE BENEFITS

Be more systematic about what and how much you buy. Use some of the better search options now available that let you source "seasonal" or "locally produced" food. Plus, many supermarkets are starting to make deliveries with electric vans. In the case of Tesco in the UK, one store's electric home-delivery fleet saves 100 tonnes of CO_2 per year.

IGNORE THE DEALS

While food prices continue to rise, the temptation to "buy one get one free" is going to be even greater but these deals are often a big factor in the amount of food that is wasted, especially when they are applied to perishable foods. Don't be drawn into buying more than you need unless you know that you are going to be able to freeze whatever's left.

USE LOCAL SERVICES

Support your community and shop locally. Many neighbourhood butchers, fishmongers, greengrocers and dairy/milk suppliers will deliver food direct to your door. Local shops offer a more personal service, they keep money circulating in the local area supporting other local businesses, and they are more energy-efficient than the big superstores.

FILL A BOTTLE

Join bottle-refilling schemes offered by some local stores and farm shops. They will fill up your existing bottles of oil, vinegar and other kitchen essentials to save you having to buy and throw away glass bottles.

SUPERSIZE ME

Buy larger packages that have a higher ratio of content to packaging. Always buying the largest available, but buying less often, will not only cut down on the number of supermarket visits, but also on the packaging you're buying.

AVOID HIGH-TECH CARTONS WHENEVER POSSIBLE

Try not to buy juice, milk and soup in cartons because they are extremely difficult to recycle, being made from a mixture of different materials. They do, however, take less energy to produce and transport than tin cans, and any that you do buy can be reused in the garden as plant pots for seedlings.

STEER CLEAR OF SIX-PACKS

Try to avoid buying cans of drinks held together by plastic yokes. Many of these end up in our oceans, where they can get trapped around the beaks and necks of birds and mammals. If you do find yourself with a plastic yoke to dispose of, make sure you cut the yokes first.

PROCESS OF ELIMINATION

Processing food expends many times more energy than the natural product. For example, a 500-g (1-lb) box of cereal requires nearly seven times as many kilocalories of energy to produce than it provides in nourishment. The greenest choice is to buy as little processed food as possible.

AVOID PLASTIC ALTOGETHER

Don't fill your cupboards with unwanted plastic shopping bags that you feel too guilty to dispose of. Invest in a couple of reusable bags, preferably made from a biodegradable material such as hessian, that can be used over and over again. If you must use plastic food storage bags, wash and reuse them as many times as possible.

ROLL ALONG

Go one better than taking your own bags to the checkout – buy a shopping trolley (shopping bag on wheels). You will be much more likely to ditch the car if you know you're not going to be putting your back out hauling food home again. And they aren't as old-fashioned as they used to be – check out www.rollser. co.uk or get a traditional willow basket on wheels at www. englishwillowbaskets.co.uk.

NEW IS NOT ALWAYS NICE

Each year the food and drink industry launches around 10,000 new products – most of which require huge amounts of the earth's resources to manufacture, package, distribute and dispose of. Don't become a slave to the industry's marketing departments – stick to the least processed and packaged foods, which have been providing good nutrition for years.

GO UNPACKAGED

Look out for stores that let you buy goods in bulk and use your own containers. In the UK, one store – Unpackaged – operates in London selling hundreds of loose products from herbs and spices to eggs and bread (http://beunpackaged.com).

IN THE BAG

About 13 billion plastic bags are given away at supermarket checkouts each year in Britain – but they take anything from 400 to 1,000 years to break down, while paper bags use four to six times as much energy to produce. For a green option, use a reusable fairtrade, organic cotton bag.

DON'T TIE YOURSELF IN KNOTS

Don't tie plastic bags too tightly – it will only mean you have to tear them open, rendering them useless. Instead, use loose knots, or seal with reusable ties if you need it to be airtight.

GET AN ONYA BAG

One of the main problems with reusable shopping bags is we forget to take them shopping! The Onya Bag is an ideal choice because it is superstrong, folds down to a tiny pouch and can be clipped onto your bag or purse (see www.onyabags.com.au).

farmers' markets

FARMING MATTERS
Farmers can now use an online tool (www.cla.org.uk) to measure their farms' greenhouse gas emissions – before you buy, ask if they are doing so.

WASTE NOT, WANT NOT
The more food you buy directly from a producer the better in terms of waste. It is estimated that 40% of food never makes it from harvest to our plates as it's lost somewhere in the distribution network, thanks to processing, storage and transportation.

FARM FRESH
There are around 550 farmers' markets in the UK and about £120 million is spent at them each year. By buying directly from farmers you will be supporting local producers and ensuring the goods you buy have not travelled miles to reach you. But remember that not all products will be certified organic and you may want to check with individual stallholders about the sustainability of their products.

GET PICKING
Look out for local "pick your own" farms and orchards. You'll be doing some exercise in the great outdoors, getting to know your local farmers and educating your children about the way in which food is grown. Plus, you can be confident in the freshness of your food. Look online for sites near you or check out www. pickyourown.org, which lists farms internationally.

BUY LOOSE VEGETABLES AND FRUIT
Avoid purchasing fruit and vegetables that come pre-packaged in lots of plastic. Much of it is totally unnecessary and simply adds to household waste. Visit shops and food markets where you can buy produce loose and avoid all packaging by taking along your own reusable shopping bags.

DOWN ON THE FARM

Many farms now have shops, in fact, there are an estimated 4,000 of them in the UK, and they are great sources of locally produced foods. They often include traditional butchers and cheese-makers, plus you'll frequently find breeds of livestock and varieties of fruit and vegetables that supermarkets overlook. You'll be reducing food miles and getting more diversity in your diet.

SAVE MONEY AT THE MARKET

County and local markets also offer a good source of fresh fruit and vegetables – often fresher than the produce you'll find in supermarkets with their ability to keep food in storage. Plus, you'll be saving some money at the market. Fruit and vegetables sold in supermarkets are around 30% more expensive than those available from street markets, according to UK pressure group Sustain.

CREATE A POCKET MARKET

In the US, a regional food cooperative has introduced the idea of "pocket markets". Smaller than farmers' markets – sometimes just two or three stalls – they sell produce from local farmers, local urban growers and community gardeners. Communities provide the location and volunteers run the stalls. See www.foodroots.ca/pmtoolkit_index.htm for ideas on getting one going in your area.

 # alternate food sources

GO WILD IN THE WILD

Look out for nutritious wild foods in your neighbourhood, whether in your garden, hedgerows, or in a local park or woodland. Your bounty could range from blackberries to wild garlic and mushrooms, but check that the plants you pick are safe to eat, are not rare or protected species and are not treated with chemicals.

DO IT YOURSELF

Whether it's brewing your own beer, curing your own ham or making your own cheese – you don't need a factory to do it for you. There's a plethora of books, websites and courses out there for the keen do-it-yourself enthusiast and you'll know more than most about the ingredients in some of your food.

 # organic food

OPT FOR ORGANIC

Studies show that, on average, organic food contains more vitamins and minerals than non-organic, and organic plants can contain between 10 and 15% more phenolics (compounds that are thought to help prevent diseases). In the case of organic fruit and vegetables, this is likely to be because plants grow in a naturally nutrient-rich soil. Another recent study found that organic fruit and vegetables contain higher levels of beneficial minerals such as iron and zinc.

SET UP A GROUP

If you know a group of like-minded people (or want to get to know some), then consider setting up a local food group. In the UK, the Soil Association has produced a toolkit to help people establish an organic buying group – see www.localfoodworks. org, while in the US, Ecotrust has released "Building Local Food Networks: A Toolkit for Organizers" (www.ecotrust.org).

LESS EMISSIONS

Eating organic could also result in lower CO_2 emissions. A recent UK Government study found that organic production led to a 26% reduction in carbon emissions; other studies have shown that CO_2 emissions from organic farming are 40 to 60% lower per hectare than conventional systems, mainly because organic farmers do not use synthetic nitrogen fertilizers.

THE BEST VEG

Eating organically grown fruits and vegetables doesn't just reduce the amount of pesticides and fertilizers released into the environment, it's also more healthy – for you, the farmers and food handlers.

GET ORGANIC JUICE

Apples can be sprayed with pesticide up to 35 times before they reach your fruit bowl, so a brief run under the tap (faucet) is not going to make much difference. Buy organic, especially for juice, where toxic residues will be concentrated.

BUY ORGANIC MILK

Organic milk takes three times less energy to produce than the non-organic version. This is mainly due to the energy used in the production of the fertilizers employed in non-organic milk production. Various studies have also found that organic milk has more health benefits with higher levels of antioxidants.

ORDER A VEGETABLE BOX

Instead of driving to the supermarket for your weekly groceries, arrange for an organic vegetable box to be delivered to your door. This has the combined benefits of supporting a local producer (check that's where the food comes from), helping to reduce chemicals used in conventional farming and reducing emissions caused by trips to the shops.

BAG A BOX

Look out for box schemes run by local farmers or groups of farmers. Many of them now stock a wide range of ethical and organic products – not just vegetables – and are often great sources of recipe ideas. Some include meat or fish, wine, juices, bread, preserves, cheese, nuts, chocolate, and more. They have the potential to transform your diet, bringing vegetables into your kitchen that you might have overlooked in the supermarket.

GM foods

GENETIC DOUBTS
GM food is being heralded as a solution to food shortages and rising prices but environmental campaigners are still adamant that it poses a huge risk to wildlife. According to Friends of the Earth, two out of three GM crops grown in UK government-sponsored farm-scale trials were more damaging to farmland wildlife than their conventional equivalents. The group also says that most GM crops have resulted in increased pesticide use.

GENES IN YOUR FOOD
Routine trials for the unexpected health effects of GM food are not required before GMOs can be sold as food or grown in the open countryside, and at least four independent studies have found negative health effects. Newcastle University research found that genes from GM soya entered the gut bacteria of those eating it.

ORGANIC TO AVOID GM
Ensuring you have a GM-free diet can be a challenge. In the US, GM foods and products are currently not labelled and roughly 70% of the foods in supermarkets have GM ingredients (see www.truefoodnow.org/shoppersguide). In the EU, products have to be labelled if they are from a GM source, but not if they have been produced with GM technology or come from animals fed on GM animal feed.

DON'T FEED THE ANIMALS GM
Nearly all the milk, dairy products and pork in UK and US supermarkets has come from animals fed a GM diet. While there are no definitive links between GM food and health risks, research is ongoing, so your best bet is to buy organic.

ROOT OUT GM
Watch for genetically modified foods hiding in ingredients lists as "modified". Modified oils, starches and flours are very common ingredients. Just because a label doesn't warn that a food is genetically modified doesn't mean that it is GM-free, and labelling standards vary from country to country.

chemicals, pesticides & additives

CHEMICAL SOUP
Being at the top of the food chain, we are particularly exposed to chemicals in food, and research has found that oily fish and fatty foods, such as meat and dairy products, contain higher levels of chemicals like organochlorine pesticides, PCBs and flame retardants. These can cause cancer and birth defects, and damage the nervous system, so reduce the chemical burden on your body by buying organic.

CONTAINER CONCERN
Avoid buying canned food and drinks in hard plastic polycarbonate bottles as they have been found to leach a chemical – Bisphenol A (BPA) – which can act like a female hormone and could be linked to breast cancer. In Canada, the use of BPA in plastic baby bottles has been banned, while recent US tests found that the lining in canned foods can leach more than double the amount of BPA than polycarbonate bottles.

"E"S AREN'T GOOD
About 400 "E" number additives and several thousand un-named flavouring agents are used in our food. There is evidence that mixtures of artificial food colourings and a commonly used food preservative can increase hyperactive behaviour in susceptible children (see www.actiononadditives. com and www.foodcomm.org.uk). Buy fresh food only, and dry up the demand for these chemicals.

PESTICIDE PERIL
Up to 40% of the fruit, vegetable and bread samples tested in the UK were found to contain pesticides, albeit at "safe" levels, while in the US, consumers can experience up to 70 daily exposures to residues through their diets. Given that more than 300 man-made chemicals have been found in human bodies, the best way to avoid chemical contact from your fruit and veg is to eat certified organic foods.

ADDITIVES TO LOOK OUT FOR

The US pressure group Center for Science in the Public Interest (CSPI) has an online guide to additives indicating whether they are safe (www.cspinet.org/reports/chemcuisine.htm). The group recommends avoiding sodium nitrite, saccharin, caffeine, olestra, acesulfame K and artificial colourings as they are among the most questionable additives.

TOP TEN TO AVOID

The charity Pesticide Action Network UK has devised a list of foods that are likely to have the highest pesticide residues. They are: flour, potatoes, bread, apples, pears, grapes, strawberries, green beans, tomatoes and cucumber. Consider buying these foods only if they are organic. In the US, the Organic Center has also produced a guide ("Organic Essentials" at www.organic-center.org).

DITCH THE FLAVOURINGS

There are around 2,700 different flavourings currently allowed in our food but they do not need to be identified, so it is impossible to know exactly what is being added to our food and drink, and how much of them we consume, according to the Food Commission. These flavourings have no nutritional value and often they replace genuine, nutritious ingredients – fooling us into believing that a fat-, sugar- or salt-laden food is in fact a fruit-based healthy option.

SUPPORT WILD BIRDS

Herbicides used on crops are damaging wild bird populations by taking away the birds' natural habitats and directly affecting feeding and nesting. Choosing organic is the only way to support wild birds.

BUY ADDITIVE-FREE

Organic meat is the best choice, but if you can't find any or you think it is too expensive for your budget, choose free range additive-free instead. Often this meat comes from farms undergoing the two-year conversion to organic, so it's basically organic meat at half the price.

PEEL YOUR FRUIT

If you buy non-organic fruit, make sure you peel it. The peel is often the most nutrient-rich part, but unfortunately it's also the part that holds onto the residue from chemicals.

SAY NO TO PLASTIC

If you're going to microwave food, don't do it in a plastic container that might release chemicals into the food when heated. It's best to avoid even those that claim to be microwave safe.

reading labels

IS IT REALLY NATURAL?

Don't be fooled by the term "natural flavourings". While the flavouring should have come from a "natural" vegetable, animal or microbiological source, an apple flavour doesn't necessarily have to come from an apple. In fact, natural flavourings can originate from unexpected "natural" sources, such as carcasses and oak wood chips. And even when the flavour has come from apples, the goodness will be lost in the production process.

BUY FAIRTRADE

Whoever does the household shopping should get into the habit of buying products that carry the FLO's International Fairtrade mark. This logo certifies that the producers are getting a fair price for the goods, including sustainable production and a premium to be invested in social or economic development projects.

LABEL QUICK-FIX

Carbon footprint labels are starting to be used on products, but assessment is complex ... Do you count how long the product sits in the store refrigerator? Do you include non-carbon, but powerful, global warming emissions such as methane from cattle? Buying less of most items is still the best thing you can do for your carbon footprint.

GET LABEL-WISE

It's easy to be mystified by the plethora of labels on foods. There's the traffic light system for fat, sugar and salt content, the Guideline Daily Amounts labels, a wide variety of food assurance schemes – such as the RSPCA's "Freedom Food", organic certification symbols and so on. Get help decoding labels – try Which?'s food shopping card (www.which.co.uk) and the Food Standards Agency guide to labelling terms (www.eatwell.gov.uk).

 # green issues

JUST GREENWASH?

If you are in search of green, nutritious food you will find yourself in a world of marketing hype, also known as "greenwash" (dubious claims to eco-friendliness). Surveys in the UK and USA show that nine out of ten of us are sceptical about green or climate change information from companies and governments. Check what's behind the claims online – see the Greenwash Guide (www.futerra.co.uk/services/greenwash-guide).

SHIPPING ISN'T SHIP-SHAPE

Picking shipped produce over air-freighted is not the answer to our environmental woes. In 2008, it was discovered that greenhouse gas emissions from shipping are nearly three times higher than previously believed. Emissions from shipping account for 5% of total annual emissions compared to the aviation industry's 2% a year.

BUY ETHICAL

Make sure the food and drink you buy has been made with wellbeing in mind. Ask for a manufacturer's and retailer's ethical policy (ideally, they will be members of the Ethical Trading Initiative). For the UK, take a look at Ethical Consumer's online guide (www.ethiscore.org), which rates companies against environmental, animal welfare and human rights issues. For the US, visit www.coopamerica.org/programs/responsibleshopper.

BEWARE ECO-HYPE

Nearly every company now claims it is becoming more climate-friendly but a lot of them aren't really making a concrete contribution when it comes to their overall impact on global warming. Supermarkets, for instance, might finally be doing something about giving away free plastic bags, but they still use huge of amounts of energy in their stores and distribution network, and their businesses are based on selling lots of processed and imported food.

MORE ON IRRADIATION

On the environmental side, there are risks of pollution from radioactive irradiation plants and the fact that irradiation allows food to be transported over greater distances. Currently, only herbs, spices and vegetable seasonings are irradiated in Europe, but in the US the list of foods is longer and includes wheat, potatoes, fruit and vegetables, herbs and spices, pork, poultry and beef. The sure way to avoid it is to buy organic, which bans irradiation. See www.organicconsumers.org/irradlink.cfm.

IS BIODYNAMIC BEST?

Biodynamic agriculture is a sustainable way in which to grow food since every biodynamic farm aims to become self-sufficient – in compost, manures and animal feeds. In 2002, a Swiss study showed that biodynamically tended soil has a higher biodiversity than either conventionally or organically farmed soil. For biodynamic produce, look out for the Demeter symbol.

BUY FAIRTRADE

Fairly traded products guarantee that disadvantaged producers in the developing world are getting a better deal by receiving a minimum price that covers the cost of sustainable production as well as an extra premium that's invested in social or economic development projects. Tea, coffee, bananas and chocolate are good examples of fairly traded products. Look out for certification by Fairtrade Labelling Organizations International (FLO).

DON'T BE FOOLED BY BIOFUEL

Did you know that biofuels are likely to do just as much, if not more, environmental harm than conventional fuels and are leading to food shortages for the poor? Huge areas of land are now being used to grow biofuels such as soya, palm and sugar cane. A recent US study found that growing biofuel on converted rainforests, peatlands, savanna or grassland created up to 420 times more CO_2 than it saved.

SAY NO TO NANO

The food industry is busy researching the use of nano-technology in ingredients, additives and packaging. There are the usual promises of environmental and health benefits – products may be able to adjust their nutrient content to meet each consumer's health needs, for example. But many scientific institutions are worried about the lack of research into the safety. For more information, see www.nanotechproject.org and http://nano.foe.org.au.

SPREADING IRRADIATION

Food irradiation – where food is exposed to high doses of ionizing radiation that kills insects, moulds and bacterium – is being promoted, especially in the US, as the answer to food poisoning and for extending food shelf life. But some believe that it can result in loss of nutrients and mask poor hygiene practices in food production by sterilizing contamination. Look at the label: US federal rules require irradiated foods to be labelled as such.

A WORTHWHILE TRADE?

International trade can bring questionable benefits but it can also result in huge greenhouse gas emissions. For example, in 2006 the amount of beer the UK sold in Spain was almost the same as the amount Spain sold in the UK. Are we demanding choice for the sake of it? Make your food and drink choices local and sustainable.

✈ food miles

IT'S THE WAY IT'S MADE

A recent US study found that food production accounts for
83% of the 8.1 tonnes of greenhouse gases that an average
US household generates each year by consuming food, while
the transportation of food led to only 11% of total emissions.
Different food groups varied widely in their emissions, with red
meat, for example, producing 150% more greenhouse gases
than chicken or fish. So it may well be better to cut your meat
consumption rather than your food miles.

THE AIR DEBATE

Aircraft emissions produce far more greenhouse gases per "food
mile" than any other form of transport – in the UK, less than
1% of imported food is air freighted but it contributes 11% of
the carbon emissions from food distribution. But, dropping all
air-freighted food from your shopping list could be disastrous
for fragile farming communities in the developing world. UK
certifier the Soil Association may offer a solution to the dilemma
– it is considering only certifying air freighted organic food if it
meets its own Ethical Trade standards or similar standards and
companies will have to develop plans for reducing air freight.

EAT SEASONALLY

The choice of fruit and vegetables at most supermarkets is
staggering. Whatever the time of year, you can pretty much
eat what you want. This exotic choice is the result of miles of
airfreighting and tonnes of CO_2 emissions. Instead, buy local
produce from farm shops and markets, which cuts emissions
and supports local producers.

GROW YOUR OWN VEG

Eliminate food miles and get back to nature by growing your
own vegetables. Even if you don't have a garden you can
still grow tomatoes and herbs inside in pots or in growbags.
Homegrown also means you can avoid the packaging that
often comes with bought groceries.

HOW FAR DOES YOUR FOOD TRAVEL?

When you are shopping for groceries, keep an eye out for food miles and reduce yours whenever possible. You might be surprised to discover that the apples you regularly buy are flown all the way from New Zealand. Try to buy local food whenever possible.

MILES AWAY

Food imported by air is a huge contributor to global warming. Kilo for kilo, a kiwi fruit from New Zealand will have created five times its own weight in carbon dioxide emissions by the time it arrives in the UK. Wherever you are in the world, try to minimize your food miles by choosing seasonal and local.

GET THE LOW DOWN

Provided that you buy locally, fruit, vegetables and crops require far less energy than meat production. So try eating lower on the food chain. Even non-vegetarians can limit the amount of meat they eat quite easily; for example, by choosing it only every other day.

CHOOSE LOCAL FRUIT

Not only does fruit flown in from around the globe have a harsh impact on the environment through fuel emissions, it also needs more protective packaging to keep it in a decent state, so it's a double whammy. Choose less packaged, local produce instead.

CLOSE TO HOME

Whenever you can, visit a local butcher, fishmonger and greengrocer, who will supply you with as much fresh, local food as possible. Or get proactive and pressure your neighbourhood shop to set up a small section selling only local food, if they don't do so already.

PRETTY PRESERVES

Don't be tempted in wintertime to buy fresh fruit flown in from across the globe. Cut down on food miles by buying local fruit when it's in season, and freezing or preserving it to keep you going when it's not.

VIRTUALLY LOCAL

For the average time-pressed person, the idea of visiting several different stores each week in order to get all you need locally just isn't realistic but there are other ways to shop locally. Local Food Shop (www.localfoodshop.co.uk) is an online service that lets British consumers search by postcode for suppliers in their region. Producers based close to each other are encouraged to team up and combine deliveries. In the US, visit www. localharvest.org to find farmers' markets, family farms and other sources of sustainably grown food in your area.

DO YOUR HOMEWORK

If you really want to make sure your food and drink choices are positive for the environment as well as for your health, then do your research and beware those that over-simplify. Buying local, for example, isn't always the greenest choice – while there are high carbon emissions associated with flying green beans in from Kenya, you might find that overall more carbon emissions come from growing green beans nearer to home due to an intensive system of agriculture used that relies on machinery, fertilizers, heating, irrigation systems and so on.

SAVVY LOCAL SOURCING

Buying local means you can find out more about the way in which your food is produced – direct from the grower – and pick the producer who is doing the most to reduce their emissions. Look online for local producer guides, such as www.bigbarn.co.uk.

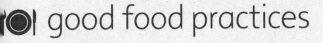 good food practices

CATERERS WHO CARE

If you are a regular user of caterers then it's time to review your sourcing. Look out for the new breed of eco-catering companies which specialize in organic, eco-friendly food and will be able to put together nutritionally balanced menus as well.

FROM HOME TO HOLIDAYS
Your interest in green eating need not stop when you take a holiday. Check out Worldwide Opportunities on Organic Farms (WWOOF – www.wwoof.org); they can put you in contact with organic farms or smallholdings that offer food, accommodation and opportunities to learn about organic lifestyles in exchange for volunteer help on the land.

GO SLOW
Find out about "slow food". The Slow Food Movement began in Italy in the 1980s as an antidote to fast food and today the "eco-gastronomy" movement has over 85,000 members in 132 countries. It seeks to retain the diverse heritage of regional food and drink and protect it from globalization, while also promoting biodiversity through its Slow Food Foundation for Biodiversity. See www.slowfood.com – and get involved.

THE MACROBIOTIC METHOD
Eating according to macrobiotic principles (developed by a Japanese philosopher in the 1920s) will bring down your carbon footprint as well as potentially your weight. The macrobiotic diet consists of foods that tend to be lacking in the average British or North American diet, such as fibre-rich wholegrains, vegetables and beans, while being low in saturated fat, meat, dairy products and sugar. It also emphasizes locally sourced, organic food.

GET ON THE LEARNING CURVE
The boom in demand for organic food and the popularity of the slow food movement show that there is a growing interest in natural and eco-friendly food. And all this interest means there's no shortage of courses out there to improve your knowledge – from residential wild food courses to cheese-making and beekeeping courses. See www.lowimpact.org/courses.htm for courses and www.slowfood.com for further education and events.

processed food &
ready-prepared meals

PASS ON THE PROCESSING
Ready meals have crept onto many people's shopping lists. In
the UK, 30% of adults eat ready-meals once a week, but they
are rarely the best nutritional or eco-friendly option. Cooking and
preservation processes ensure the nutritional content of most
are low, while packaging and transporting them huge distances
releases large amounts of carbon into the atmosphere, to say
nothing of their contribution to our waste mountain.

WHEN PROCESSING IS GOOD
Occasionally processed food can improve the nutritional
benefits of food – take tomatoes, for instance. They contain
a powerful antioxidant – lycopene – but the body can access
more of this nutrient if the tomato has been cooked. Indeed,
there's five times more available lycopene in tomato sauce than
in an equivalent amount of fresh tomatoes. But pick an organic
ketchup or sauce and, if at all possible, one made locally.

REDUCE EMPTY CALORIES
Eat fewer empty calories and you will find you require less food,
and therefore less packaging. Most additives in processed foods
are chemicals that lack nutritional value so if you eat lots of
processed foods, chances are you'll have to eat more of them
to get the nutrition you need.

SANDWICH SOLUTIONS
If you routinely buy pre-prepared sandwiches from a
supermarket then it's time you thought about making your
own. Apart from saving on the packaging waste and food miles
(a recent study showed prepacked sandwiches sold in England
often came from France), you will be able to liven up your
taste buds by packing homemade sandwiches with nutritional
goodies such as sprouts and avocado.

CHEW IT UP

Choose mastic-based gum for your chewing habit – normal chewing gum takes many years to biodegrade and can cause problems for wildlife because of its stickiness. Mastic gum is made from the resin of the Aegean mastic tree and is 100% natural.

restaurant dining

CERTIFIED GREEN

In the US, a Green Restaurant Association has been established since 1990 to help restaurants become more environmentally sustainable. Check out its Certified Green Restaurant Guide, which lists those that meet its standards at www.dinegreen.com.

ALL BAR NONE

The refreshments on offer in most pubs and bars aren't known for their health-giving properties but some places are trying to change all that. Look out for organic "gastropubs" that offer seasonal, organic, locally sourced food along with locally brewed beers and organic wines and spirits.

NOT SO FAST

Britons eat almost 2 billion takeaway meals a year while in the US nearly half the money spent on food goes on food prepared away from home. But while many fast-food chains are making improvements to their menus and practices, as with supermarkets, the scale and the way they operate means they are never going to be the best eco-friendly option.

FISHY FARE

Many restaurants are starting to realize that customers care about the sustainability of their food and this includes the fish on the menu. Look out for those that include details of how the fish is caught (always opt for line-caught fish) and seek out restaurants that carry the Marine Stewardship Council (MSC) eco-label.

USE YOUR OWN CUP

The fast-food industry giants such as Wendy's and McDonald's are some of the largest consumers of paper products in the US and much of the paper is coming from the forests in South America, where many species of plant are endangered due to habitat loss. The next time you want a coffee, take your own cup along and say no to napkins and cup holders. See nofreerefills.org for more ideas.

GASTRONOMICALLY GREEN

A growing number of restaurants are starting to take responsibility for the planet, and in London they have formed a network called Ethical Eats. For example, the Acorn House restaurant in London has a green roof for growing the herbs used in their dishes and their own water-purification system. And the reason it matters? Recent research found that the CO_2 produced by a selection of restaurant meals in London, based on imported ingredients from non-European countries, is on average more than a hundred times higher than that of ingredients produced in Britain.

CAFÉ CULTURE

Many local cafés and quick-stop restaurants are still bastions of deep-fried food but there are healthier alternatives for a quick meal. Juice bars are great options for healthy salads and fresh-pressed drinks, or choose vegan or vegetarian cafés. Some specialty restaurants, such as VitaOrganic in London, focus on raw foods and food cooked at a low temperature to optimize vitamin content.

WHERE'S THE INFO?

Fast food is often high in fat, additives, sugar and salt, but you'd be hard-pressed to find out just how high. A recent National Consumer Council study in the UK has found that leading takeaway chains still offer little, if any, nutritional information to help customers make healthy choices. Buy food from somewhere that is happy to shout about the nutritional content of its meals.

fruit & vegetables

FEELING FRESH

Produce that is fresh and ripe will contain more nutrients than that which is stored for weeks, or even months, in energy-hungry refrigerated containers. A good way to buy fresh is to buy local, directly from producers, and also to buy seasonally – such as apples in autumn or strawberries in summer.

LETTUCE GROW

Don't think that lettuce is impossible to grow if you don't have a garden – it's the perfect crop for windowsills as they prefer sheltered, sunny spots. Simply plant out the seedlings and watch them grow.

SAVE YOUR PEELINGS

Don't throw away fruit and vegetable peelings. If you don't compost, they can make great food for local wildlife. Contact your local council or wildlife trust for advice on where they can be left to benefit animals without attracting pests.

EAT YOUR WEEDS

Don't overlook the green stuff in your garden, even if it is just weeds. Some weeds make tasty additions to salads, so give nettles, dandelion, purslane and lamb's quarters (*Chenopodium album*, also known as wild spinach) a try when the plants are young and tender. You'll find more information and recipes online.

PICK YOUR VEGETABLES

Help is at hand when it comes to finding out which vegetables are in season. The website www.thinkvegetables.co.uk lists those that are in season in the UK and ranks veggies according to their value in terms of particular vitamins or phytochemicals. In the US, search www.sustainabletable.org/shop/eatseasonal for a state-by-state directory of crops in season.

USE IT QUICKLY

Minerals and vitamins in fresh vegetables are gradually lost over time no matter how carefully vegetables are transported and stored, so it is vital to eat them as quickly as you can after purchase – another good reason to buy locally and frequently!

AN APPLE A DAY

A non-organic apple can be sprayed up to 16 times with 36 different chemicals, many of which cannot simply be washed off. British government tests, carried out in 2005, found pesticides in 80% of non-organic apple samples. Choose organic to cut out chemicals in your diet or research pesticides used on fruit at www. pesticides.gov.uk or www.epa.gov/pesticides/about/types.htm.

PEEL ALERT

According to the WWF, orange production requires more intensive use of pesticides than any other major crops. If pesticide residues do remain on the fruit (and in 2007 the British Pesticides Residues Committee found residues from more than one pesticide on all 37 samples of soft citrus fruits tested), then they are likely to be on the peel. So avoid using non-organic peel in your recipes and buy organic marmalade.

GROW IT, DON'T BUY IT

Cultivate your own vegetables and fruit without using pesticides and herbicides and you will know that your food is as fresh and natural as possible. From a selection of herbs on your windowsill to a raised bed filled with tomatoes, strawberries and runner beans – you can grow at the scale that suits you.

FROZEN IN TIME

Frozen vegetables are usually processed within a few hours of harvest and there is little nutrient loss in the freezing process so frozen vegetables are likely to have a higher vitamin and mineral content than some fresh vegetables, which often take days or weeks to reach the dinner table.

HERBY HOMES

As well as fruit and vegetables, be sure to grow some herbs – if only on a windowsill. Chives, mint, basil, parsley – start with those you use regularly and experience the thrill of snipping minutes before eating. It'll also save you buying costly vacuum-packed, pesticide-laden herbs that have been flown in to a supermarket near you.

BUCK THE TREND

Just a few varieties of fruit and vegetables are grown and sold commercially, chosen by supermarkets and their suppliers for regularity of shape, colour and flawless appearance, rather than flavour or continuity. This has led to the loss of many tasty, nutrition-packed varieties, which is bad for biodiversity and potentially leaves us exposed to future pests and diseases. So look for unusual varieties, support retailers that are bucking the trend and plant your own heritage seeds.

EAT HERITAGE VEGETABLES

Purchase or grow heritage produce to preserve genetic diversity. Britain's organic growing charity, Garden Organic, looks after over 800 varieties of rare and heirloom vegetables in its Heritage Seed Library, and is offering people the chance to "Adopt a Veg" (www.gardenorganic.org.uk), which conserves a variety by paying for the seed handling, storage and propagation facilities.

GIVE IT A SCRUB

Wash your fruit and vegetables, especially if you don't buy organic, since your produce is likely to have been sprayed with pesticides or other chemicals. A good scrub will help remove some of these, although be aware that many agricultural chemicals are trapped under a wax coating added to resist water and prolong shelf life. There are several products out there that can help, such as Organiclean or Veggie-Wash, or you can try soaking produce for five minutes in a 50/50 solution of white vinegar and water. But remember to always fill a bowl with water rather than to wash produce under a running tap (faucet).

GET SPROUTING

You don't need much space to grow your own nutrition-packed sprouts. Use on old jar or invest in a sprouter, buy organic, non-GM sprout seeds (try your local health food store for these) and off you go (remembering to soak and rinse them first). They could be ready to eat in as little as 12 hours for quinoa and five to six days for most others.

GO RAW

By eating a lot of raw fruit and vegetables you will be saving power, have fewer pans to go in the dishwasher and be doing your health the world of good by reducing the amount of cooked, processed or highly refined foods in your diet.

DON'T SEEK PERFECTION

Bent carrots, odd shaped spuds … nature doesn't go in for standardization. Yet, every year thousands of tonnes of perfectly tasty fruit and vegetables are thrown away by supermarkets because they don't look good. The retailers say their customers won't buy any produce that is less than perfect … prove them wrong!

SURPRISE BENEFITS

You may be routinely throwing away beneficial parts of your vegetables. Take the leafy tops on beetroot, for example, or salad onion leaves. Before cutting and binning, take a look online for recipes and cooking tips: you may be surprised to see what you could have been eating for all these years. But don't be tempted to give rhubarb leaves a try – these really are very poisonous when eaten raw or cooked.

SALAD DAYS

If you are a sucker for those pre-washed and bagged salad leaves in the supermarket, then stop and think again. According to the World Wide Fund for Nature (WWF), they are often immersed in chlorine at concentrations up to 20 times higher than the average swimming pool. Dump the plastic bags of leaves and give growing your own a try – salad leaves are incredibly easy and fun to produce.

DRESS IT WELL

It's a health crime to make a beautiful salad using organic leaves, sprouts, veggies or fruits and then smother it in a highly processed, unhealthy dressing. Make your own using just a few ingredients – you can get away with just one part vinegar to two parts good-quality olive oil, with a dash of mustard or garlic for taste – and experiment with flavours.

GET WITH THE BEET

Don't overlook traditional, seasonal vegetables such as the humble beetroot. It is one of the best dietary sources of folate and is a good source of vitamin C, potassium, manganese and fibre. Deep red varieties are rich in anthocyanins, which may reduce cancer risk and you can also eat beetroot's green leaves, which contain betacarotene, calcium and iron.

TIME FOR SOME SPUDS

Britons eat 94 kg (207 lb) of potatoes each a year – and for good reason; they are packed with potassium, iron and other nutrients such as vitamins C, B6 and B1. In fact, one portion of spuds can provide 19% of the recommended daily intake of iron compared with pasta's 7%. Rather than flying your pasta in from overseas, pick potatoes for your next meal.

MUSHROOM MAGIC

You can grow your very own mushrooms by purchasing a mushroom growing kit. The easiest culinary mushrooms to grow at home are oyster, shiitake, wine cap and portobello, but many more possibilities exist. Mushrooms are low in salt and fat, and provide dietary fibre, some protein and significant quantities of B vitamins. They are also good source of minerals, including iron.

GO BANANAS

It's official … bananas are the world's most popular fruit with almost 5 billion US dollars' worth sold each year. But the banana business has caused widespread deforestation, the pollution of coral reefs and waterways, and contamination from toxic agrochemicals. It also has a history of exploitation when it comes to paying a fair price to growers. Look for organic, fairtrade or Rainforest Alliance certified bananas.

LOCAL CARROTS

Carrots are Britain's second most popular vegetable after potatoes and almost all of the carrots we buy are grown in the UK, but there are still issues relating to food miles. According to Sustain, carrots, like other foods, are travelling nearly 60% further on the UK roads than in the 1970s due to the centralization of food distribution. Buy your carrots loose from local, preferably organic growers.

PEEL IT

Pesticide use on carrots has been such a matter of health concern that the British government actually advises consumers to peel and top carrots before eating, which will remove about four-fifths of the residue – unfortunately it also removes nutrients in the peel. This is just another good reason to buy organic!

GET A GROWBAG

Tomatoes are taking a heavy toll on our environment. The World Wildlife Fund says that tomato production uses high levels of agro-chemicals, such as methyl bromide for disinfecting soil, which damage and pollute rivers and cause soil erosion. They are another easy crop to grow for anyone with a small amount of space in a sunny spot and you can buy organic growbags to make life really easy.

BERRIES FROM HEAVEN

The superfruit trend has seen a soaring demand for products like goji berries (which come from a vine that grows in China, Tibet and other areas of Asia) and the Brazilian palm tree super-berry acai, based on their high nutritional value. But while they may be high in vitamins and antioxidants, so are many other fruits grown nearer to home.

CHEERS TO CHERRIES

Cherry orchards are going the same way as apple orchards in the UK – in 50 years 90% of cherry orchards have been lost and 95% of cherries eaten in the nation are now imported. Benefit from a better local supply of this healthy fruit by supporting Cherry Aid, and even renting your own cherry tree for a year (see www.foodloversbritain.com).

SUPPORT FOR ORCHARDS

Since 1970, over 60% of UK apple orchards have been lost and, although there are around 6,000 varieties of dessert and cooking apples and hundreds more cider apples, today just ten types of apple account for 92% of the UK's area of eating apple orchards. In the US, only 15 varieties account for 90% of total production. Seek out traditional or "heirloom" types, and look out too for unusual varieties of damson, plums, cherries and pears. Heirloom apple farms will often sell cuttings from their trees as well as the fruit.

DRIED FRUIT DANGERS

Dried fruit is full of fibre and vitamins but there are some health fears linked to the use of sulphur dioxide as a dried fruit preservative. In some sulphites may cause allergic reactions such as breathing difficulties, hives and migraines. Ten years ago the World Health Organization (WHO) warned that up to 20–30% of childhood asthmatics may be sensitive to sulphite preservatives and recommended their use be reduced or phased out. Seek out organic non-sulphured apricots and avoid the many over-packaged dried fruit snack products for children.

DON'T PEEL

If you buy organic fruit and vegetables, then peeling is mostly unnecessary from a health perspective and could reduce the nutritional value of your food. Rather than waste a vitamin- and fibre-rich part of your diet, keep the peel on and just give it a quick scrub in a little water. For those items that need peeling, a banana or orange say, make sure the peelings go on a compost heap and not in the garbage bin.

DEGRADABLE DOUBTS

You may think that the greenest packaging for your fruit and veg is the latest kind of degradable plastic, but it is causing a number of concerns. Some types require light to degrade, so if they end up buried in a landfill site they won't break down, while others that biodegrade may cause an increase in the greenhouse gas methane if they end up in landfill as opposed to a hot compost heap.

dairy products

A LOT OF BOTTLE
Britons now consume about 85m litres (180m pints) of milk a
week, at least two-thirds of which is sold by supermarkets in
plastic bottles, which either end up in landfill or are shipped
hundreds of miles for recycling, mostly in China. Find and
support a local milk delivery service – they often use electric
vehicles and will pick-up and re-use the bottles. Look online
at www.findmeamilkman.net or www.winderfarms.com/
homedelivery/milkmenacrossamerica.

MILK IT
European research has found that organic milk has nearly 70%
more essential fatty acid omega-3 than its non-organic equivalent
and other studies have also shown organic milk contains
significantly more vitamin E and beta-carotene. This is likely to be
due to the cows' diet – organic cows graze freely on fresh grass and
clover while most non-organic cows eat a more grain-based diet.

HORMONE-FREE
In the US, cows are commonly injected with an artificial,
genetically engineered growth hormone (rBGH) in order to
increase the per-cow milk yield. But these hormones have
been linked to increasing risks of developing breast and colon
cancers. Milk from hormone-treated cows doesn't have to
be labelled, so look for milk labelled "No rBGH" or check
online for a list of those hormone-free milk producers
(www.organicconsumers.org/rBGH/rbghlist.cfm).

ARTISAN ICE CREAM
Some non-dairy ice creams contain palm oil – listed as
"vegetable fat", while other ingredients might include
chemical colourings, emulsifiers, stabilizers and partially
hydrogenated fats, as well as a lot of air to add bulk
(up to 120% air in cheap ice cream). Look for artisan
dairy ice creams made using natural, organic and
authentic eggs, milk and cream.

CONSIDER UHT

It could be greener to buy UHT (Ultra High Temperature) milk – milk that has been heated to a higher temperature than pasteurized milk – as it doesn't require storing in large energy-guzzling refrigerators. UHT milk is popular in Europe, accounting for over 90% of milk consumption in France, Spain and Belgium, but in Britain it makes up only 8.4% of the milk market. In the US, Parmalat UHT milk is sold, and many food products are made using UHT milk.

A BAG OF MILK, PLEASE

In Canada, 40% of milk is delivered in bags and now British consumers are getting the same opportunity. The bags, or packs, use 75% less plastic than a standard one-litre plastic milk bottle. You buy a jug to keep in the fridge and top it up with the bags. The idea is to stop 100,000 plastic milk bottles hitting our landfill sites each year. But in order to offset the energy used to make the non-recyclable jug, you need to keep using it.

YUMMY YOGURT

Yogurt is rich in protein, B vitamins and calcium but pick an organic brand in order to avoid artificial additives, flavourings, sweeteners, and so on. You can also benefit from the higher omega-3 fatty acids and antioxidants commonly found in organic milk.

GET READY FOR CLONES

Regulatory authorities in the US and Europe have decided that meat and milk from cloned cattle is safe. Already claims are being made for cloning, such as the possibility of cloning a cow that produces lower-fat milk, but others argue that there isn't enough evidence to be certain about the long-term health effects and that cloning reduces biodiversity.

EAT YOUR CHEESE

There are around 700 cheeses produced in Britain alone, but they account for only 65% of the cheese eaten in the UK. Instead of driving up demand for imported food, seek out local cheese makers and support their businesses. Goat's and ewe's milk cheeses are likely to have the lowest carbon emissions since cows have a bigger carbon footprint. You could also try making your own – www.cheesemaking.co.uk has advice on how to get started.

cereals & grains

A TRADITIONAL LOAF

Almost all of the bread industrial bakers sell is made with enzymes. These don't have to be declared as an ingredient as they are deemed to be a "processing aid" and there is currently no safety evaluation of food enzymes at European level, but there are concerns that they could cause allergies. Find a traditional artisan baker and ask how they make their bread.

FAT IN YOUR BREAD

Of the 9 million loaves of bread eaten each day in the UK most will come from vast industrial bakeries where vegetable fat is used to keep the loaf fresher for longer. Not only is this more saturated fat that your body could do without, it could also be at the expense of the world's great forests. Millions of hectares of tropical rainforest are being cleared yearly for the planting of palm oil crops and it is often palm oil that is being used in bread.

BAKE BREAD

Go back to a simpler time when bread was made of flour, salt, water and yeast – bake your own. There are many recipes available and plenty of advice online. You will be able to avoid additives and preservatives such as sodium stearoyl lactylate and diglycerides so common in shop-bought breads, as well as feel empowered by creating nutritious and delicious food from the wholesome ingredients you have chosen. For more on why it's worth the effort, see www.breadmatters.com.

DO YOU KNEAD IT?

Unfortunately, far too many people think the first step to baking bread is a dash to their nearest electrical store to buy a bread-maker. But over the past ten years electricity consumption from consumer electronics and domestic computers in the UK has increased by 47% and is expected to rise by 82% by 2011. Cut back on your power consumption and get kneading – it will be good for toning your arms as well – but start with a simple recipe first.

BE ADVENTUROUS

You don't just have to stick with brown rice and oatmeal – there's a whole world of healthy grains out there, including amaranth, emmer, farro, grano (lightly pearled wheat), spelt, triticale, bulgur (cracked wheat), millet, quinoa and sorghum. But always opt for organic and support local farmers, where possible.

WHEAT CONCERNS

More land is used to grow wheat than any other crop in the world, which is why the way in which it is grown matters so much for biodiversity. Unfortunately, conventional wheat farming uses large amounts of artificial fertilizers, is a big user of chemicals such as herbicides, soil fumigants, insecticides and fungicides, and demands a lot of water – it is the second most-irrigated crop globally.

BECOME A MUESLI MIXER

Save money and gain peace of mind by mixing your own muesli. You'll also be able to ensure that the nuts, fruits, seeds and grains you choose are produced ethically and in a sustainable manner. Plus, by buying in bulk you'll be saving on packaging and reducing the carbon emissions that would have resulted from frequent purchases of pre-packed muesli.

LOOK FOR LOCAL GRAINS

To cut your food miles and ensure you are getting a good mix, look into locally produced, ideally organic, grains – likely to be oats, barley and rye for those living in northern Europe. Buy wholegrains to ensure the least amount of energy has been used in their production and to maximize nutritional content.

BARS ARE NOT THE ANSWER

More than half the UK population purchases a cereal bar every six weeks but replacing a nutritional breakfast with a cereal bar is unlikely to be helping you or the planet. Tests on cereal bars found them to be high in saturated fat and sugar. Then there's the packaging – each bar is individually wrapped – plus the energy used to process them.

KEEP IT REAL WITH YOUR CEREAL

Beware the big brands and their child-friendly breakfast cereals – these products are often loaded with teeth-decaying sugar. Consumer group Which? found that out of 275 cereals tested, 52 were found to directly target children and 88% of these were found to be high in sugar. A good number of them are among the saltiest of children's foods. Look for healthier options that are GM-, sugar- and salt-free.

MORNING GLORY

Scientists have found that people who eat breakfast every day are a third less likely to be obese compared to those who skipped it, and are half as likely to have blood-sugar problems. It's also crucial to get the content of your breakfast bowl right since some cereals contain as much sugar as a chocolate bar and as much saturated fat as a portion of cake. The best option is to make your own porridge, using organically-grown oats sourced locally.

CUT BACK ON RICE

More than 90% of the world's rice harvest is grown and consumed in Asia, which means that unless you live there your rice has probably notched up quite a few food miles. It is also likely that it will have been treated with chemicals – Asian rice growers use 13% of global pesticides, according to the World Wildlife Fund – and a great deal of water (it takes 3,000–5,000 litres of water [790–1,320 gallons] to produce 1 kg [2¼ lb] of rice).

TRY QUINOA

A "superfood" that is classified as a grain but which is actually a seed, quinoa is high in protein, calcium, iron and lysine, an amino acid. Not only is it nutritionally beneficial but it contains saponin, a bitter, resin-like substance that is a natural insect repellent – this keeps the crop nearly untouched by birds thus limiting the pesticides needed to grow the crop. It is also easily cultivated and has a long growing season. The saponins must be removed by soaking the grain in water before cooking.

 # fish & seafood

FISH FACTS

Atlantic cod stocks are currently at historic low levels and the species is now threatened with commercial extinction in UK waters. Only buy cod that has been line-caught from a sustainable fishery or choose alternatives such as rock salmon. Cod, hake, halibut and plaice are usually caught by bottom trawling, which destroys the seabed.

HAVE A FISH SUPPER

When you eat seafood, steer clear of endangered species. In the case of salmon, for example, choose a sustainably fished species, such as wild Alaskan, over farm-raised (which pollutes watersheds) or wild Atlantic (which is at historic lows). If in doubt, check for Marine Stewardship Council certified products and their Fish to Eat and Fish to Avoid lists.

BE FISH FRIENDLY

Fish, and especially oily fish, is a great option for your health. But over half of fish stocks are being fished at their maximum biological capacity and, of all the world's natural resources, fish are being depleted the fastest, according to the United Nations. So buying sustainably is imperative.

GO LOW ON THE FOOD CHAIN

Avoid bigger fish such as tuna, swordfish, shark and sea bass, as these accumulate toxins and heavy metals in their flesh. Opt instead for smaller "schooling" fish such as sardines, herrings and anchovies.

KNOWLEDGE IS POWER

Overfishing has affected oceans in every part of the world, making it a global concern. Educate yourself to be a sustainable seafood consumer. There are some great resources out there, such as the pocket fish guides from the Marine Conservation Society (www.fishonline.org), the Environmental Defense Fund (www.edf.org) and the National Audubon Society (www.seafood.audubon.org), which tell you which species to avoid eating.

EAT LESS FISH

In the UK, the Food Standards Agency recommends that people should consume at least two portions of fish a week, of which one should be oily, based on its nutritional benefits. However, if 49 million adults in the UK complied with this advice it would require an extra 33 million portions of oily fish per week. Look into getting the nutrients, vitamins and oils in fish from other sources. For example, high levels of omega oils can also be found in walnuts and linseed and flax oil.

GET AN MSC

The Marine Stewardship Council (MSC) runs the only widely recognized environmental certification and eco-labelling programme for wild capture fisheries, so look for the blue MSC logo on the fish you buy. There are over 1,100 seafood products sporting the logo to show they have come from well-managed and sustainable fisheries (visit www.msc.org).

TUNA TIPS

Canned tuna is a good source of omega-3 fatty acids and it is hugely popular in the US. But there are health concerns regarding mercury contamination. Of the two main kinds – canned light (chunk light) and albacore tuna (solid/chunk white) – the latter averages three times the amount of mercury as that found in other canned tuna.

CATCH OF THE DAY

The way your fish is caught could have cost the environment dearly. Bottom trawling can destroy sensitive marine environments while longline fishing is responsible for the death of thousands of other animals and fish caught alongside. It is estimated, for example, that 250,000 seabirds die each year because of longline fishing, including around 40,000 albatross in the Southern Ocean.

CANNED SALMON

If you are looking for a healthy alternative to tuna, consider opting for canned wild salmon which contains up to four times as many omega-3s as chunky light tuna, according to the USDA (US Department of Agriculture). The fish are usually low in contaminants but still ensure that they are sustainably caught.

"DOLPHIN-FRIENDLY" TUNA

The term "dolphin-friendly" on tuna labels generally means very little, according to Greenpeace, since there is no legal standard or minimum criteria applied to the term. So, while the tuna may have been fished using methods less likely to catch dolphins, it could have come from overexploited tuna stocks or have been caught using a method that has other adverse impacts. If you must buy tuna, choose line-caught skipjack tuna.

SUSHI SAFETY

For health and environmental reasons, steer clear of ordering sushi made with bluefin tuna. Demand from the global sushi market is driving this large fish to the brink of extinction. A recent *New York Times* report found that much of the bluefin sushi served in New York City restaurants exceeds the US FDA's "action level" for mercury. For safe and sustainable sushi, check out the Environmental Defense Fund's Seafood Selector (www.edf.org).

THE COST OF SHRIMP

Shrimp fisheries have the world's highest bycatch rate—about 5 kg (10 lb) of marine life is killed for each kilo of shrimp harvested and an estimated 10 million tonnes of finfish is thrown away each year in shrimp trawl fisheries. Look instead for northern coldwater prawns that have been sustainably caught, particularly pot-caught.

FARMING FISH

A large amount of the fish we eat comes from fish farms— indeed in the US, over one-third of all fish eaten is farmed. But these farms can be terrible for the surrounding environment. For example, wild fish are used as feed for some farmed fish, so these farm operations actually consume more fish than they produce. Other farms may pollute the surrounding ocean with faeces from the huge populations of penned fish and toxic chemicals used to kill off algae on nets.

OILY BENEFITS

To get all the health benefits of oily fish without costing the environment dear, choose wild salmon from Alaska that is certified by the Marine Stewardship Council, or Scottish and Irish wild salmon. For cheaper choices, try mackerel and herring.

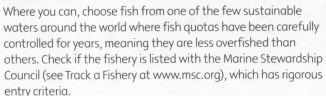

ABOVE WATER

Where you can, choose fish from one of the few sustainable waters around the world where fish quotas have been carefully controlled for years, meaning they are less overfished than others. Check if the fishery is listed with the Marine Stewardship Council (see Track a Fishery at www.msc.org), which has rigorous entry criteria.

SHELLFISH OPTIONS

Shellfish farms tend to be more eco-friendly than fish farms as shellfish don't need extra feed and are not concentrated in pens. Choose from farm-raised oysters, clams and mussels for a more environmentally friendly seafood option.

THE ORGANIC CHOICE

You can buy organic farmed fish from farms which will have met high environmental standards, including limits and restrictions on the use of medicines and chemicals, plus feed is sourced sustainably and stocking densities are limited. But for many, even organic farms aren't great – they can still use lots of the same chemicals as conventional farmers and they still pollute the ocean with sewage – it has been estimated that an organic salmon farm can produce the same amount of untreated sewage as the population of a small town.

SEAWEED SOLUTIONS

Seaweeds, such as kombu, wakame and nori, are becoming popular worldwide due to their nutritional and medicinal benefits. In fact, seaweeds provide all of the 56 minerals and trace minerals required by the body and contain 10 to 20 times the minerals of land plants. Buy from a company that supports traditional seaweed farming and harvesting practices, and avoid hijiki – there have been concerns over high levels of the toxin arsenic found in this seaweed.

WALK THE LINE

When buying wild fish such as tuna and marlin, make sure you choose fish caught by long lines rather than nets. This ensures that no dolphins or other aquatic species have been harmed to get you your dinner.

FARM YOUR FISH
Don't worry about buying farmed fish as long as it's organic – organic fish farming processes are humane and overfeeding of fish is not allowed. Fish are kept in natural river habitats without the use of dyes.

PRAWN PROBLEMS
Annual sales of prawns (shrimp) are growing at an average of 9% a year but this demand is driving environmental destruction around the world. Nearly 40% of world mangrove loss has been attributed to shrimp farming and mangroves are among the most productive ecosystems on the planet. If you do buy them, look out for organic or Madagascan tiger prawns as Madagascar is working toward making all its prawn fisheries sustainable.

beef, lamb & venison

A MEATY MATTER
Eat less meat. A report for the United Nations, "Livestock's Long Shadow", has found that the meat industry is responsible for 18% of greenhouse gases – more than all forms of transport put together – and leads to deforestation, acid rain and desertification. According to Environmental Defense, if every American skipped one meal of chicken per week and substituted vegetarian foods instead, the carbon dioxide savings would be the same as taking more than a half-million cars off US roads. See www.meatlessmonday.com for support and ideas.

FEED THE HUNGRY
Raising livestock uses a disproportionate amount of the world's resources which could be better employed in feeding the hungry. For example, in the US it is estimated that 70% of all grains, 80% of all agricultural land, half of all water resources and one-third of all fossil fuels are used to raise animals for food. When you hear about global food shortages, ponder the fact that there is already enough grain grown on earth to feed 10 billion vegetarian people but much of it is fed to cattle.

DON'T SEE RED

Red meat is a rich source of protein, iron, vitamin B12 and zinc, but some clear links are emerging between the consumption of red meat and certain diseases such as bowel cancer. By cutting back on red meat you will doing your body a favour and helping the environment – the world's 1.5 billion cattle are among the greatest threat to the climate, forests and wildlife.

GO FOR GRASS

Producing red meat really does cost this planet dear – for example, scientists have found that producing 1 kg (2.2 lb) of beef results in the same CO_2 emissions that would be released by a European car every 250 kilometres (155 miles) and the energy consumption is equal to a 100-watt bulb being left on for 20 days. But in 2003, a Swedish study found that raising organic beef on grass, rather than feed, reduced greenhouse gas emissions by 40% and consumed 85% less energy.

A QUESTION OF BREEDING

If you decide to have a meat treat then go for local traditional breeds such as Sussex cattle, one of the oldest English breeds. You will be doing your bit to support biodiversity, reducing food miles (especially if the meat came via a local abattoir) and traditional breeds are often farmed less intensively.

CHOOSE PORK OVER BEEF OR LAMB

According to a comparison report by Defra, the British government's environmental authority, beef and lamb received the poorest marks of all meats in terms of energy usage, global warming and eutrophication. Pigs, however, don't expel methane from their digestive tracts throughout the day, they breed more efficiently and they eat less to reach their weight, making pork a greener choice.

DIP INTO A DIRECTORY

Help is at hand if you want to get the health benefits of grass-fed meat. In the US and Canada Eatwild's Directory of Farms has a listing of more than 800 pasture-based farms (www.eatwild.com) while in the UK, Seeds of Health lists grass-fed meat producers (www.seedsofhealth.co.uk).

DON'T BE TEMPTED BY CHEAP MEAT

To produce beef, pork and poultry cheaply in large quantities, industrial farmers cut corners that harm the environment and result in a lower quality of meat. Most intensively-reared animals are given antibiotics daily and this use has been linked to the rise of antibiotic-resistant superbugs such as the *Staphylococcus aureus bacterium*, MRSA. In the US, cattle is commonly injected with hormones to increase the growth rate.

CHECK YOUR INGREDIENTS

If you are buying meat from a supermarket, make sure you check your ingredients list carefully. There should be nothing but meat in it. Anything saying "meat protein" means you're buying heavily processed food.

GO FOR GRASS

Look for beef from cattle fed grass-based diets as American research has found it has up to 500% more of two types of conjugated linoleic acids (CLAs) than beef from animals fed high cereal-maize diets. These CLAs are believed to protect against cancer, and red meat and milk from grass-fed animals are the richest dietary sources. All organic cattle in the EU have grass-based diets.

LAMB CHOICES

Sheep don't lend themselves to intensive farming, so whether you buy organic or not, your lamb is likely to have been naturally produced with sheep grazing freely in open countryside. Organic sheep fed mostly on pesticide-free grass will have received far fewer veterinary treatments than non-organic sheep. In Britain Soil Association organic standards ban the use of organophosphorus sheep dips to control infestation as they have serious health implications for animals and humans.

EAT LEAN MEAT

Whenever you can, eat lean meat. Chemicals from animal feed, antibiotics or fertilizers in grass are stored more in fat than in muscle, accumulating to high levels. Making sure you trim fat off meat could lessen your chances of ingesting it.

GET BUTCHER'S BLOCK

One of the best things you can do to make your meat a green choice is cull the supermarket and visit a butcher who will source meat locally and will be able to tell you the origin of what you're buying. They often have long-established connections with specific farms and will know about the raising of the animals. Packaging is kept to a minimum, too.

A MEATY MATTER

Buy free-range, organically raised meat and poultry products. The animals will have been raised humanely and on untreated feeds, resulting in chemical-free food. You can also be assured that the soil from these farms is treated well, reducing the impact on wildlife habitats.

PICK ECOLOGICAL

It doesn't have to be organic to be an ecological option. These days you can pick from a variety of meat and cheeses that have come from sheep and cattle grazed on biodiverse pastures, such as moorland and salt marshes, rich in wild plant species. Research has shown that not only does this kind of grazing assist the biodiversity of the sites, there are also health and taste benefits for the consumer. Look online for suppliers.

VEGGIES BEWARE

While it is a great idea to give beefburgers a miss, replacing them with veggie burgers may not be the best alternative. Many of these are made with soya-based Textured Vegetable Protein, which needs a lot of energy to produce and is far from a traditional natural product. Choose organic varieties made with rice, beans and/or vegetables.

V IS FOR VENISON

Venison might be a more eco-friendly red meat option than beef since there are a number of small, sustainable providers of wild venison who are actually helping to protect endangered species, such as bluebells, that are under threat from a recent rise in the number of deer. Like most red meat, it is a good source of protein and iron, but as a bonus it is fairly low in fat, including saturated fat.

UPLAND ISSUES

In the UK, almost two-thirds of sheep are in hill and upland areas but overstocking and overgrazing have caused widespread ecological damage; this leads to barren landscapes that can no longer absorb all the rain that falls, increasing the risk of flooding in towns and cities. But a recent change in agricultural subsidies is seeing a decline in hill farming which is resulting in too little grazing and therefore a loss of habitat for some birds. Support hill farmers that are managing the land sustainably.

CUT BACK ON PROCESSED MEAT

Researchers from the US National Cancer Institute found that both red and processed meats increased risks for bowel and lung cancer, and between them raised the risk of developing other cancers such as throat cancer and pancreatic cancer (in men). In the case of processed meat, there are concerns that additive sodium nitrite – used as a preservative and to fix the colour of the meat – is carcinogenic.

 # poultry & eggs

A GOOD LIFE

Treating animals well brings benefits for you, too. For example, studies have shown that factory-farmed chickens contain more fat and less iron than traditional breeds that are usually farmed in free-range or organic conditions, with ample space to roam. Intensively farmed chickens are given high-energy foods and are inactive, so a typical supermarket chicken in the West contains more fat than protein, with 2.7 times as much fat as in 1970.

RAISE YOUR OWN

If you want to be certain that your eggs come from happy, healthy, truly free-range chickens, then consider keeping your own, but check with your local regulating body whether you need permission. Try www.mypetchicken.com for advice, and remember to feed them your food scraps and use their manure on your compost.

BEWARE WASHED CHICKEN IMPORTS

The US chicken industry widely uses antimicrobial washes for poultry meat but there are concerns that this masks the underlying cause of bacterial contamination in the first place and could lead to further antibiotic resistance in humans. The EU banned antimicrobial washes for poultry meat in 1997, but there is pressure to lift the ban in order to allow trade. Find out if the chicken you've been buying has been washed.

BATTERIES ARE BAD

Battery cages give laying hens less space than a sheet of paper. As well as leading to psychological and physical suffering for hens, recent scientific research has found that battery eggs are more likely to carry salmonella than free-range or organic eggs. Europe is banning the use of battery cages by 2012 but currently more than 75% of European hens are kept in them, while in the US nearly 280 million laying hens are confined in cages (according to the Humane Society).

ALL IN AN EGG

Eggs contain 13 essential vitamins and minerals, are a good source of high-quality protein and are rich in antioxidants. But buy your eggs from pasture-raised chickens which have been allowed to roam freely. Numerous studies have found that eggs from poultry raised on pasture have been shown to have higher levels of vitamins A, B12 and E and far higher amounts of omega-3 fatty acids than conventional eggs. Plus, it uses less energy as there is no need to transport feed and animal waste.

nuts, seeds & pulses

TRADITIONAL PRACTICES
When buying soya products, such as soya sauce or miso, select those that have been made according to traditional methods from Japan and China, whereby the soya has been fermented for months. This process reduces the levels of the phytoestogens by two- to threefold and saves on fossil fuels used in modern factory processing. Plus, Japanese or Chinese strains of soya have lower levels of isoflavones. Beware non-brewed soya sauce, which is made in just two days and will have salt, caramel and chemical preservatives and flavourings added to provide colour and taste.

PROTEIN FROM PULSES
Substituting pulses (legumes) for meat could bring down the climate cost of our diets. Choose from a range of beans, peas and lentils and add them to stews, casseroles, soups and sauces or use them in salads. They are high in fibre, which may help lower blood cholesterol, and a good source of iron (although try to drink orange juice or eat foods high in vitamin C with them in order to help absorb the iron).

SUNNY SIDE OF SEEDS
Whether it's from your sunflowers or pumpkins, remember you can harvest the seeds to make a nutritious snack. In the case of the sunflower, once it has finished flowering tie a paper bag over the flower to catch the seeds as they dry. Try roasting the dry seeds or, if you have enough of them, remove the hulls and crush them to make a tasty nut butter.

SOYA SAGA
Soya, in its various forms, can be found in more than 60% of processed food such as breakfast cereals, biscuits, cakes, gravies, pastries and sauces. But growing demand has led to the destruction of large swathes of precious South American habitat and is one of the main threats to the Amazon rainforest. So cut out processed food and cut back on cheap meat too – the demand for soya in animal feed is also driving deforestation.

SOYA RISK

Being high in omega-6 fatty acids, soya is thought to be one of the reasons why our balance of omega-3 to omega-6 essential fatty acids is so out of kilter, plus it has a high content of phytoestrogens, which can mimic or block the action of the human hormone oestrogen. Those with a thyroid problem and women with oestrogen-dependent breast cancer are particularly at risk from a diet high in soya.

NUTS ABOUT NUTS

Research has shown that eating nuts five or more times a week can reduce the risk of heart attack by 60% and there are many other health benefits. They may be high in fat, but people who regularly eat nuts are also more likely to be lean than those who don't. But check the nuts you buy are organic, as pesticides are commonly used in production.

BEANS AT HOME

Grow and dry your own pulses and enjoy an incredible array of beans in all sizes and colours. First, source varieties marked as "suitable for drying" from heritage seed suppliers such as www.heritageharvestseed.com. Once the plants have grown, just leave the pods on the plant – when they're brown, dry and rattling, the beans can be removed from the pods and packed in airtight jars.

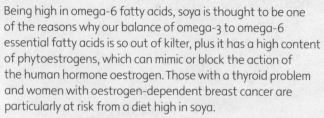

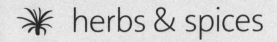# herbs & spices

HERB YOUR ENTHUSIASM

Don't buy packaged fresh or dried herbs in the supermarket when you can grow them in pots indoors. They are easy to grow, last much longer than shop-bought herbs and make your kitchen smell good, too. Some supermarkets sell growing herbs for this use.

GROW YOUR OWN FLAVOURFUL HERBS

Even if you're not at all green-fingered or don't have a garden you can still grow a few herbs in small containers to help liven up your diet. Indoor pots (try recycling cans and yogurt pots) may be used to grow herbs such as basil, thyme and parsley – you'll be saving energy and reducing emissions, too.

GROW YOUR OWN SPICES

Spices usually come from tropical countries, but it is perfectly possible to grow some of your own and cut down on your food miles. Coriander seed, chilli peppers and curry leaf – *Murraya koenigii* – will all grow in temperate climates if you can find a suitably sunny spot and keep the plants frost-free.

SPICE UP YOUR LIFE

Spices not only add flavour, they can also provide valuable health benefits. Turmeric, for example, has antioxidant, anticancer and anti-inflammatory properties, while cinnamon is thought to protect against type II diabetes and heart disease. Buy whole dried spices and grind them yourself in an energy-saving pestle and mortar to get the best flavour.

BEST SPICES

Seek out organic and fairtrade spices. Not only will you avoid pesticide residues and be certain the growers are receiving a fair price for their labour, but you will also be sure that the spices have not been irradiated. Irradiation of spices on a commercial scale is practised in over 20 countries and in 2000, 80,000 metric tonnes of spice were processed worldwide using irradiation, yet there have been no studies on the long-term effects of eating irradiated food.

 fats & oils

IS BUTTER BETTER?

Butter is a less-processed product since it must be at least 80% fat and the only additive allowed is salt, whereas margarine can be a mixture of oils and fats along with a range of additives; many also contain the health-harming hydrogenated vegetable oils to extend their shelf life.

OILY ISSUES

Over 70% of all oils and fats consumed in the world come from vegetable crops – but campaign group Sustain has found that most are made by companies that do little to protect the environment or consumer health. Of particular concern are palm oil, olive oil and rapeseed oil. Groundnut (peanut) and safflower oils are better choices.

CHECK FOR PALM OIL

Avoid food containing palm oil, which is found in one in ten supermarket products including chocolate, bread and crisps. Not only is it a saturated fat, but the growing demand for palm oil is driving the deforestation of the earth's rainforests. Check if your food retailer is buying from a sustainable source and ask if it is present in your products (often it's labelled "vegetable oil").

OLIVE HAS DOWNSIDE

Olive oil contains monounsaturated fat, which may lower cholesterol, and polyphenols which can help to ward off cancer. But intensified olive farming in the Mediterranean region "is a major cause of one of the biggest environmental problems affecting the EU today," according to WWF. To protect the environment, buy organic or from small cooperatives.

HEMP HELPS

Hemp seed oil is packed with healthy goodies, such as minerals, proteins and omega-3, -6 and -9, and it is said to help with eczema, asthma, heart disease and high blood pressure. It is a sustainable crop, since it requires very few agro-chemicals, is fast-growing and nearly all of the plant can be used in some way.

RAPESEED ISSUES

Rapeseed oil is lower in saturated fat and has a higher vitamin E content than olive oil. But it may be not so good in other ways. It is a winter crop and part of the big switch from spring-grown crops in the UK, which has dramatically reduced farmland biodiversity such as birds, which rely on spring crops for nesting sites. Plus, it relies heavily on fertilizers so has a poor record among arable crops for leaching nitrates into waterways.

HYDROGENATED NIGHTMARES

One of the worst health hazards in processed foods comes from trans fats – formed when liquid oil is turned into solid fat through a process called hydrogenation. Trans fats increase the risk of coronary heart disease and are likely to have worse effects on the body than saturated fats found in butter. Both Denmark and Switzerland have banned these fats in food, but in the UK they don't even have to be listed in the ingredients. Avoid food containing hydrogenated vegetable oil.

salt, sugar, sweets & condiments

GO EASY ON THE SALT

Too much salt raises your blood pressure and thus increases your risk of heart disease and stroke so it's best to cut back. But avoiding salt can be tough – 75% of the salt we eat is already in the food we buy, such as breakfast cereals, sauces, soups and ready-meals, according to the Food Standards Agency. The best tip is to read the label and avoid processed foods in the first place, with the additional benefit of saving on the packaging and carbon emissions associated with these foods.

SALT OF THE SEA

Consider buying unrefined natural sea salt. It's higher in minerals and trace elements that are lost in the processing of table salt, and as it has a better flavour, less is needed in your food. Avoid all salts with anti-caking agents.

IS IT SO SWEET?

Most people in the developing world are eating too much sugar – it is rotting our teeth and contributing to the obesity epidemic. But it isn't just our health that is suffering. A WWF report shows that sugar may be responsible for more biodiversity loss than any other crop. Cut back the amount you eat by avoiding cakes and biscuits (cookies), and drinking fewer sugary, fizzy drinks.

CHOOSE YOUR CHOCOLATE

There are so many organic products to choose from nowadays that it's often hard to know where to start and stop. The cocoa plant is one of the most heavily sprayed in the world, so keep chocolate on your organic list. Many good organic brands use cocoa sourced in Central and South America. Make sure, however, that the manufacturer certifies that all of the cocoa they purchase is produced without the use of forced labour.

SWEET BAKING

When buying sugar for home baking, choose those that are certified as both organic and fairly traded to be sure that the environment and those working with the sugar are being protected from exploitation. Opt for unrefined raw cane sugar as this will not have been refined using chemicals and bleaching agents – even "brown" sugar is just refined white sugar that has been coloured with caramel or raw cane molasses.

LOW-CAL CAUTION

For those seeking to reduce their calorie intake without giving up treats, artificial sweeteners appear to be the answer. But while they may be more or less calorie-free, they involve carbon-hungry manufacturing processes and are full of chemicals linked to health risks. Artificial sweeteners are not allowed in organic food.

SWEET AS HONEY

For thousands of years, honey has been used as a natural remedy for ailments – from sore throats to burns and cuts – because of its antiseptic properties. And this is one product that most of us can source locally. Supporting local, small-scale beekeepers will cut your food miles and ensure bees continue to play their vital role in pollinating crops in the countryside near you.

CHOCOLATE HEAVEN

Research has shown that eating small amounts of chocolate with a high cocoa content could bring nutritional benefits such as lower blood pressure and a reduced risk of death from cardiovascular disease because the chocolate is rich in antioxidants (flavonoids) and trace minerals. However, chocolate is also high in sugar and saturated fat, so consume high-cocoa-content chocolate in moderation.

SAVE THE TROPICS

Over 18 million acres (7.5 million hectares) of tropical land is used to grow cocoa so the way it is produced effects a big chunk of habitat. Like coffee, it is best for biodiversity to buy cocoa that has been grown under the shade of native canopy trees in a landscape similar to natural forest. It is also good to purchase organic and fairtrade chocolate as cocoa crops may be heavily sprayed with agrochemicals, while plantation workers can be working in conditions akin to slave labour.

EXOTIC IMPORTS

If you can't source locally produced honey, then opt for fairtrade and/or organic honey from overseas rather than mainstream commercial products. Commercial beekeepers may use synthetic pesticides and antibiotics to combat pests, while organic bees can't be treated with antibiotics as they must be able to forage in organically cultivated areas or areas of natural vegetation free from pesticides.

BEE FRIENDLY

Honeybees are big business – in the UK, bees contribute £165 million a year to the economy through their pollination of fruit trees, field beans and other crops, while in the US bee pollination services are worth an estimated $15 billion. But they are currently disappearing – almost two million colonies of honeybees have disappeared in the US. Pesticides are likely to be part of the problem, so help by supporting organic agriculture. Along with insect diseases, environmental stresses and other factors, pesticides are thought to be behind Colony Collapse Disorder, where worker bees from honeybee colonies suddenly disappear (see www.aworldwithoutbees.com).

GO FOR JARS

Ignore the ads enticing you to pick "easy squeeze" plastic bottles for your condiments and spreads. It is better to go for glass jars, especially those with a high recycled content (ask the manufacturer or retailer). In most countries, they can be recycled more easily than plastic and you can re-use them.

GET SAUCY

There's been a shift away from glass bottles to plastic bottles in the world of sauces and condiments. Packaging already represents the largest single sector of plastics used and, even if your local authority will recycle plastic, the recycling process is more complex and energy intensive than it is for glass. Whether it's ketchup or mayonnaise, avoid adding to the plastic mountain and stick to glass bottles. Even better – make your own condiments.

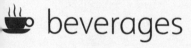

beverages

GET JUICING

Give your body a treat and invest in a juicer. It's a great way of getting your five-a-day of fresh fruit and vegetables and ensures you have a concentrated source of minerals, vitamins and enzymes. In fact, liquidizing or juicing can increase the availability of some substances, such as carotenoids from carrots. Make sure you include a mix of ingredients such as beetroot, spinach and carrots, or apple, celery and lemon; remember to put the waste pulp and skin on your compost heap, too.

THE TRUE COST OF OJ

Chances are your orange juice will have travelled miles before it ends up in your fridge – 80% of orange juice consumed in Europe comes from Brazil, and Brazil and Florida now grow between them nearly half the world's oranges, 95% of which are juiced. As well as all those transport emissions, a study has found that for every glass of Brazilian orange juice drunk, 22 glasses of processing water and 1,000 glasses of irrigation water are required. Choose juices made from local fruits instead.

DRINK TAP WATER

Tap water costs a fraction of the price of bottled water and creates no waste. If you are concerned about the chlorine used to disinfect tap water, simply fill a jug and place it in the refrigerator to allow the chlorine to evaporate. Remember to keep the water covered and replace it every 24 hours.

KEEP WELL WATERED

The recommended amount of water to drink in the UK and US is approximately 1.8 litres (6 to 8 glasses or 3 pints) of fluid every day to prevent dehydration. Ideally, this fluid should be tap water – it's better for teeth than sugary drinks, contains no calories and is free. Keep a jug of water in the fridge if you like to drink it cold, since you can waste a lot of water running the tap (faucet).

BAN WATER BOTTLES

Bottled water is a cause of major environmental headaches. Empty bottles create thousands of tonnes of plastic waste – 90% of which is not recycled. Around 1.5 million barrels of oil – enough to run 100,000 cars for a year – are used to make plastic water bottles. Tap water costs a lot less and is often required to meet stringent standards.

ARE YOU GETTING FRESH?

Most shop-bought juices have been pasteurized – a process which kills bacteria and germs but which many believe can destroy vitamins, minerals and enzymes. Plus fruit sugars in the whole fruit are less damaging to teeth than those released during processing. A manual juice press or simple juice squeezer needs no electricity and you will get a fresh, vitamin-packed drink.

MAKE A LITTLE TEA

Don't boil more water than you need for one cup of tea (but make sure you cover the heating element completely). The energy wasted boiling a kettle full of water instead of one cup's worth just three times a day could be enough to power one energy-saving light bulb for nine hours.

GROW YOUR OWN JUICE

Wheatgrass is packed with vitamins, minerals, enzymes and chlorophyll, and makes a healthy, cleansing and energizing juice. Chlorophyll has been shown to build red blood cells quickly, regulate blood pressure and promote higher metabolism. Try growing wheatgrass to prepare your own juice – you can purchase kits with organic seeds and compost online to make it even easier.

FIT A FILTER

If you're unhappy with the taste of tap water or worried about its quality then it's still better to filter your water rather than buy bottled. You can fit a house water filter to your tap (faucet) and the filter will usually last up to six months, or buy a jug water filter system but look out for those with refillable cartridges, so you won't have to throw away plastic outers. Some manufacturers are also now installing recycling bins in retailers to ensure spent filters don't end up in landfill.

A HEALTHY CUPPA

Researchers have indicated that tea could be just as good, if not better than water as it rehydrates the body and also provides valuable antioxidants, some minerals and is a natural source of fluoride which can help teeth. Drinking tea has been linked to a reduced risk of heart disease and some cancers, but don't drink it with a meal or just before or after as it can block the absorption of iron from food.

THINK ABOUT WATER

You need to take water into account when looking into the environmental impact of your food. According to the Food Ethics Council (www.foodethicscouncil.org), the world uses 200 million litres (53 million gallons) of water a second to grow its food but, by 2025, an estimated 1.8 billion people will be living without enough water to survive. In fact, agriculture uses 70% of the world's water, rising to 90% in many developing countries, and wastes 60% of the water it uses each year. Read the World Wildlife Fund's report on "Thirsty Crops" at www.wwf.org.uk.

SAY NO TO SODA
Fizzy drinks or sodas account for over 28% of all drinks consumed in the US and it is thought that the average American teenage boy drinks 3.5 cans of soda each day, while one in ten drinks 7 cans a day. But soda is empty of nutritional value and high in sugar and potentially harmful chemicals, such as the preservative sodium benzoate. Plus, even if you recycle the can, the energy and resources gobbled up by the soda industry is still incredibly wasteful. Have a glass of water instead.

CHECK THE BACTERIA
Those little plastic bottles of probiotic health drinks are popular, but they may not always be accepted for recycling, and there are concerns about some less well-known brands. Studies have found that one in two probiotic health drinks tested do not have the healthy bacteria claimed on the label, while others contain a type of bacteria that's unlikely to survive in the gut. Look for those containing lactobacilli or bifidobacterium, and a minimum of 10 million bacteria per bottle.

OPT FOR ORGANIC
When it comes to tea it's best to buy organic and fairtrade or teas that have met other high certification standards, such as those set by the Rainforest Alliance. Non-organic tea plantations are heavy users of pesticides and will often pay workers below a minimum wage. Plus, of the 132 million children estimated to be employed in agriculture by the International Labour Organization, many are working on tea plantations.

MILK YOUR LOCAL FARMS
Organic dairy produce is a good choice because you can be sure it's free from antibiotics and pesticide residues. But local milk from named farms bought through farmers' markets and independent stores can also be a good choice.

CARRY A CONTAINER
Use a stainless-steel thermos to carry drinks with you instead of buying bottles and cans. There are many varieties available, some which can be customized with "skins". A few companies, such as Sigg (mysigg.com) support water-saving programmes.

LOOSEN UP

It is better to buy loose tea than tea in bags because there is less packaging involved and ultimately fewer resources are used. There may also be a case for saying that loose-leaf teas are often better quality than those teas that make it into bags. But if you do buy tea bags, look for those produced with unbleached paper.

HEALTHY HERBALS

Herbal teas or infusions have been used to treat a huge variety of ailments for centuries. Made from the roots, flowers, bark, seeds, stems or leaves of herbs and spices, they contain no caffeine. But many herbal infusions may contain residues from agricultural chemicals while others might have been unsustainably harvested from the wild. Opt for organic with as little packaging as possible, or, better still, make your own by infusing the leaves or flowers in boiling water for 3 to 5 minutes.

FRUITY FACTS

Fruit teas or infusions aren't always packed full of the fruits that appear on their labels. For example, the Food Commission found that some cranberry, strawberry and raspberry tea bags contained only 0.2% berry. Ask the manufacturers where the flavour is actually coming from and don't be fooled into thinking you'll get the same benefits as you would from actually eating a piece of fresh fruit.

SIP A BREW

You might think you're choosing the healthy option by going for herbal tea, but make sure you choose organic – otherwise the herbs used to make them could have been heavily drenched with pesticides. Herbal teas also have a poor environmental record because herbs are commonly grown in greenhouses and in soil-free substrates.

DON'T BE A MUG

If every coffee-drinking American used a refillable instead of disposable mug, it would save close to 3 million kg (7 million lb) of carbon dioxide emissions every day.

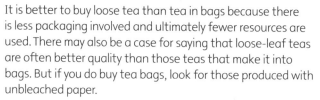

THE BEST CAFFEINE FIX
Coffee's contribution to carbon dioxide emissions is minimal because the plant captures and holds carbon in its woody stem and roots throughout its life. It's the chemicals used to grow it and the large amounts of water used to extract the beans from the pods that are the environmental bad guys.

SEEK OUT THE SHADE
Coffee is farmed on about 12 million hectares (30 million acres) worldwide and most of these farms are in areas where conservation is a key concern. Buy shade-grown coffee, traditionally grown under the leafy canopy of native rainforest trees, as it provides a great habitat for wildlife, protects the soil from erosion and uses fewer agrochemicals. Look out for brands certified by the Rainforest Alliance.

LOOK AT TEA LABELS
Buy tea and coffee with the organic label where you can. If you can't afford organic, choose fairtrade, which limits the use of chemicals to ensure a non-toxic environment for workers.

COFFEE CAUTION
Like tea, coffee is another commodity that brings big profits to the brand owners but barely a living wage for many of the 25 million people in the tropics who depend on coffee farming. A good way to be sure that growers get a fair return is to buy products labelled "fairtrade" – this not only guarantees a minimum price for suppliers, but also pays an extra premium for farmers to invest in community projects and encourages sustainable methods of farming.

GREEN ORIGINS?
Make sure your coffee supplier and local coffee shop really know where their beans have come from. The World Wildlife Fund recently found that some coffee brands contained coffee that was illegally grown inside one of the world's most important national parks for highly endangered tigers, elephants and rhinos. In its report, "Gone in an Instant", WWF said that most of the companies buying the coffee were unaware of its illegal origins.

alcohol

DON'T THROW AWAY THE PLONK
Reduce wine waste with a vacuum cork, so you don't have to throw away surplus wine if you don't finish a bottle. Opened bottles should be used within three days and kept sealed in the refrigerator to slow down the oxidation process. You can also buy special champagne stoppers to help preserve the bubbles.

DON'T BE A WHINER
Organic wine is a great choice because it contains fewer sulphur deposits and chemicals, although you'll have to do without a huge variety. Make sure you choose single estate wines, where you can be more sure of quality.

ENJOY IN MODERATION
There's no denying the terrible impact alcohol can have on people's health – it has been linked with an increased risk of mouth and throat cancers; it can also cause ulcers, liver disease, high blood pressure … the list goes on. Yet, recent Danish research found that people who led an active lifestyle and drank moderately (at least one drink per week) were less prone to heart disease.

DRINK A LOCAL TIPPLE
The export of beers and wines all over the world comes at a cost in terms of CO_2 emissions. Seek out your local breweries and vineyards. In England and Wales there are nearly 400 commercial vineyards (find them on www.english-wine.com), while in the US there are more than 1,300 independent, traditional "craft" breweries (www.beertown.org).

WILD GIN
In many areas wild sloes – the fruit of the blackthorn (*Prunus spinosa*) – are readily available and can be used to flavour gin. Just prick the skins with a needle, add 250 g (½ lb) sugar for each 500 g (1 lb) sloes, fill a bottle halfway with the sloes and top up with gin. Shake, store and turn occasionally and the gin should be ready in a couple of months. Strain first, then drink as an after-dinner liqueur or mix with white wine or champagne.

FINE WINE

A study by the European Pesticides Action Network (PAN) has found that wines on sale in the EU may contain residues of up to ten different pesticides potentially harmful to human health. According to PAN, grapes receive a higher dose of synthetic pesticides than almost any other crop. To avoid guzzling pesticide residues in your wine, buy organic.

A LIGHTER DRINK

Some retailers have started using lighter glass bottles for wines, which need less energy to transport, while other wines are packaged in cartons made from renewable materials, which are also a lighter load. Given that in most countries a large proportion of the wine is imported, choosing the lightest possible packaging will help reduce your carbon footprint. Look out too for imported wines that are bottled closer to home, so cutting needless transport emissions.

RAISE YOUR SPIRITS

Even hardened liquor drinkers can be eco-friendly by opting for organic and ethically sourced spirits. In the case of rum, it is sugar that is the principle ingredient and which should come from a sustainable source, while with vodka the grain that is used could have been drenched in pesticides. Check the brand's website to see if they state the source of their key ingredient.

AN ORGANIC ALE

Your regular beer could be made with hops that have been sprayed up to 14 times each year with an average of 15 pesticide products. Organic beer is made from organic malt and hops using farming methods that rule out this kind of chemical saturation. Look out also for "carbon neutral beer" – Adnams brewery in the UK uses an Energy Recovery System that recycles 100% of the steam created during the brewing process and uses it to heat 90% of the following brew.

WHAT'S IN YOUR GLASS?

As well as possible pesticide residues, most wines contain additives which, unlike food, do not have to be listed on the label. These include fining agents, such as isinglass, which is made from fish bladders, clay or silica as well as sulphur, which is used as a preservative, ascorbic or tartaric acid, and sugar to increase the alcohol content. Certified organic wines add less sulphur dioxide to the wine – on average, organic producers use just one quarter of the legal maximum for conventional wines.

HAVE A CORKING TIME

Make sure your wine has a real cork, rather than a plastic one or screw top. You will be supporting the cork industry, one of the most environmentally friendly industries, which helps to maintain endangered wildlife such as the Iberian lynx, Spanish Imperial eagle and Barbary deer, while also cutting back on your plastic consumption.

cooking

TEACH YOUR FAMILY TO COOK

If you are the main cook, encourage the other members of your family to learn how to put together a few basic meals. Cooking from fresh ingredients saves money and resources, particularly packaging. It may also mean that you get to have a night or two away from the kitchen.

BE A HOME COOKER

Home-cook whenever you can. With fresh food, very little or no processing is involved. This minimizes the energy used to get it to your plate and therefore also the cost to the environment.

PUT A LID ON IT

Save energy by cooking more efficiently. Putting a lid on a pan you are using speeds up the cooking time by around 6%. Always choose a hob size that matches the diameter of the pan and keep the centre of the pan over the element.

ALL THAT REMAINS
Peelings from your vegetables, the remains of a roast, or washed trimmings ... all of these can be used to make a mineral-rich stock which is itself a part of many other dishes such as soups. It saves on food waste and will help you to avoid processed stock cubes or powders, many of which contain flavour enhancers and loads of salt.

SPEED UP COOKING TIME
Save energy while you are cooking by using a pressure cooker. They work by cooking food under high pressure in a short period of time, thereby speeding up the cooking process and saving energy. Although using a pressure cooker does result in more nutrient loss than steaming, it is still better than boiling or microwaving your food, and as it cooks three or four times more quickly than a conventional cooker, it will save energy.

REACH FOR THE MICROWAVE
If you are simply reheating food rather than cooking a meal it is more energy-efficient to use the microwave rather than the oven. However, don't use the microwave to defrost food: think ahead and put it in the refrigerator to defrost overnight before you need it.

MAKE THE MOST OF YOUR OVEN
When cooking, try switching off your oven a few minutes before the food is ready and let the food cook in the remaining heat. Don't preheat your oven on a higher temperature than you need to cook the food – it won't get it hotter any faster.

DON'T GRILL IT, TOAST IT
Always use a toaster when possible rather than the grill (broiler), which uses more energy. Toasters also require less time to do the job than a grill and don't need heating up, so it's worth investing if you don't already have one.

KEEP A LID ON IT
If you are boiling food then keep a lid on your pots and pans. This will speed up the cooking time and allow you to use less water, which also benefits the nutritional content of your food.

COOK IN BULK

Prepare more than you need of your favourite dishes and freeze the excess. You will be saving energy and will be far less likely to reach for an over-packaged, processed ready meal when you are next short of time – you'll have your own stock of healthy dinners in the freezer.

GREEN STEAM

Steaming your vegetables and fish will minimize nutrient loss, especially vitamin C, vitamin B1 and mineral salts. For example, a study has found that when steaming fresh broccoli 11% of flavonoids were lost compared to 47% lost when pressure cooked, 66% lost when boiled and 97% lost when microwaved. Plus, if you use a layered steamer, it will ensure you make the most of the energy used to cook your food.

HOB OF CHOICE

A gas hob is considered more energy efficient than electric, (and is preferred by chefs because of the control you can achieve over the heat), with the exception of induction hobs. They are more expensive than traditional hobs, but consume half as much electricity as electric hobs and are more efficient in heat transfer. Manufacturers estimate that power savings of 40–70% are achievable.

USE LESS WATER

Valuable nutrients, such as the water-soluble B vitamins and vitamin C, can be lost by using too much water when preparing and cooking your fruit and vegetables, and of course we are all being asked to save as much water as possible. So instead of soaking your produce, just give it a quick rinse, use less water when boiling or microwaving and cook until just tender.

GIVE IT A SPRAY

Use a hand-pump oil spray if you need to fry food and especially when browning meat and vegetables. Spray the pan lightly and you will reduce the amount of oil absorbed by the food, and ultimately reduce the volume of oil you need to buy. To make your own oil spray, simply decant olive oil from a large container into a spray bottle.

STIR-FRY TO GET YOUR VEG
Fried food is invariably high in fat and best avoided; however, stir-frying food over a high heat for a short period of time and using minimal oil will not result in a fatty dish and can be a good way to eat more vegetables, along with other traditional, healthy stir-fry ingredients such as ginger, garlic and tofu.

BBQ WITH CAUTION
Don't be tempted by too many barbecues this summer. The smoke not only produces hydrocarbons but also tiny soot particles that pollute the air and can aggravate heart and lung problems. Also, meat cooked on a barbecue can form potentially cancer-causing compounds – the hotter the temperature and the longer the meat cooks, the more compounds produced.

GREEN BBQS
If you do indulge in a bit of barbecue action, then make sure you use locally produced charcoal from sustainable sources; avoid briquettes (the US Environmental Protection Agency says charcoal briquettes release 105 times more carbon monoxide per unit of energy than propane and a lot of toxic volatile organic compounds) and ditch the disposable – it's a massive waste of resources.

kitchen tools & appliances

DELIGHTFUL DISHES
Hand-washing your dishes might not be the most eco-friendly option. One study has found that a dishwasher uses only half the energy and one-sixth of the water as hand-washing. Hand-washing typically uses about 63 litres (16 gallons) of water, rising to 150 litres (40 gallons) if dishes are rinsed off under running water, whereas a modern dishwasher can use just 10 litres (2 gallons) of water per cycle. But buy the most energy-efficient model on the market, fill your dishwasher right up and use phosphate-free, eco-friendly detergents.

AVOID TEFLON PANS

There is growing concern that over-heated Teflon and other non-stick pans release toxic fumes; also concern about the pollution caused during the manufacturing process of Teflon. Use stainless steel saucepans or iron-bottomed pots instead.

AVOID ALUMINIUM

According to the Food Standards Agency in the UK, it's best not to use aluminium pans, baking trays and foil, or other cookware made of aluminium to cook foods that are highly acidic, such as tomatoes, rhubarb, cabbage and many soft fruits. A study has found that about 20% of the aluminium in our diet comes from aluminium cookware and foil.

REUSE OLD FOOD CONTAINERS

Rather than throwing them out, recycle old food containers such as ice-cream tubs and jam jars to store food leftover foods and small household items. Jars with screw-top lids are a great way to store dried goods such as lentils, as well as old screws and nails.

CHOOSE WOOD IN THE KITCHEN

When buying utensils for your kitchen try to avoid plastic, wherever possible. Wooden washing-up brushes and stainless steel utensils are widely available and a greener alternative to plastic, which has a big environmental impact during its production and disposal.

CUTLERY OF STEEL

Stainless steel has a high proportion of recycled content – on average around 80%. Items made from stainless steel can be melted down and reformed into a new product, which makes it a good green choice for kitchen equipment such as cutlery; it is also hardwearing.

DON'T BUY PLASTIC FOR PICNICS

It may be tempting to invest in a brightly coloured picnic set for days out or simply for use in the garden, but from an environmental perspective you should avoid buying plastic, if at all possible. A picnic is a good reason to bring out old crockery and cups that you might otherwise throw away.

DON'T USE PLASTIC CUPS FOR SPECIAL EVENTS

If you're having a party or a special event and need extra cups, don't be tempted into buying "disposable" plastic ones that are simply destined for landfill. Many off licences (liquor stores) and supermarkets offer a glass hire service, which is a far greener option.

HAVE A FLASK ON HAND

Make sure your home has at least one thermos flask that can be used to hold hot drinks and soups. This will help reduce waste from plastic cups and take-away food containers. A flask can also be a good idea if you work from home because it saves having to brew up fresh cups.

SIZE MATTERS

When buying new gadgets for the home such as can openers, only purchase one big enough for the job in question. Larger items use more resources during their manufacture. The only time a larger gadget is preferable is when it lasts twice as long as this saves resources in the long run.

FRIDGE FRESH

In most households, the fridge is the single biggest energy-consuming kitchen appliance. But are you sure everything in your fridge needs chilling? Many foods need only be stored in a cool, dry place – especially if you plan to eat them reasonably quickly. It may be time to bring back the old-fashioned larder!

reducing food waste

FREEZE IT

One of the best ways to limit the amount of food you waste is to freeze it – check the "use by" dates and freeze anything that you may not need in the next few days. It won't drastically reduce the food's nutritional value and will give you flexibility.

USE WHAT YOU'VE GOT

We all waste a terrible amount of food – in the UK, for example, 6.7 million tonnes of food hits the bin each year, roughly a third of everything we buy. But not all of this waste is out of date or inedible. Organize your cooking so that you are eating food while it's fresh and use your imagination when it comes to using up the odds and ends in your fridge. You will also find ideas online – try www.lovefoodhatewaste.com.

CREATE A COMPOST

A heap of rotting food scraps, newspaper and green waste from your garden might not sound like a nutrition tip but it is if you use the resulting compost on your vegetable garden or allotment. Around 30% of each household's waste could be composted, but much of it ends up in landfill where it produces the powerful greenhouse gas methane. Throw it all on a compost heap and in around six months' time you'll get your very own natural fertilizers, mulch and soil conditioner. There are loads of online tips for would-be composters out there, including those on www.recyclenow.com or www. howtocompost.org.

BUY A DIGESTER

For your food waste consider investing in a food digester, which doesn't produce compost – it just breaks the food down until there is minimal residue. A digester can accept all types of food including raw and cooked meat, dairy products, bread, pasta, fish and bones. Because they are sited outdoors and break up the food underground, odour is minimal. Some food digesters need sun, while others work better in the shade. Or try a Green Johanna "hot" composter, which does produce compost.

USE YOUR LEFTOVERS

One-third of food ends up getting thrown away without being composted, so don't over-buy in the first place and use up leftovers by incorporating them into new dishes. When mixed with other materials in landfill sites, food waste can produce polluting liquids along with methane gases, which contribute to the greenhouse effect.

GET PLANNING
Reduce food waste and get the most out of your food by planning a series of meals which follow on from each other. For example, start with a roast chicken, and the next day use any leftover chicken in a stir-fry (making sure it is hot all the way through). The day after that, use the last bits of chicken from the carcass in a stew bulked out with root vegetables. This will also help cut down on the amount of meat you are buying.

REDUCE FOOD WASTE AT HOME
Make sure you are not throwing away lots of leftover food by following a few simple rules. Always try to incorporate leftovers into other meals, and freeze or bottle surplus fruit and vegetables. Grind leftover bread into breadcrumbs to make fat balls for birds.

storing food

NO NEED FOR PLASTIC WRAP TO STORE FOOD
The production of the polyethylene used to produce plastic wrap is wasteful in terms of energy, raw materials and pollution. There is also research to prove that some of the chemicals found in clingfilm (plastic wrap) may actually leach into foods causing health problems, so try to avoid it.

WRAP IT WELL
Don't wrap fatty foods, such as cheese, fried meats, pastry products and cakes with butter icing or chocolate coatings, in clingfilm (plastic wrap) since tiny amounts of chemicals can leach into these foods from the wrap. Better to choose butcher's paper or recycled aluminium foil, which can both be further recycled, or, in the case of the paper, added to your compost heap.

LEAVE IT ALONE
Don't let plastic wrap come into contact with food. Make sure you don't buy clingfilm (plastic wrap) made from PVC or vinyl – it is more likely to leach harmful substances into food and be more damaging to the environment.

SORT IT OUT

It's great to recycle but make sure you do it properly or it could be a waste of everybody's efforts. Don't include plastics that can't be recycled locally – in Britain this includes margarine tubs and yogurt pots – and wash all items thoroughly to avoid contamination. Lastly, don't mix the new breed of degradable plastics in with your recycling.

GO GLASS

When storing food, choose glass containers instead of plastic. Plastic is a petroleum-based product, results in a great deal of pollution from its creation to disposal and there are concerns that freezing or heating plastic can release toxic carcinogens. If you must buy plastic containers, look for a "1" or "2" inside the recycled arrow symbol on the package as these containers are more likely to be accepted for recycling.

USE RECYCLED FOIL

If you can't do without aluminium foil (which has a major environmental impact during its production), make sure you use 100% recycled aluminium foil. This product can be recycled over and over again. Producing recycled foil uses 95% less energy than is used when making primary aluminium.

ALUMINIUM FOILED

Although aluminium foil can be reused over and over with no loss of quality, this generally isn't what happens and so vast quantities end up in landfill each year. Rather than reaching for the foil, store food in the refrigerator in old ice-cream tubs and wrap packed lunches in greaseproof (waxed) paper, which can be composted.

SAVE YOUR BREAD

If you find you waste a lot of bread because it goes mouldy in your bread bin, put a dab of vinegar on a tissue or cloth inside the bread bin. The acetic acid in vinegar kills moulds, so your bread stays fresher and you'll waste less. Alternatively, buy large amounts, but freeze a third or half the loaf.

feeding babies & children

AVOID SOYA FORMULA
With growing demand for soya leading to deforestation around the world it is a good idea to avoid soya-based formula milk but there are other good reasons for this too. There are concerns that it could affect babies' reproductive development due to the high levels of plant hormones or phytoestrogens in soya.

BREAST IS BEST
There is no doubt that breast milk is the most complete nutritional option available to babies, helping protect them against a myriad of infections in the early years while also providing a range of nutrients that formula milks still aren't able to match. But think too of all those plastic bottles and teats, the packets of formula and the energy used to sterilize ... breast is best for the planet, too.

JUNK THE JUNK
A British study has found that eating a diet of fatty, processed food when pregnant or breastfeeding may result in children with high levels of fat in their bloodstream and fat around the major organs, potentially leading to the development of type II diabetes and heart disease in the future.

PUREE POWER
The best introduction to nutritious and eco-friendly eating habits for babies is homemade baby food. You can be sure that the food you give them is fresh, made from organic ingredients with no pesticide residues and doesn't contain additives. Cook in bulk, purée in a blender and freeze in ice-cube trays – simple.

PACK LIGHT
All too often, packed lunches are heavy on packaging and light on nutrition. Make them a lesson in green living by using reusable containers, ditching the individually wrapped items and learning about healthy options. There are lots of ideas online – see www.wastefreelunches.org and www.schoolfoodtrust.org.uk.

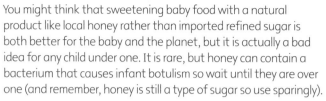

HONEY FOR YOUR HONEY

You might think that sweetening baby food with a natural product like local honey rather than imported refined sugar is both better for the baby and the planet, but it is actually a bad idea for any child under one. It is rare, but honey can contain a bacterium that causes infant botulism so wait until they are over one (and remember, honey is still a type of sugar so use sparingly).

SNACK ATTACK

Encouraging children to snack on fresh fruit will not only help their health, it will also help cut down on the packaging mountain that comes from crisp packets, sweet wrappers and so on. Given that around seven out of ten items of litter are food related, this should also help reduce the waste on our streets, beaches and green spaces.

DIY CRISPS

A 35 g (1¼ oz) single-portion bag of crisps (potato chips) contains two-and-a-half teaspoons of oil, and is also three times as salty as sea water – containing half the recommended daily salt intake for a six-year-old. Choose versions made with unpeeled potatoes, as these will have a higher fibre content. Best of all, make your own from root vegetables, such as parsnips or beetroot.

vitamins & supplements

SAVE ON SUPPLEMENTS
A well-balanced diet, one that is high in fruit and vegetables, should be enough to keep most of us healthy. Occasionally, there may be an advantage to taking a supplement – folic acid when pregnant, for example, but otherwise save on the natural resources and energy needed to produce, package and distribute them.

BUY NATURAL SUPPLEMENTS
If you do need to take a food supplement, beware those made with synthetic nutrients that are manufactured using chemicals. In the US, the Organic Consumers Association says that 90% or more of the vitamins and supplements now on the market labelled as "natural" or "food-based" are actually spiked with synthetic chemicals. It is developing a new set of Naturally Occurring Standards (NOS), which will lead to the certification of genuinely natural products – see www.organicconsumers.org/nutricon.cfm.

FISH-OIL FEARS
Fish oils are not only sold as supplements, but are also added to animal and farmed fish feed. But some can contain potential pollutants such as dioxins and polychlorinated biphenyls (PCBs) and they can also come from unsustainable fishery operations. Check the purity and sustainability of any fish oils you buy and consider safer options such as flaxseed oil or algae-derived sources of omega-3s.

RADIATION CONCERNS
A few years ago a UK government survey found that nearly half the food supplements sampled were completely irradiated or contained an irradiated ingredient, but were not labelled as such. Several studies link irradiation with a reduction in nutritional value, but it's also a reminder that supplements are essentially processed products.

SUSTAINABLE SOURCING
The demand for herbal remedies
in North America and Europe has
been growing by about 10% a
year for the last decade, but it
is now threatening to wipe out
10,000 of the world's 50,000
medicinal plant species, according
to Plantlife International. Ask the
retailer where the raw material for
your herbal remedy comes from
and how it's harvested.

Health
Matters

LEADING A HEALTHY LIFE and living an eco-friendly lifestyle often go hand in hand – what's better for you is usually best for the planet, too. This chapter is full of suggestions on how to improve your health by avoiding exposure to toxins and chemicals in the world around you. It also explores healthy-living ideas that won't cost the earth and the benefits of using natural remedies for minor ailments.

traditional medicine

BEWARE OF TAKING TOO MANY MEDICINES
A large amount of any medicine we take is excreted in our urine. This means that there is a risk of pharmaceuticals ending up in our waterways and adversely affecting the ecosystem. To protect yourself and the environment, avoid taking more medication than you need.

DON'T REACH FOR THE PILL
Try to modify your lifestyle or choose homeopathic remedies when you're suffering from minor illnesses rather than reaching for that headache tablet or tummy treatment. Many common ailments such as headaches, colds and indigestion are the result of poor nutritional or healthcare habits. Medicinal treatments for minor problems should be used only after all other avenues have been exhausted.

SEEK A GREEN DOCTOR
More GPs are getting interested in green medicine, which addresses the interplay between healthcare, the care of patients and the physician, and how sustainable development can factor into the practice of medicine. Choose one with these ideals in mind, as they may have green programmes underway.

PHARM AROUND
Choose pharmaceutical companies who invest in green chemistry, whereby chemists are encouraged to develop environmentally friendly products alongside their normal product lines. Ask them about their green schemes and choose accordingly.

QUESTION TIME
Pharmaceutical companies have historically been very bad at releasing damaging compounds. Don't be afraid to ask your pharmaceutical company what they are doing to reduce the release of solvents and other poisons into the environment.

DISPOSE OF DRUGS CAREFULLY

Many people flush expired medication down the toilet, thinking it's safer to do this than to dispose of it where it might be found by children or pets. Unfortunately most sewage treatment plants aren't designed to filter these drugs out, so the ingredients make their way into rivers and drinking water. Expired medication should be returned to suppliers. Pharmacies take back expired medicines, which are in turn collected by medical-waste companies that dispose of them in a responsible manner, usually by burning.

PUT SOME PRESSURE ON

Hospitals are among the worst offenders when it comes to producing rubbish. Put some pressure on your local hospital to do a waste count, and then encourage them to come up with ways to minimize their rubbish.

GO PVC-FREE

PVC-free intravenous and blood bags are widely available, as are alternatives for disposable PVC gloves. Likewise, PVC-free or DEHP-free tubing is on the market for most medical applications. Encourage your local hospital not to use PVC, if it can be avoided.

CHOOSE A SAFER OPTION

Glutaraldehyde disinfectants, which can cause asthma and skin problems as well as poisoning the environment, are often used by hospitals because they are economical and available in large quantities. Often used to kill viruses on surgical instruments that are too delicate to be heat-treated, they are, however, harmful if inhaled or swallowed and can cause irritation to the eyes and skin. Encourage hospitals to swap to safer options instead.

NOW WASH YOUR HANDS

Encourage your doctor and other health care professionals to use alcohol-based hand-rub gels to stop the spread of germs, rather than antimicrobial products.

GET GOOD GLASS
Whenever you can, opt to buy medicines stored in glass rather than plastic. Some pharmacists even run bottle reusing schemes, where you can take back your empty pill bottles.

SAY NO TO CHLORINE
Look for pharmaceutical products using the new techno ingredient of supercritical carbon dioxide as solvents for medicines, instead of chlorine and fluorine compounds, which have historically been used to carry other materials in solution.

SMALL STEPS IN THE RIGHT DIRECTION
Some smaller pharmaceutical companies are promoting environmental stewardship, investigating new ways to move the industry forward with respect for the environment. Choose them for your medicines.

✳ alternative medicine

GROW YOUR OWN
Try growing your own herbs to use medicinally at home. A herb garden or even a couple of plant pots on a windowsill will enable you to brew up fresh herbal teas. Try feverfew for headaches and peppermint to aid digestion. There are many herbalism guides available for growing, harvesting and storing medicinal plants, as well as making remedies for home use.

TRY NATURAL ANTIBIOTICS
There are reports of pharmaceutical antibiotics occurring in our wastewater. They have also been linked to breast cancer, Crohn's disease and childhood asthma. Avoid using them when possible by opting for natural alternatives, such as garlic, a natural antibiotic, or echinacea to build up your immunity.

CHOOSE ORGANIC MEDS
Wherever possible, pick up organic varieties of medicines. The manufacturers will have put some thought into the production process and packaging to minimize effects on the environment.

CHOOSE COMPLEMENTARY MEDICINES
These are environmentally friendly if they're sourced from properly cultivated organic stock rather than harvested from wild habitats, which can disrupt the ecosystem and deplete natural resources. Make sure any treatment you get from a homeopath or naturopath is sourced in this way – not all are.

GO HERBAL
If you're not growing your own herbs or plant medicines, then purchasing herbal remedies or complementary medicines that are grown locally and packaged in recycled containers is better than buying an imported product, because they do less harm to the environment.

SIMPLE HOMEOPATHY
Keep your treatments in as pure a form as possible. Homeopathic remedies are made from simple substances that, for the most part, come from the plant, animal and mineral kingdoms. Because of the method of preparation used, only small amounts of any substance are necessary to produce high-quality remedies, which means the process is unlikely to strip the earth of resources or harm animals.

NATURAL HERB HELP
Instead of using conventional pharmaceuticals, try herbalism – 80% of the world's population uses it for some aspect of primary health care. Organic herbal tinctures are free of pesticides and some are extremely effective for everyday health problems, such as feverfew for migraines.

RELAX WITH REIKI
Reiki is a healing therapy that originates from Japan and involves a form of touch therapy to stimulate the life force, or chi. It has been found to boost relaxation and reduce stress, headaches, insomnia and improve general wellbeing.

TEST YOUR REFLEXES
Reflexology is a natural therapy that may help a wide range of health problems without the use of pharmaceuticals. Visit a qualified practitioner first and then, if it works for you, try learning some of the pressure points yourself so you can self-treat.

TRY SCENT THERAPY

Based on aromatherapy principles, these are mood-balancing patches you wear on your wrist. All-natural and easy to use, you simply bring the patch to your nose and breathe deeply three or four times. Patches are available for stress, curbing nicotine cravings, dieting and more.

WELL ORIENTED

If you use Chinese medicine, ask your doctor to ensure that none of the remedies you are prescribed are sourced from endangered species like tigers and turtles. Most doctors are willing to find a plant alternative.

DISCOVER YOUR DOSHA

Ayurvedic medicine has been used in India for centuries. It works on the principle that we all fall into one of three "doshas" or body types. A holistic, traditional form of medicine, Ayurveda treats the whole body, not just the symptoms, with a combination of herbal formulations, nutrition, yoga and massage.

USE AROMATHERAPY

Treat minor aches and ailments with aromatherapy. This is the practice of using the therapeutic benefits of essential oils to ease symptoms such as headaches, stress and fatigue. Visit a qualified practitioner to find out which oils are best for you, and then self-administer at home.

REACH FOR THE RESCUE REMEDY

Bach flower remedies are a natural way of treating a wide range of emotional conditions, from anxiety to fear. The 38 remedies are derived from plants and flowers and the best known is Rescue Remedy, a combination of five flower essences: impatiens, rock rose, cherry plum, star of Bethlehem and clematis, which treats stress, anxiety and panic attacks.

TAKE UP YOGA

Yoga is the eco-friendly way to unwind, tone muscles and increase flexibility. It is better than going to the gym in terms of emissions and is fantastic for your health. Studies have shown that people who practise yoga regularly are less stressed, too.

GET AN OIL BURNER
Burning essential oils can improve your health and wellbeing. Use organic clove oil for mild depression and rosemary for relaxation. Peppermint essential oil can be burnt to ease nausea and stimulate the mind.

BOOST HEALTH WITH MEDITATION
Research has shown that regular meditation is thought to have a broad range of benefits for the mind and body: it boosts the immune system, improves sleep and is beneficial for insomnia, obesity and depression.

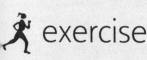# exercise

PLAY BALL
When your training shoes are worn beyond use, don't throw them away. Because of their high rubber content and the fact that rubber is easily recyclable, old trainers (sneakers) are now being used to make new sports surfaces. Nike is one brand that operates this function by producing it's Nike Grind material.

A WEIGHTY MATTER
Ten treadmills in the average gym use the same amount of electricity in a day that it would take to run your hairdryer non-stop for a year. Stick to weights and non-electric machines such as spinning bikes.

TAKE UP SPORT AS A HOBBY
The best way to improve your health is to incorporate some regular exercise into your lifestyle. Taking up a sport as a hobby can help improve your fitness without any negative impact on the environment. Look out for local swimming, yoga or Pilates classes that you can walk to.

DON'T TEE OFF AT RANDOM
Be discerning about your choice of golf course – choose one that tries to reduce or eliminate the use of poisonous pesticides on greens and fairways by using non-toxic alternatives.

LEAD A LESS SEDENTARY LIFE

By getting out into the countryside you will be improving your health and wellbeing, and as long as you use public transport, cycle or walk, you will not be harming the environment. Research has found that the more time we spend in nature, the more likely we are to try and protect it.

MIND HOW YOU GO

Walk your next journey rather than hopping in the car. Walking has been shown to improve mental health by boosting self-esteem, relieving symptoms of depression and anxiety, and offering opportunities for relaxation and social contact. It is also environmentally friendly.

GO FOR A WALK

Improve your health and boost your fitness by going for a walk, every day if possible. Research has shown that regular walking is associated with reduced mortality for older and younger adults, as well as a reduction in the risk of cardiovascular disease and bone strength.

TURN OFF THE COMPUTER

Research has found that only half of 11- to 16-year-olds currently walk for 10 minutes in a day. Children walk significantly less than they did 50 years ago and there are considerably more overweight and obese children. Encourage them to switch off and get out – it will save energy and improve their health.

GET SOME FRESH AIR

Spend time in nature. Taking a walk, having a picnic or simply sitting outdoors and watching the sky deepens our connection to the natural world, motivating us to be better stewards of the earth.

ON YOUR BIKE

Leave the car behind and get on your bike. A 30-minute commute by bike will burn 8 calories a minute or 11 kg (24 lb) of fat a year, according to the international non-profit Friends of the Earth. You will also be helping the environment because you will save around 1 kg (2 lb) of carbon dioxide for every 8 km (5 m) trip taken by bike rather than car.

GO NATURAL

Choose natural fabrics to exercise in rather than highly engineered versions that require lots of energy to produce. If you must buy the latest hi-tech fabrics, make sure you purchase quality so you won't have to replace them soon.

AVOID THE GYM

Unless you live next door, avoid the gym. Instead, improve your health and fitness by walking or running. Gyms have a significant impact on the environment due to the energy they use for lighting, air conditioning and heating. There is also the added environmental impact of people driving to the gym and then home again.

GET ACTIVE EARLY

One of the best things you can do to improve your children's health and the environment is to get them active early on. If children experience walking as part of a fun activity, they will want to do it again. Aim for something that will appeal to them, such as a few hours at a playground or boating pond.

SCRAP THE SCHOOL RUN

For the sake of your and your children's health, and the impact on the environment, try a different approach to the school run. If you can, walk or use public transport. If these are not practical, pool resources with other parents and take it in turns to drop off and pick up the children to cut back on multiple car journeys.

MAKE SPORT A FAMILY AFFAIR

Rather than heading out to the shops or even the cinema, why not go for a bike ride as a family outing? This will improve your whole family's health, provide some quality time together – and it will have a minimal impact on the environment.

SET A GOOD EXAMPLE

Research has shown that children who grow up with parents who exercise regularly are much more likely to take part in sports themselves. Set a good example to your children by walking to the shops rather than driving, and you will improve your health and your children's for years to come.

HEALTH MATTERS

JOIN A CONSERVATION GROUP
A good way to help improve the environment and your health is to join a local conservation group. This will ensure that you spend time outside helping to maintain the environment at the same time as improving your health and general wellbeing.

CYCLE TO SCHOOL
Get your children on their bikes and cycling to school. This will help improve their health as well as reduce carbon emissions. Make sure they take part in a cycling course first to ensure that they are proficient and confident on the roads.

JOIN A GREEN GYM
The Green Gym project is a scheme to encourage people to get fit at the same time as improving the environment. It offers 3-hour sessions of physical activity in the outdoors. There are Green Gym groups in the UK, Australia and the US, and there is always scope to set one up yourself locally.

WORK YOUR COMPOST
Reduce waste and make your own compost for your garden. It takes around six months for food and garden waste to break down to form usable compost; however, the process can be helped along by turning the compost over regularly. This will provide regular exercise and help to improve your general fitness and muscle strength, too.

DIG IN
By growing your own food you will be reducing your carbon emissions and be getting fit at the same time. Gardening can burn off calories, and tasks such as digging and mowing are excellent cardiovascular workouts.

BURN GREEN CALORIES
Go green and burn off more calories by gardening than visiting the gym. Research has shown that almost a third more calories can be burnt in an hour of gardening than would be done in a step aerobics class. Other household tasks, such as washing dishes or painting the house, also burn calories effectively.

CHOOSE AN ECO-FRIENDLY SPORT

There are plenty of sports and activities that will improve your health and boost your appreciation of the environment without having a negative impact on it. Surfing, climbing, walking and cycling are all about being outside and being in harmony with the environment.

BECOME A RAMBLER

Spend your spare time rambling – regular brisk walking can improve your heart rate and circulation as well as lower blood pressure and reduce cholesterol levels. Some research has found that it can dramatically reduce the risk of heart attack.

BUILD UP MUSCLES

The kind of physical activity needed for gardening, for example digging and weeding, has been found to help build muscle strength, which is particularly important for older people. By spending a couple of hours tending your green spaces you may even put years on your life.

GET A DOG

Having to walk a dog is one of the best ways to ensure that you get out and about in the countryside. A daily walk is extremely beneficial for your health, improving cardiovascular fitness; as long as you don't drive the dog to its walking spot, it's eco-friendly, too.

first aid

GREEN FIRST AID
Having natural remedies on hand will help prevent you from
choosing medicines that may harm the planet. Include aloe
vera for wounds and burns; arnica for bruises, sprains and sore
muscles; calendula for its anti-inflammatory, astringent and
antiseptic qualities, and for inhibiting bleeding; camomile for an
anti-inflammatory and digestion; echinacea to help fight off
colds and flu; lavender oil for burns or stings; and tea tree oil
for a natural antiseptic.

GET A HOMEOPATHIC FIRST AID KIT
Homeopathy is a natural remedy that is based on the principle
of treating like with like. Because it is safe to use on children
and babies, keeping a homeopathic first aid kit in the house
is a good way to look after the family without reaching for the
medicine cabinet first.

ARNICA AWAY WOUNDS
Help your wounds heal with arnica instead of highly packaged
and produced creams designed to do the same job. Arnica
soothes muscle aches, reduces inflammation, reduces bruising
and is great for skin problems such as acne and insect bites. It
should not be used on broken skin or by those who suffer from
skin sensitivity.

BANDAGE IT UP
When you're choosing bandages and plasters for your home
medical box, look for those with solvent-free adhesives. They
are kinder to skin and you can be sure that the environment
has not been harmed during their manufacture.

TEA TREE FOR CUTS
Tea tree oil is a great alternative to chemical healing ointments
and balms. A natural antiseptic, it's great in emergencies for
cuts and grazes. Either dab on diluted tea tree essential oil or
use a specially formulated tea tree ointment. It can also be
applied to insect bites.

HEAL BURNS WITH CALENDULA

The herb calendula has natural anti-inflammatory properties and is ideal for soothing skin problems. Calendula gel is an excellent natural remedy for burns. First cool the wound under cold water and then apply the calendula gel. Repeat until the skin has healed.

USE ARNICA FOR BRUISES

If you use just one homeopathic remedy, make it arnica. Well known for its ability to improve the healing process after injury, it can be beneficial for bruising. It is the ideal remedy to administer to children after bumps to aid recovery.

SAY ALOE TO STINGS

Don't invest in chemical creams for stings and bruises when natural products will do just as well to help you heal quickly. Aloe vera is a great soothing product that can be used on itchy skin. It also helps bites and stings to heal and can ease the pain of burns. Aloe vera produces around six different antiseptics, which can kill mould, bacteria and fungus.

TAKE THE STING OUT

Use sodium bicarbonate (baking soda) dissolved in a small amount of water as a poultice to neutralize ant and bee stings. Tea tree oil and lemon juice can also be effective at easing the pain of an insect sting. Wasp stings are best treated with a vinegar solution.

GET RID OF ATHLETE'S FOOT WITH TEA TREE

Tea tree oil is a natural antifungal and can be used to fight infections such as athlete's foot. Simply dab some diluted tea tree oil onto the affected area twice a day. It can also be used to prevent attacks by adding a few drops to your bath or a foot soak.

TREAT CUTS WITH FRESH GARLIC

Traditionally garlic has been used to help heal cuts and wounds as it has natural antiseptic properties that boost the healing process. Rub a cut clove of garlic over the area, or place finely cut slivers onto the affected area as a poultice.

REPEL MOSQUITOES WITH ESSENTIAL OILS
Bites from mosquitoes can itch badly and become infected; avoid mosquitoes by dabbing the edges of your clothing with lavender or citronella essential oil. Another effective way to avoid mozzie bites is to eat Marmite (yeast-extract spread) – some sources say it's the lingering smell that repels them, while others say it's the folic acid in the spread.

GET AN ALOE PLANT
The aloe vera plant is a fantastic natural cure-all. The gel can be used as an alternative to shaving foam, and it can also be applied straight to cuts and scrapes for instant relief. It has natural anti-inflammatory and skin-softening properties, which also makes it the perfect after-sun treatment.

sprains & sports injuries

SPORTS INJURY HELP
One of the best anti-inflammatory painkillers for the joints and for sports injuries is bromelain, which is actually an enzyme from fresh pineapple juice. Bromelain reduces inflammation by first breaking down fibrin, a substance that would otherwise work in the body to cause local swelling. It has also been shown to be as effective as antibiotics in treating a variety of infectious and painful conditions, from bronchitis to pneumonia.

PEAS, PLEASE
For sprains and bruises, a great way to reduce bruising and swelling is to make the area cold, thus reducing blood flow. Even better than shop-bought ice packs are bags of frozen peas, because they mould around the body part to ensure equal distribution of the cold. Place a tea towel next to your skin first to prevent ice burn.

MAKE A COMFREY POULTICE

Comfrey works as a healing agent due to allantoin – a substance that speeds the production of new cells and aids healing. Grind fresh leaves in a mortar and pestle with enough water to form a paste. Warm in a saucepan over a low heat, stirring constantly, then remove from the heat and cool slightly. Apply to the bruise or sprain and bandage to secure.

 # aches & pains

TREAT BACK PAIN WITH THE BOWEN TECHNIQUE

The Bowen technique is a holistic therapy that is reportedly most successful for treating problems such as back pain, frozen shoulders and neck pain – all which can be brought on by long hours in front of a computer. It is also thought to be beneficial for hay fever, asthma and migraines. The therapist uses fingers or thumbs to manipulate muscles with a gentle rolling motion.

RELIEVE PAIN WITH ACUPUNCTURE

One of the most researched natural therapies is acupuncture, which has been found to have great success in treating everything from aches and pains to infertility. Make sure you visit a registered practitioner with a good track record.

HERBAL HELP

Make your own relaxing herbal pillow to help relieve aches and pains. Use an old pillowcase or a thick pair of tights (pantyhose) and fill with a mixture of dried pulses, such as lentils, and herbs – lavender is ideal. Stitch or tie up the end securely and, when needed, heat it for a minute or two in the microwave.

TURN ON YOUR HEAD

Relieve aches and pains with inversion therapy. It may sound odd, but hanging upside-down can relieve aches and pains, stiffness and stress. It is also thought to help the body detox by speeding up the flow of blood and lymphatic fluids that clear out waste.

SPICE IT UP

Research has found that cayenne pepper and turmeric can be beneficial for pain relief from joint and muscle strain. Topical creams containing cayenne are best for sore muscles but it can also be taken in tincture form for fast-acting relief, and may be included as a spice in food. Turmeric can also be used in food or taken in a capsule form.

REDUCE YOUR IRONING AND VACUUMING

A surprising number of cases of repetitive strain injury (RSI) are caused not by computers but by vacuuming and ironing. If there was ever a case for cutting back on two of the most tedious household chores, this is it – and you have the added bonus of saving energy, thereby cutting your carbon footprint.

SWAP BUBBLES FOR SALTS

Bath salts are natural and have restorative properties to relieve stress and muscle aches. They are a much greener alternative to bubble baths. Dead Sea salts have been found to help both eczema and psoriasis, and to ease sore and broken skin.

◎ headaches & migraines

REMEDY HEADACHES

Tension headaches, caused by stress, nervous tension, eyestrain or muscular strain, can be irritating, but try a natural remedy before a painkiller. Lavender and valerian are good herbal choices, or you can try immersing your feet in hot water for 15 minutes while, at the same time, applying a cold ice-water compress to your forehead, temples, back of neck, or where you feel the pain. This will increase blood flow to the feet while constricting blood vessels in the head.

USE TIGER BALM

If you have a headache, try Tiger Balm before reaching for the paracetamol. This blend of Chinese herbs is a mild analgesic, which helps to promote blood flow and reduce irritation. It is also good for muscular aches and pains.

RELIEVE MIGRAINES WITH GINGER

Due to its natural anti-inflammatory and pain-relieving properties, ginger may be beneficial in preventing a migraine from developing. At the first symptom, either chew on a piece of ginger root or alternatively mix a small amount of ground ginger in a glass of water and drink.

GET AHEAD

Boost concentration and ease headaches and eyestrain with an Indian head massage. This is a traditional technique designed to invigorate and stimulate the senses as well as to relax and heal aches and pains. Because it is thought to help boost concentration levels and sharpen the mind, it is an ideal pre-exam or pre-interview therapy.

MASSAGE AWAY HEADACHE PAIN

Place your fingers at the top of your spinal column, where your neck meets the skull. Then move your fingers out 5 cm (2 in) along the base of your skull until you find a little indentation. Apply firm pressure with your fingers, making a small rotating motion. Breathe deeply while you massage for one to three minutes, and let yourself relax.

 # colds, coughs & sore throats

WARMING UP NATURALLY

Heat your house naturally as much as possible to avoid the health problems associated with central heating, such as colds and sore throats. Get as much warmth as possible during the day from the sun by pulling curtains wide, but be sure to draw them at dusk to keep the warmth in.

BLOW YOUR NOSE ON COTTON

Use cotton handkerchiefs that can be washed after use instead of disposable tissues. This will not only help save trees, but the cotton will be softer on your nose.

WRAP UP

Instead of flicking on the central heating as soon as the weather gets cold, which has been reported to increase your chances of developing a blocked nose and nose bleeds, put on some extra layers of clothes. Wrapping up is a healthier way of staying warmer.

EASE STUFFINESS WITH EUCALYPTUS

Dilute a few drops of eucalyptus essential oil in a bowl of hot water and use as a steam inhalation to help clear nasal and sinus congestion. A few drops of eucalyptus on a handkerchief or even a pillow can aid sleep. The main ingredient of eucalyptus oil, cineole, has been studied as a treatment for sinusitis, and the oil is said to act on receptors in the nasal mucous membranes, leading to a reduction in nasal stuffiness.

REDUCE SNUFFLES WITH WATER

If you are feeling stuffy from a cold, place a bowl of water by the bed overnight. This will help increase the level of humidity in the room, which prevents your nasal passages from drying out and should make it easier to breathe. When you close the windows and turn the heat on in the winter, you reduce humidity in your home, so keep air circulating to increase humidity and prevent dry skin and scratchy throats.

NATURAL SOOTHERS

Ease a sore throat and cough with a homemade drink of lemon, honey and ginger, rather than reaching for a bottle of medicine. This natural remedy will soothe the throat while giving you valuable nutrients to help boost your immunity.

CHOOSE CHYWANAPRASH

Chywanaprash is a traditional Indian food supplement, which is thought to help boost health during the winter months. It is made from fruit, spices, herbs and honey, and contains the amla fruit, which is a rich natural source of vitamin C and antioxidants. Often referred to as Indian gooseberry, the amla fruit contains 30 times the amount of vitamin C found in oranges, making it useful for treating throat and respiratory tract infections. Chywanaprash can be mixed with water to drink as a tea, it may be taken by the teaspoon, and it can be spread on toast.

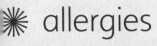

allergies

KEEP YOUR BULBS DUST-FREE

Dust in the home can trigger allergies and lead to respiratory problems. Make sure you keep your light fittings dust-free, as this will create a healthier environment and it will also make each bulb more efficient, thereby saving energy.

EAT HONEY, AVOID HAY FEVER

There is some evidence that eating locally grown honey may desensitize you to local plant allergens, which cause hay fever. The added benefit is that buying local will reduce food miles and help support producers and the economy in your community.

HELP HAY FEVER WITH EUCALYPTUS

Eucalyptus will protect you against respiratory complications and help boost your immune system during the hay fever season. Like the oil, eucalyptus hydrosol is the first line of defence against respiratory problems, coughs, colds, chest infections and hay fever-type allergies. It makes a good gargle or cough syrup on its own or combined with essential oils.

high blood pressure & heart disease

HAVE A CUP OF ORGANIC TEA
Research has found that the antioxidants in regular black tea can help to improve heart health and may even protect against cancer. Tea is a natural product but choose an organic variety to help protect the environment against over-use of pesticides and fertilizers.

DON'T OVERDO THE MINERALS
Despite it being marketed as the ultimate healthy drink, a recent study has shown that some mineral waters contain too much sodium and should be avoided by people with high blood pressure. Other contaminants including benzene have been found in bottled water.

LOWER BLOOD PRESSURE WITH TAI CHI
Studies have found that the traditional Chinese practise of tai chi can help to reduce blood pressure in women. It was also found to improve balance, reduce anxiety and stress, and improve flexibility. Tai chi is considered to be a particularly beneficial exercise for middle-aged adults.

arthritis

TRY CELADRIN TO EASE ARTHRITIS PAIN
Derived from all-natural, esterified oils, Celadrin is a natural pain reliever and "cellular lubricant" that has been found to be particularly beneficial for arthritis and joint pain caused by inflammation. It is a healthier but effective alternative to the non-steroidal anti-inflammatories that are normally prescribed, which often cause side effects such as headaches and heartburn.

A GREEN CURE FOR JOINT PAIN

Celery is a good choice for joint pain because it helps reduce inflammation. Crunching celery sticks is helpful, but consuming the extract of celery seeds is more powerful. Available from health food stores, the liquid extract should be taken with plenty of juice or water at mealtimes. The recommended dose is ½ teaspoon of the extract three times a day.

TAKE THE STING OUT OF ARTHRITIS

Because they are a natural diuretic and have blood-cleansing properties, stinging nettles are good for relieving the painful inflammation caused by arthritis. Drink nettle tea on a daily basis or brew your own from fresh nettles.

GET OUT THE OLIVE OIL

Warm olive oil is a great way to help reduce arthritis pain. Simply cover warm hands in warmed olive oil and massage the affected area gently, applying gently upward pressure to help reduce pain. Better still, add a few drops of lavender, rosemary or thyme oils to add scent and aid relaxation.

 # eye health

CLEAR CONJUNCTIVITIS WITH CALENDULA

The herb calendula (*Calendula officinalis*) has antiviral and anti-bacterial properties, which make it ideal for treating conjunctivitis. It also has a natural cooling action, which reduces soreness. Make a compress from calendula tea and bathe the eyes.

SOOTHE SORE EYES WITH FENNEL

Eyes that are overtired or strained from working on a computer can be soothed with a solution of the herb fennel. Mix a teaspoon of fennel seeds in a cup of boiling water, allow to cool, then strain. Soak a cotton wool ball in the solution and apply the compress to the eyelids for 10 minutes. Fennel is also helpful for digestive ailments and relieving water retention.

WEAR GLASSES WITH PRIDE

Contact lenses are great when it comes to practicality, but the chemicals used for hard lenses and the amount of packaging for disposables make them a bad environmental choice. Save them for sport and special occasions and wear glasses whenever you can.

 # circulation

SCRUB UP

Detox naturally with a body brush. Use a wooden brush with natural bristles to give your body a good brush – this will improve circulation and aid detoxification, with very little impact on the environment.

BOOST YOUR WARMTH

Drinking a cup of warming tea can help boost blood circulation to your extremities (as opposed to caffeinated drinks, which can actually reduce circulation). Infuse fresh ginger and cayenne pepper into hot water and drink to boost blood flow.

GO FOR GINSENG

Ginseng is a great supplement to take if you suffer from circulation problems – not only does it help regulate sugar levels to assist in diabetes, it also reduces cholesterol and has anti-clotting properties.

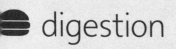 # digestion

REDUCE BLOATING WITH GENTIAN

A digestive tonic, the plant *Gentiana lutea* contains one of the most bitter substances known, and bitters are used in herbalism to improve appetite and digestion. Gentian is believed to aid digestion by increasing salivary flow and easing bloating; it also has the added benefit of strengthening the pancreas and spleen. It can be taken as a tincture or brewed into an herbal tea.

INDIGESTION AND STOMACH PAIN

Stomach discomfort is often caused by inflammation of the lining of the gut. The single best natural healing agent is aloe vera, which is available in juice form. It is rich in mucopolysaccharides, which help block pain, and it alleviates symptoms of irritable bowel syndrome (IBS).

BOOST DIGESTION WITH PROBIOTICS

If you have digestion problems such as bloating and flatulence, avoid over-the-counter medicines and treat the condition naturally with probiotics instead. Natural live yogurt is ideal for increasing the healthy bacteria in your system on a day-to-day basis and if you need a boost, for example after a course of antibiotics, try supplements as well.

NATURALLY ON THE MOVE

If you suffer from constipation, avoid traditional laxatives, which can sometimes exacerbate the problem, and get moving with natural laxatives such as psyllium husks. A tablespoon of these or ground flaxseeds sprinkled on cereal in the morning should ease the problem quickly.

hair & scalp problems

TREAT DANDRUFF NATURALLY
Anti-dandruff shampoos contain a cocktail of chemicals, so
avoid these and make your own herbal remedy. Simmer some
garlic, nettles and thyme in a pot for five minutes, then cool
and strain. Use the mixture as a final rinse every time you
wash your hair.

AVOID VOCS IN LICE PRODUCTS
Conventional head lice treatments are insecticides and
contain chemicals including organophosphates – a volatile
organic compound (VOC). VOCs have been linked to lots of
health problems including fatigue, joint and muscle pain and
depression. Use a lice comb to remove lice and their eggs.

HERBAL HELP FOR LICE
Use shampoos made from natural plant-based ingredients, which
contain essential oils such as neem to combat head lice. Try adding
essential oils such as thyme – a natural insecticide – and rosemary
to natural neem shampoo for an extra boost. Saturating the
hair with olive oil before combing through with a lice comb is an
alternative method. The oil is meant to smother the lice.

mouth & dental care

GO LARGE FOR TOOTHPASTE
Buy your toothpaste in the largest tube size possible to
maximize the ratio of toothpaste to packaging, but avoid the
pump-action plastic bottles. They are heavy on packaging and
difficult to recycle.

GET VEGGIE TEETH
If you want to be even greener when it comes to your dental
hygiene, choose a toothpaste based on vegetable products
rather than the more common chemically manufactured
versions. You'll need less for each application too.

FRESHEN BREATH WITH ALOE VERA
Serious cases of bad breath, or halitosis, may be caused by
stomach disorders. Daily gargling with aloe vera juice will help
to reduce toxins in the digestive system as well as relieving
any inflammation. Look out for an organic variety, however, to
ensure it is toxin-free and kind to the environment.

BE CHOOSY ABOUT FILLINGS
Make sure your dentist isn't using mercury-based fillings or ones
that contain heavy metal ions. Go for the safer option of gold or
ceramic fillings. If you have mercury fillings removed, make sure
they are disposed of with care so they don't poison waterways.

PICK A PLANT-BASED TOOTHPASTE
Toothpaste is a daily essential so it makes sense to choose the
healthiest, greenest option to reduce exposure to chemicals.
Pick a paste made from natural ingredients to avoid exposure
to artificial colourings and flavourings as well as unnecessary
chemicals such as triclosan.

TREAT MOUTH ULCERS WITH GINGER
Mouth ulcers can be relieved by chewing on a piece of fresh
ginger root which will help to speed up the healing process and
prevent infection of the sore. Aloe vera gel can also be dabbed
onto mouth ulcers to aid recovery of the area.

CHOOSE A HOLISTIC DENTIST

Mercury in the amalgam used in traditional dental fillings has been associated with a wide range of health problems, including headaches and even depression. If possible, choose a holistic dentist who uses homeopathic techniques and avoids mercury amalgam fillings altogether. You could also consider getting your existing amalgam fillings replaced with a mercury-free, white-composite alternative.

DON'T FORGET TO FLOSS

Flossing has been shown to be very effective for good oral health, but many conventional flosses contain colourings and flavourings as well as harsh antiseptic ingredients. Look out for flosses coated in beeswax, or vegetable waxes for vegans, rather than ingredients derived from petrochemicals. Some consist of nylon whereas others are based on pure silk strands (which may involve chemical sterilization), Teflon or other manmade fibres.

CHEW PARSLEY

Instead of using harsh mouthwashes to freshen your breath, chew on some fresh parsley. Traditionally used to disguise the smell of alcohol on breath because of its natural breath-freshening properties, parsley contains high levels of chlorophyll, which helps prevent toxins from accumulating in the digestive tract.

USE A TOOTHPASTE-FREE BRUSH

Because fluoride poses health risks, especially for bone health, avoid using toothpaste altogether with an ionic eco toothbrush. These work by releasing ions, which then blend with saliva to attract positive ions from the acid in the dental plaque. The acid is neutralized, the plaque disintegrates and there is no need for any toothpaste.

RINSE WITH SEA SALT

Avoid using conventional mouthwashes, which contain harsh ingredients such as alcohol and have been linked with an increase in throat and mouth cancers. Make your own rinse instead using a teaspoon of sea salt dissolved in a cup of warm water. Sea salt has natural antiseptic properties to protect the gums.

TAKE MORE CARE BRUSHING

Rather than relying on lots of foaming toothpaste to get your teeth clean, it would be better to ensure that you are brushing your teeth thoroughly. It is the brushing action rather than the toothpaste that gets your teeth clean, so make sure your brushing technique is up to scratch.

USE A HERBAL MOUTHWASH

Conventional mouthwashes may contain harsh ingredients and some have even been linked with an increased risk of throat and mouth cancers. Use a natural, herbal mouthwash instead, or make your own using a few drops of sage or peppermint oil added to water.

USE A TONGUE SCRAPER

Rather than relying on harsh mouthwashes to maintain fresh breath, try using a tongue scraper. The bacteria that causes bad breath is often found at the back of the tongue. Regular scraping can reduce bad breath and help prevent the build-up of plaque.

USE A WOODEN TOOTHBRUSH

A wooden toothbrush is kinder for the environment because it is made from a sustainable material and no plastics are involved in its manufacture. It is also easier to dispose of – you can compost or burn it in a wood burning stove. Natural bristles are also gentle on the gums, making them suitable for even very young children.

PUT THE FREEZE ON COLD SORES

At the first tingle of a cold sore, try zapping it with an ice cube rather than reaching for the medicine cabinet. If you catch it early enough, this may prevent a breakout.

USE CLOVES FOR TOOTHACHE

Try using oil of cloves to relieve toothache. Dab some of the oil onto the affected area and it should numb and reduce pain, as well as helping the healing process. This may enable you to avoid taking painkillers until you have time to visit a dentist.

PREVENT GUM DISEASE WITH SAGE

Regular rinsing with a solution of sage and sea salt may help protect against gum disease. Both sage and sea salt have mild antiseptic properties and have been found to reduce inflammation and promote healing. The tannins in sage are thought to help kill the bacteria that cause gingivitis.

TREAT COLD SORES WITH TEA TREE

Both cold sores and warts can be treated with tea tree essential oil. It has powerful antiviral properties, which help dry up the blisters and eliminate warts. Mix it with an equal amount of vegetable oil to prevent irritation of the surrounding skin.

BEAT ULCERS WITH SEA SALT

Sea salt is a mild antiseptic that stimulates saliva flow and promotes self-cleaning. It also has natural healing properties, which make it good for relieving mouth ulcers. Simply gargle with a solution of sea salt in water several times a day until the ulcers have healed.

urinary tract infections

SOOTHE CYSTITIS WITH CRANBERRIES
Drinking cranberry juice is a natural way to prevent and ease
the pain of cystitis without having to resort to antibiotics.
Research has found that as much as 80% of all the bacteria
in the body is resistant to conventional treatment – generally
antibiotics – which may also cause other problems such
as thrush. It is thought that the cranberry juice works by
preventing bacteria from adhering to the walls of the bladder,
so preventing infection from taking hold.

CURE WITH FRAGRANT JASMINE
The jasmine plant flowers have been used in Ayurvedic medicine
for hundreds of years and are regarded as a sattvic tonic, which
encourages the principles of light, harmony and increased
perception. Tea made from the flowers reduces fever, treats
urinary inflammation and aids the immune system. Jasmine
flower compresses can also be made to treat heat stroke,
headaches or anxiety.

 # skin problems

SUNSHINE FOR PSORIASIS
Sunshine is a natural healer for skin conditions such as psoriasis.
Moderate exposure to the sun can help to heal the scaly
patches that afflict sufferers, but be very careful not to burn
the skin. Always avoid the sun in the middle of the day.

GET A BAMBOO COVER-UP
Make sure your children have the best sun protection by slipping
on a bamboo cover-up when you are at the beach. Bamboo
is a sustainable, fast-growing crop, which also provides a sun
protection factor of around 50.

EASE ECZEMA WITH SUPPLEMENTS
Research has found that low levels of zinc and calcium may be linked to an increased risk of eczema, so boost levels naturally by increasing your intake of organic leafy greens and supplementing with zinc or calcium tablets.

EFAS FOR ECZEMA
Research has also found that essential fatty acids (EFAs) may play a significant role in keeping skin healthy and can help to ease the symptoms associated with eczema and psoriasis. Boost levels of essential fatty acids by increasing the amount of fatty fish, such as salmon or linseeds, in your diet.

FIGHT ACNE WITH OILS
Squeezing can make pimples worse; try treating spots with a dab of tea tree oil instead. A mixture of tea and lavender essential oils can also be dabbed directly onto blemishes a few times a day – the lavender helps to heal blemishes while the tea tree fights infection.

SOOTHE SKIN WITH CAMOMILE
The herb camomile is known for its cleansing and cooling properties, and it is good for easing irritated skin caused by eczema or psoriasis. As a natural antihistamine and a good substitute for hydrocortisone in cases of eczema, camomile cream will help reduce irritation and itching.

ALOE EASES SUNBURN
Take away the sting of sunburn with aloe vera gel. Use the purest, organic gel you can find, which will relieve pain and act as a disinfectant to protect against possible infection. Lavender oil diluted in water can also be used to clean sunburnt areas and help healing.

SCREEN SUN WITH EDELWEISS
The alpine plant edelweiss (*Leontopodium alpinum*) has its own built-in UV light-absorbing substance. Look out for plant-based sun lotions containing edelweiss extract for natural protection in the sun.

CHOOSE A NATURAL SUN BLOCK

Avoid unnecessary exposure to petrochemical-based ingredients and apply a natural sun protection cream. Lots of the chemicals commonly used in sun creams are known skin irritants and some have even been found to have hormone-disrupting effects. Choose a sun cream that contains plant- and mineral-based ingredients instead.

LEAVE NO TRACE

Avoid exposure to the chemical residue left on clothing by conventional detergents. This has been linked to health problems, including skin irritations and allergies. Some chemicals found in detergents are unnecessary because they don't increase the washing or hygiene effects.

USE A NATURAL STAIN REMOVER

Reduce unnecessary exposure to the chemicals in conventional stain removers, which have been linked to a number of health problems ranging from skin irritations to cancer. Mix up your own natural stain removers using common kitchen items such as lemon juice and salt instead.

GET A HAT

The most natural and healthiest form of sun protection is to cover up. Avoid exposure to the sun, particularly during the hottest part of the day. Wear a hat, which gives good coverage to your face and neck to prevent damage to the delicate skin from the sun's rays.

boost immunity

A TASTE OF HONEY

Eating honey is good for your health because it is high in antioxidants, which help to boost the immune system, and rich in vitamins and minerals. Bees themselves are good for the environment because they pollinate over 60 different types of crop, including fruits and vegetables.

CUT CAFFEINE FOR BETTER IMMUNITY

For a healthy immune system, avoid caffeine and alcohol. Coffee, tea and colas are stimulants and known to compromise the immune system, making you more susceptible to viruses, coughs and colds. Caffeine increases the heart rate and elevates blood pressure, plus stimulates the excretion of the stress hormones cortisol, epinephrine and norepinephrine. Drink health-promoting herbal teas instead.

GET SOME SLEEP

Making sure you get enough sleep is a good way to stay healthy and boost your immune system. Lack of sleep puts extra pressure on your body and makes you susceptible to viruses. Try a cup of camomile or valerian tea at bedtime if you have trouble sleeping. Cinnamon sprinkled onto hot milk is another good natural sleep aid.

BOOST IMMUNITY WITH ASTRAGALUS

Although less well known than echinacea, the Chinese herb astragalus is very beneficial for boosting immune health. Traditionally used in Chinese herbal medicine, it is thought to stimulate white blood cell production, which supports the immune system by fighting infections.

BOOST YOUR IMMUNITY NATURALLY

The herb echinacea is well known for its immune-boosting properties. Research has found that it can help reduce your chances of developing a cold and will lessen the severity of symptoms if you do become ill. Take a few drops of tincture in some water on a daily basis at the start of the cold season.

hangovers

SPEED RECOVERY WITH VITAMIN C
Vitamin C is an excellent nutrient for speeding up recovery from a hangover. Foods naturally high in vitamin C include oranges, papaya, mango, red or orange pepper and broccoli, or you could take a vitamin C supplement instead. Avoid smoking as this will reduce levels of vitamin C in your body.

NATURAL RELIEF FOR HANGOVERS
Rather than reaching for painkillers the morning after overindulging, try getting rid of your hangover naturally first. Bananas are an excellent source of potassium, which helps to keep the body fluids balanced, so they help remedy dehydration. They also help to control blood-sugar levels, which drop the day after a drinking session. Eggs are also good as they contain cysteine, which is said to mop up the destructive chemicals that build up in the liver when it's metabolizing alcohol.

DETOX WITH MILK THISTLE
Detoxing your body is a great way to stay healthy and rejuvenate your whole system. Before you embark on a detox programme, however, give the process a kickstart by supplementing with a tincture of the herb milk thistle, which is thought to aid detoxification by supporting the liver-cleansing process. Milk thistle has been used medicinally for over 2,000 years, most commonly for the treatment of liver and gallbladder disorders.

 # addictions

B AN ADDICT
Addicts – particularly alcoholics - are commonly deficient in the B vitamins, particularly thiamine. Thiamine is available from quorn, brewers' yeast, pork products, wheatgerm, roe and breakfast cereals, so make sure you get the recommended daily amount.

STOP SMOKING
If you haven't already, quit smoking. Research has shown that it takes ten years for a cigarette butt to decay. The health implications of smoking such as premature ageing are well known, as are the effects of passive smoking, so stop now for the sake of your health and that of the planet's.

STAY RELAXED WITH VALERIAN
Studies have shown that one of the main reasons for giving in to addictions is anxiety – fight yours with valerian tea (the natural source of valium), which helps detoxify as well as calm nerves and induce calmness.

stress & depression

EASE STRESS WITH SOUND THERAPY
Sound therapy works by using brass or crystal bowls to produce sounds that are thought to aid relaxation. It is believed to benefit a number of health problems including stress, insomnia, depression and even irritable bowel syndrome.

GARDEN AWAY STRESS
Research has shown that gardening is a great way to relieve stress and may help combat depression. There are even claims that a harmless bacteria normally found in dirt, *Mycobacterium vaccae*, has been found to boost the production of serotonin, a mood-regulating brain chemical.

NATURAL STRESS RELIEF
Stress is the modern ailment that can have long-reaching effects on the body and mind, causing chronic health and mental-health conditions. To de-stress naturally, you can try meditation, massage or breathing techniques – all have a good proven track record. Take responsibility for your wellbeing, too, by making sure you are getting regular exercise, nutritional food with enough vitamin B in your diet, and a good night's sleep.

BEAT EXAM STRESS WITH RHODIOLA

The herb rhodiola (*Rhodiola rosea*) has been found to improve mental health naturally. It is an adaptogenic herb, which means it helps the body cope with stress and a demanding lifestyle. This makes it ideal for exam times, the menopause or simply busy periods in your life.

PACK IN THE PANIC ATTACKS

If you suffer from panic attacks and anxiety, you may like to try the natural dietary supplement 5-HTP (hydroxytryptophan). Found in minute amounts in such foods as turkey and cheese, 5-HTP is an amino acid and works by increasing the serotonin in the brain in a similar way to antidepressants and beta-blockers, but without the side effects. It may also be beneficial as an appetite suppressant and sleep aid.

TREAT DEPRESSION NATURALLY

Antidepressants do have some side effects and there are concerns about them being overprescribed. Research has found that the herb St John's wort (*Hypericum perforatum*) is as effective at relieving mild to moderate depression as antidepressants, but without the side effects.

BRIGHTEN UP

Combat Seasonal Affective Disorder (SAD) and save energy by making the most of natural light in your home. Natural daylight is an important trigger for the production of serotonin, a brain chemical that controls mood.

GET OUTSIDE

Try to spend 30 minutes a day outdoors, no matter what the weather is, and exercise regularly. This will help to lift your spirits due to the release of endorphins, boost your fitness levels and save energy on usage of household appliances at the same time.

 # relaxation

TREAT YOURSELF TO A MASSAGE

Massage not only provides relaxation and relief for muscle strain and fatigue, it may also have emotional, physical and physiological benefits. It has very little impact on the environment – especially when done by candlelight – and has been found to be extremely beneficial for overall health and wellbeing.

UNWIND NATURALLY

For a relaxing bath, make your own bath milk. You will be able to have a long soak without worrying about exposing yourself to unnecessary chemicals, which may actually irritate and dry out the skin. Mix 2 cups of powdered milk with ½ cup of finely ground oats, and add straight to the bath for a gentle, soothing exfoliation.

LAVENDER FOR RELAXATION

Add five drops of organic essential oil lavender to a bath of warm water and relax for 20 minutes. Lavender promotes relaxation and has been found to help induce a sense of calm and improve sleep.

CHEMICAL-FREE MASSAGE

Wooden massage tools are another way to de-stress naturally without the addition of lots of manufactured lotions and potions. Massage has been found to reduce anxiety and stress, as well as boost circulation.

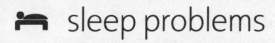
sleep problems

COMBAT INSOMNIA WITH CAMOMILE
If you suffer from insomnia, avoid taking sleeping pills, which have a range of side-effects. Try natural alternatives such as camomile tea, which has traditionally been used to improve sleep. Put some camomile tea bags in the bath for a sleep-inducing soak.

VACUUM YOUR MATTRESS
Mattresses are home to some pretty unpleasant things – including sweat from our bodies and dust mites. It is estimated that mattresses contain anything from 100,000 to 10 million dust mites, depending on their age and use. Try to air your bed as often as possible and vacuum it regularly.

GET A SLATTED WOODEN BED BASE
Choose a slatted wooden bed base rather than a divan. Wooden bases allow air to the underside of the mattress, which helps to reduce the number of dust mites your mattress may harbour. Try to make sure the wood is from a sustainable source.

USE ORGANIC COTTON
According to reports by Pesticides Action Network (PAN), conventional and GM cotton accounts for 16% of global chemical pesticide use, more than any other single crop. Sleep easy and avoid exposure to these chemicals by choosing organic bed linen.

SLEEP NATURALLY
Don't reach for the sleeping tablets next time you're having trouble dropping off – not only can you become reliant on using them to get to sleep, but many also give you an unpleasant hangover feeling the next day. Try natural sleep enhancers like lavender essential oil and camomile tea.

WARMING UP
Warm your bed up with a hot water bottle rather than an electric blanket. Electric blankets use unnecessary energy and have been linked with health problems. The blanket can also be a fire hazard if it develops a fault.

SLEEP EASY
If your mattress is reaching the end of its life, why not replace it with a natural one? Natural, organic mattresses are free from chemicals and, as we spend roughly a third of our lives in bed, will significantly reduce your exposure to potentially toxic substances that are routinely used to treat mattresses, such as fire retardants, petroleum-based foams, plastics, vinyls, fungicides and pesticides.

improving concentration

BEWARE OF ALUMINIUM PACKAGING
Avoid buying foods packaged in aluminium or using aluminium cookware, as some reports have linked aluminium foil to low zinc levels and to premature senility and memory loss. It is estimated that the average person takes in between 3 and 10 milligrams of aluminium per day, and it can be absorbed into the body through the digestive tract, the lungs and the skin.

DRINK MORE WATER
Most of us could do with drinking more water. Being dehydrated adversely affects your mental performance. When dehydrated, your attention and concentration decrease by 13% and short-term memory by 7%. Make sure you drink filtered tap water rather than bottled to reduce bottle waste.

women's health

GET FIT WITH PHYTOESTROGENS
Plant phytoestrogens are natural hormone balancers and they may improve hormonal health in women going through the menopause. Soya, legumes, seeds and lentils all contain phytoestrogens, which balance hormones naturally as well as offering protection against breast cancer and heart disease.

BALANCE HORMONES WITH BLACK COHOSH
The herb black cohosh was used by Native Americans as a traditional folk remedy for women's health conditions, such as menstrual cramps and hot flashes, arthritis, muscle pain, sore throat and indigestion, and today is used by some women to help them through the menopause. It balances hormones without the health risks associated with HRT.

USE ORGANIC SANITARY PROTECTION
Avoid exposure to the chemicals used in conventional sanitary protection such as chlorine, which has been linked to toxic shock syndrome, and dioxins, which are known to be carcinogenic. Choose 100% organic and GM-free cotton products, such as those by Natracare, which will be kinder to you and the environment.

WRAP IT UP
When it comes to that time of the month, it's difficult to think of being green, but simple steps can be taken. Purchasing sanitary towels (napkins) that are not individually wrapped is a good start to reducing your environmental impact.

WHAT A WASTE
Instead of using sanitary towels (napkins) that are thrown away after a few hours, consider changing to reusable sanitary towels that can be washed. This will cut down your monthly waste by a considerable amount. Organic cotton tampons without applicators are another green choice as they won't have any of the chlorine, dioxins, synthetic chemicals or fragrances of ordinary tampons.

DON'T APPLY

When you're choosing tampons, avoid unnecessary packaging like applicators. Disposable plastic is a bad environmental choice. If you have to use disposable tampons, those you apply yourself are best.

DON'T FLUSH YOUR FLOATERS

Don't flush your used tampons down the toilet. Wrap them in a small amount of toilet roll and place in the bin to avoid your personal waste finding its way into public water systems. It takes about six months for a tampon to biodegrade.

CUP YOUR FLOW

The most environmentally friendly option when you've got your period is the use of a silicone menstrual cup that is available commercially. It is worn internally like a tampon but collects menstrual fluid rather than absorbing it. The fluid can be flushed away and the cup washed and reused.

BIN THE WIPES

Feminine wipes are totally unnecessary and may even be damaging to your health. Save money, reduce waste and avoid exposure to potentially toxic chemicals such as fragrances and preservatives, which are often derived from petrochemicals, and go natural instead. If you must use them, seek out organic cotton wipes.

CRAMPING RELIEF

If you suffer from menstrual cramps, try evening primrose oil, which is rich in gamma-linoleic acid (GLA), an anti-inflammatory prostaglandin that can counter the hormones causing pain. Niacin (vitamin B3) is also often recommended for dilating the blood vessels and improving blood flow to the uterus.

HELP HOT FLUSHES WITH SAGE

Research has shown that one of the main symptoms of the menopause, hot flushes, can be helped by supplementing with sage. This herb is a natural product that may be taken in tincture or capsule form and helps the body to rebalance the sweat-regulating mechanism in the brain naturally.

DON'T HAVE A MID-LIFE CRISIS

Approach the menopause naturally and avoid hormone replacement therapy (HRT), if possible. Hormones from medicines have been detected in waterways and HRT has been linked to ovarian and breast cancer. Prepare yourself for a healthy menopause by eating a balanced diet and reducing stress.

HAVE SAFE, GREEN SEX

Use a biodegradable condom from the manufacturer Condomi. Condoms pose a waste problem and, when they are not disposed of properly, they end up polluting our public places and marine environments. So choose green and ethical condoms – they are also vegan – for safer, eco-friendly sex.

A MAGNETIC FORCE

Avoid taking unnecessary drugs for hormone problems by using a magnetic device known as Ladycare. A magnet that clips onto underwear over the abdomen, it has been found to reduce menopausal symptoms as well as PMS and other hormonal-related problems.

FIGHT NAUSEA WITH GINGER

Ginger is one of the best known natural remedies for nausea. It is particularly beneficial for morning sickness in early pregnancy. Pour boiling water over fresh ginger root to make a tea and drink it first thing in the morning. Alternatively, nibble on stem ginger.

CUT OUT THE CHEMICALS IF YOU ARE PREGNANT

Recent research found that children born to women who used lots of cleaning products and air fresheners during pregnancy were more likely to have symptoms such as wheezing. It may sound obvious, but try opening windows to freshen rooms rather than using air fresheners.

CURE THRUSH WITH YOGURT

Natural, live yogurt is good for lots of minor health problems, including thrush. The yogurt contains *Lactobacillus acidophilus* which, like yeasts, naturally live in the human body, and its presence helps keep Candida yeast populations in check. It can be eaten or applied topically to the affected area.

BOOST FERTILITY WITH FLOWER ESSENCES

Avoid medical procedures such as IVF and boost your fertility
naturally with flower remedies. The Australian bush flower
remedy, she oak (*Casuarina glauca*), is thought to be especially
beneficial for fertility. The plant produces fruit the same size
and shape as human ovaries and has traditionally been used
to boost fertility.

EASE PERIOD PAIN WITH YOGA

Gentle exercise helps the body get rid of excess hormones
and flush them out of the body. Yoga in particular also helps
to balance the endocrine system and has the added benefit
of reducing stress and improving mood. Twists and inverted
positions (such as headstands and shoulder stands), however,
are not suitable during menstruation because they reverse the
blood flow and can intensify cramps.

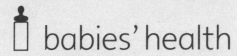
babies' health

CAMOMILE FOR COLIC
Add some drops of camomile essential oil to a warm bath to help ease a colicky baby. Camomile is a gentle sedative and anti-spasmodic so will help to calm and soothe. If you prefer, add a couple of drops of oil to a carrier oil, such as almond oil, and massage your baby instead.

POLYCARBONATE WARNING
There are concerns about plastic baby feeding bottles made with polycarbonate plastic. A report in 2000 by the World Wildlife Fund highlighted the dangers posed by bisphenol-A (BPA), a hormone-disrupting chemical contained in polycarbonate that is particularly risky for children. Polycarbonate can be identified by looking on the packaging for PC7, or inside the recycling triangle for the number 7.

NATURAL TEETHERS
Instead of giving your baby plastic teethers, why not try offering them pieces of frozen banana – it will disintegrate as they chew. Other natural teething aids include crusts of toast and strips of organic dried fruit such as mango.

HOMEOPATHIC HELP
Homeopathy is really helpful for treating health problems in babies and young children because it is safe. For a teething baby, use the homeopathic remedy Chamomilla (made from German camomile). Either dissolve a pill in water and give teaspoonful by teaspoonful until the symptoms subside, or alternatively use homeopathic teething granules, a product that mothers highly recommend.

EASE TEETHING WITH AMBER
If your baby is teething, avoid plastic teething rings. Instead, try an amber teething necklace. These are designed to be worn, not chewed, and act as a natural analgesic, easing the pain of teething when worn on the skin. However, babies must be supervised at all times while wearing the necklace.

USE OLIVE OIL ON CRADLE CAP

If your baby has cradle cap, rub some olive oil with a couple of drops of tea tree oil added onto the scalp and leave it overnight. In the morning the loose flakes can be gently brushed away with a soft baby brush. Repeat regularly until the scalp is clear.

GIVE YOUR CHILD WOODEN TOYS

Choose wooden toys made with child-friendly paint for your children. Wooden toys are made from a sustainable source and will not harm your child's health. Just check that they are painted with water-based, non-toxic paints.

SOOTHE SKIN WITH CALENDULA

The herb calendula has antiviral properties and is good for soothing irritated skin. Calendula cream is ideal for use on babies with nappy (diaper) rash. Alternatively, make a soothing tea by pouring hot water over dried calendula and use the strained liquid to dab onto minor skin infections.

DRESS YOUR BABY IN ORGANIC WOOL

Organic merino wool is non-allergenic, so as well as being kinder to the environment (and the sheep), it is also better for your little one. The wool helps regulate body temperature, enabling your baby to maintain a safe temperature, whether the weather is hot or cold.

CHOOSE TO BREASTFEED

If you are having a baby, choose to breastfeed if you are able. Breastfeeding offers a significant number of major health benefits for you and baby. Environmentally, it's better too, because it requires no sterilizing solutions or equipment, and no plastic bottles, teats or containers.

GIVE BABIES A BREAK

Don't sterilize baby equipment using chemicals. Babies need to be able to develop their immune systems, so washing equipment with hot, soapy water and then rinsing with boiling water is sufficient. This simple method also reduces the amount of chemicals entering the waterways.

AVOID HARSH DETERGENTS
If you use washable nappies (diapers), avoid cleaning them with harsh detergents, which have been to linked to an increased sensitivity among some children. Choose a natural detergent, which is free from dyes and fragrances and is made from plant-based ingredients.

HOMEOPATHY FOR KIDS
Avoid exposing your children to unnecessary medicines. Instead of reaching for painkillers such as Calpol or Tylenol, try homeopathy instead. It can be very effective for teething and colic pain, which are common reasons for administering painkillers for children, and it is safe enough to be used on babies.

USE A TALC ALTERNATIVE
Research suggests that using talcum powder may increase your risk of developing cancer. Look for natural alternatives or make your own using cornstarch mixed with a few drops of essential oils, particularly if you are considering using it on an infant or child.

USE WASHABLE NAPPIES
Protect your baby's health by ensuring that they don't come into contact with any chemicals from disposable nappies (diapers). Washable nappies help reduce the number of chemicals your baby is exposed to and they are better for the environment.

MAKE YOUR OWN BABY FOOD
To cut back on waste and the energy used in production and distribution, making your own baby food is by far the greenest option. It is also the healthiest because although there is a wide range of organic baby foods available, home-cooked is always going to be the most nutritious option.

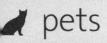

pets

AVOID HARSH PET SHAMPOOS
Research has found a link between pet shampoos that
contain a type of harsh detergent called pyrethrins to autism
in children. The research, published in the *New Scientist*, found
that mothers of children with autism-spectrum disorder were
twice as likely to have reported using pet shampoos as those of
healthy children.

USE BORAX FOR FLEAS
If you find your pet has fleas, try using borax instead of
reaching for a powerful insecticide. To get rid of fleas on
furnishings, sprinkle a thin layer onto carpets, leave overnight
and vacuum away in the morning.

TRY A MAGNETIC COLLAR FOR YOUR PET
A magnetic collar can be used on cats and dogs to help improve
their general wellbeing and reduce aches and pains. They
are thought to work by putting a charge in the bloodstream,
encouraging the blood to accept more oxygen.

USE GARLIC TO BANISH FLEAS
Try mincing fresh garlic into your dog's food several times a week
as a natural flea repellent. Garlic has the added benefit of being
an immune booster and so may help prevent other illnesses, as
well as protecting against fleas and ticks.

toxins & chemicals

LOOK OUT FOR TRICLOSAN
Triclosan can be found in many household products including toothpaste and hand soap. Linked with cancer, it has been found to cross over into breast milk. It is also particularly un-environmentally friendly because it converts to dioxins when exposed to sunlight and is known to be toxic to aquatic organisms.

BEWARE OF "GENDER BENDING" CHEMICALS IN YOUR HOME
A number of chemicals found in a huge number of household items, from paint to detergents, have become known as "gender benders". This is because they have been found to mimic the female hormone oestrogen. They have been linked to infertility and one group, dioxins, are known carcinogens.

CHOOSE FRAGRANCE-FREE PRODUCTS
Phthalates have been linked with a number of health problems, including infertility and liver damage. They are commonly used in a wide range of beauty and bodycare products and are best avoided. Choose "fragrance-free" rather than "unscented" products, which often means that one scent has been used to mask another.

AVOID SLS FOR BETTER HEALTH
Sodium laurel sulphate (SLS) is a common ingredient in many household products from shampoo to detergent, but it has been linked to a number of health concerns including cancer and is a known skin irritant. Avoid it by making sure you use plant-based products, which are also kinder to the environment.

GREENER CLEANERS
Reducing your reliance on chemical cleaners can improve your health as well as the environment. Research has found that only around 14% of the most heavily used chemicals have basic safety data publicly available, so it's difficult to know exactly what you and your family are coming into contact with.

MAKE YOUR OWN TOILETRIES
Avoid exposure to toiletries containing harsh detergents, which can cause skin sensitivity and other health problems, by making your own. Store-cupboard staples such as honey and olive oil can be mixed with an egg yolk to create a home-made conditioner, or try avocado mashed with natural yogurt for a facemask.

BEWARE PEGS
Look out for ingredients called polyethylene glycol (known as PEGs) in bodycare products. Polyethylene glycol is a commercial polyether used in many skin creams, toothpastes and sexual lubricants. Studies have highlighted that some PEGs may cause dermatitis and other skin irritations, while research has found that a carcinogen may be formed as a by-product during manufacture.

AVOID OVEN CLEANERS
Conventional oven cleaners often contain a number of highly toxic chemicals including sodium hydroxide, and contact with these chemicals could cause serious damage to your health. To avoid any risk, use a homemade combination of salt and bicarbonate of soda (baking soda) mixed with a little lemon juice or vinegar.

HEALTH MATTERS

REACH FOR THE RHUBARB

Avoid using harsh detergents which have been linked to a number of health problems including asthma, and which are damaging to the environment. Instead, remove burnt-on food and grease from the bottom of pans by boiling up rhubarb stalks, which will do the job just as well.

FORMALDEHYDE WARNING

This is a common ingredient in lots of different household and body-care products. A suspected human carcinogen, it has been found to cause lung cancer in rats. It has also been linked to asthma and headaches. Formaldehyde is often found in disinfectants and is used as a preservative in deodorants and hand wash.

AVOID ORGANOCHLORINES

Organochlorines are compounds often found in synthetic chemicals such as those used to make household cleaners and air fresheners. They include polychlorinated biphenyls (PCBs) and polyvinyl chloride (PVC), and chloroform and chloramines. They have been linked with skin irritation, depression and headaches.

 # healthy home

MAKE SURE YOU'RE INSULATED

Living in a cold, damp environment is not good for your health, and there will be times when the central heating is necessary. Make sure you're not wasting any of the energy used to heat your home by increasing the insulation in your loft.

VENTILATE YOUR HOME WELL

A cold, draughty house is not very welcoming, but it is important to ventilate your home properly as well as to draught-proof it. Inadequate ventilation in kitchens and bathrooms can cause health problems due to a potential build-up of mould.

KEEP YOUR WINDOWS OPEN

If you have been decorating with paint or varnish, make sure you keep your windows and doors open to reduce air pollution in your home. Conventional paints can emit possible carcinogens such as toluene and xylene, as well as hormone-disrupting chemicals. Opt for natural, ecological decorating materials, but still make sure the room is kept ventilated.

AVOID VINYL FLOORS

PVC or vinyl flooring creates environmental hazards, mainly because one of its main constituents, chlorine, can lead to the creation of dioxin – a toxin linked to cancer – when it is manufactured. Chemicals called phthalates can also leak out of PVC floors and these have been linked to asthma. A study from the American Journal of Public Health found that children raised in houses with PVC flooring were 89% more likely to develop bronchial obstructions.

GET A DEHUMIDIFIER

Dehumidifiers work by removing the moisture in the air, which can cause mould, which in turn exacerbates allergies and helps to increase the dust mites in your home. A wide range of dehumidifiers are available and are suitable for every space, from a box room to a three-bedroom house.

GO NATURAL WHEN YOU INSULATE

If you do decide to add extra insulation to your home, use natural products such as sheep's wool or cellulose, if possible. These will be safe to handle and help keep humidity levels stable, maintaining a healthy environment.

PROTECT YOURSELF WITH SOLVENT-FREE PAINT

Ecos Organic Paints are made using natural ingredients and are VOC-free. They also do a range of specialist paints to help you create a healthier home, such as their radiation-shielding wall paint and the MDF passivating primer, which is designed to absorb formaldehyde from the wood.

REDUCE CONDENSATION

An ideal way to reduce condensation problems in kitchens and bathrooms, which may lead to health problems and allergic reactions, is to use a wind-operated extractor fan. This ensures that there is a steady supply of fresh air without having to open any of the windows.

AVOID SICK BUILDING SYNDROME

Indoor air pollution, or Sick Building Syndrome, has been linked to all sorts of health problems such as headaches, nausea, asthma and even cancer. Try to keep your interiors as natural as possible and make sure your home is well ventilated to reduce pollution.

DISPOSE OF FITTED CARPETS

Wall-to-wall carpets may look comfortable but they harbour dust, which may lead to a build-up of dust mites and act as a trigger for asthma and other allergies. Replacing fitted carpets with natural flooring, such as wood, will reduce your exposure to potential allergens.

SAND YOUR FLOOR

A wooden floor is a green and healthy option, especially if you are sanding existing floorboards, and it is the natural alternative to synthetic carpets and vinyl. It will reduce your exposure to toxic chemicals such as volatile organic compounds (VOCs) that may be emitted by floor coverings.

WAX AWAY

If you do decide to sand your floorboards, make sure that you choose an environmentally friendly way to finish them. Waxing floorboards is the most eco-friendly option. Lots of floor varnishes contain high levels of VOCs that have been linked with asthma and other health problems.

BEWARE OF PLASTIC

Our homes contain plastic in a huge variety of different forms – furniture construction, paint, food containers and cleaning products. Not only is it a by-product of the energy-intensive petroleum industry, it has also been linked to health problems due to the chemicals it contains, such as Bisphenol A.

WATCH OUT FOR FORMALDEHYDE

Formaldehyde has traditionally been used as a binder and preservative in hundreds of household items including furniture upholstery, bed linen and cosmetics. It is known to release toxic vapours at room temperature and is a suspected carcinogen.

LOOK OUT FOR LEAD

Lead can cause poisoning and is extremely energy-intensive to produce. Avoid any exposure by taking extra care when stripping old paint, which may contain high levels of lead. Use a mask to protect your nose and mouth, and make sure the room is well ventilated.

CHOOSE SHUTTERS INSTEAD OF CURTAINS

Although curtains are good for blocking out draughts and insulating windows, they also absorb toxins and dust. They are likely to have been treated with flame-retardants and other chemicals to meet current fire safety regulations. If you are lucky enough to have them, wooden shutters are a better option and they are easier to clean, too.

AVOID TOXIC PAINTS IN YOUR HOME

Conventional paints contain solvents that give off volatile organic compounds (VOCs). These have been linked to a number of health problems including damage to the respiratory system and headaches. Always choose plant-based decorating paint made using natural ingredients.

 health at work

REDUCE YOUR USE OF THE PRINTER

Only switch on your printer when you need it. New research has found that printers can cause a form of indoor air pollution because they release tiny particles of toner-like material into the air, which could be inhaled into the lungs.

REDUCING STATIC

Home computers and other electrical equipment produce radiation, which has been linked to miscarriage and facial rashes. Reduce the amount of time you spend in front of your PC by switching off and going for a walk, rather than sitting at your desk with it on standby.

BALANCING IONS

Electrical equipment such as PCs produce positive ions, which have been reported to cause atmospheric pollution and linked to health problems such as hayfever and stress. To neutralize the positive ions, place some plants or a water feature near your computer.

OPEN THE WINDOW

Reduce the amount of static produced by your PC by improving ventilation. Opening a window will help to prevent the build-up of static electricity. Using natural materials, such as wood, near your PC will also help the static to disperse.

PUT A PLANT ON YOUR DESK

Research has shown that having a plant on your desk at work can help reduce your risk of getting a sore throat and stuffed-up nose. A study by researchers in Norway found that nose, throat and dry skin symptoms were 23% lower in offices with greenery.

HAZARDS IN THE WORKPLACE

You may be aware of the environmental risks to your health in your own home, but what about your workplace? Many employees are exposed to waste materials and toxins without being fully aware. Check your company's health and safety guidelines, as well as your national standard; for example, the Occupational Safety and Health Administration (www.osha.gov) in the USA, or try the Health and Safety Executive (www.hse. gov.uk) in the UK.

GET OUT AT LUNCHTIME

A staggering number of workers spend their lunch hour in the same position as the rest of their day – eating in front of their computers. If this applies to you, try switching off and going for a walk instead. A 10-minute walk will boost circulation and has been found to improve brain power, too.

AVOID EMFS FROM PCS

To reduce your exposure to electromagnetic fields (EMFs) and save energy, limit your time on your computer. EMFs and low-frequency electromagnetic fields (ELFs) have both been linked to problems such as eyestrain, headaches, high blood pressure and stress.

UNPLUG ELECTRONIC EQUIPMENT

Although there is no proof that EMFs and ELFs are harmful, the amount of research is growing. You can reduce the levels you and your family are exposed to by switching off electrical equipment such as computers and televisions, which will also help to save energy.

TAKING THE STRAIN

Prevent eyestrain from your monitor by buying one with a liquid crystal display (LCD) screen. The LCD monitors cause less strain than those with cathode ray tubes (CRT) because they are higher resolution. Plus they emit much less radiation and are slightly more energy efficient.

STRIKE OUT ON YOUR OWN

Consider going freelance! It's a lot easier to be green if you are working alone from home rather than in an office – there's no carbon emissions caused by the commute for a start. Research has shown that self-employed people report higher levels of job satisfaction and less stress.

TURN YOUR OFFICE GREEN, LITERALLY!

Studies have shown that offices painted white, blue or green are conducive to better mood and job satisfaction than other colours, particularly red. Just make sure you use a plant-based, low-VOC (volatile organic compound) paint.

WATCH OUT FOR RSI

Repetitive Strain Injury (RSI) is a computer-related health problem caused by working on a PC for long periods of time. Improve your health and reduce energy consumption by taking regular breaks away from your computer and stretching your arms and shoulders.

TAKE A BREAK

Save energy by switching your computer off and taking regular breaks throughout the day. We waste a huge amount of energy by leaving appliances on standby, so turn your computer off and have a rest. Long periods in front of the machine can lead to carpal tunnel syndrome and even deep-vein thrombosis.

USE THE STAIRS

Instead of using the lift (elevator) at work, walk up the stairs. This will cut energy use and improve your health instantly. Studies have shown that people who use the stairs have lower cholesterol, better breathing capacity, healthier hearts and also weigh less.

RESTRICT YOUR USE OF LAPTOPS
Although laptops use up to 80% less energy than desktop computers, they may be responsible for more health problems. There is evidence that they can cause injuries from bad posture and they have also been linked to fertility problems. So if you have a laptop, try not to use it for extended periods on your lap.

SCRAP THE AIR CON
Lobby your boss to eschew energy-guzzling air conditioning for more simple methods, such as installing blinds and opening the windows. Air conditioning has been linked with minor ailments such as colds and coughs; it also means you have to adjust to the temperature outside every time you leave your office.

USE A CERAMIC MUG FOR YOUR TEA
Avoid using polystyrene cups for hot drinks when you are out and about. The waste problem they pose is considerable, especially when you consider that polystyrene cups never biodegrade. Also, there is some evidence that chemicals from the polystyrene may leach into the contents.

travel & holidays

WIND DOWN YOUR WINDOW
Air conditioning has been linked with a number of minor
health problems. Avoid switching it on in your car when you
are travelling at lower speeds. Tests have shown that it is more
environmentally friendly to open your windows under speeds of
96 kph (60 mph) than it is to use air conditioning, which boosts
fuel consumption.

TAKE ADVANTAGE OF LOCAL AMENITIES
Rather than driving somewhere for a walk or a day out, take
advantage of your local sports facilities, such as tennis courts. As
long as you can walk or cycle to your local tennis court or swimming
pool this is a very eco-friendly way to improve your health.

STAY LOCAL
Instead of travelling for hours, explore areas of beauty nearby.
This will reduce carbon emissions and give you a fresh outlook
on your neighbourhood. Improve your health by visiting local
beauty spots on foot with the help of public transport.

PLAN A HEALTHY AND GREEN HOLIDAY
Decline the two-week package to the islands and make your
holiday healthy and green. Pack up your camping equipment
and explore the coastline by bike or foot (with the help of public
transport for longer distances). Children love camping and it's
a very low-impact way to take a vacation.

LEAVE THE CAR FOR SHORT JOURNEYS
Nearly 40% of journeys of less than 3 km (2 m) are made by
car, even though they are the kind of distances that could
be cycled quite easily. Short car trips result in higher levels
of emissions because engines are not operating at their
optimum temperature.

TAKE A GREENER COMMUTE

If you are one of the many people who travel to work in
a vehicle on your own – the majority of work commutes
are done by car – then leave it at home for a couple of days
of the week. Walking or cycling to work, or to the train station
for longer journeys, will boost your cardiovascular health and
help the environment.

AVOID AIR TRAVEL

Air travel is one of the biggest contributors to global warming
– in the UK it accounts for more than 6% of total carbon
emissions. New research has also found that flying could be bad
for the health due to contaminated air being pumped around
the aircraft. The air absorbs fumes from the engine oil, and can
cause nausea and headaches.

CHOOSE A LOW-IMPACT ACTIVITY HOLIDAY

Why not combine getting healthy with taking your summer
break? Rather than sitting back and having it all done for
you, get active. Canal boat trips, hiking excursions and surfing
vacations will be fun and improve your health and fitness at
the same time.

Beauty
&
Fashion

FROM COAL TAR IN HAIR DYES to formaldehyde in nail varnishes, the average woman is exposed to as many as 175 chemicals from her beauty products every day that can cause conditions as mild as skin irritation or as serious as cancer.

It's not just the toxins in beauty products that are bad for the health either; synthetic chemicals from these products find their way from your home into waterways and soil, contaminating food and water supplies for all living things. The following tips highlight the environmental and health problems associated with lots of ingredients commonly found in beauty and bodycare products to help you make well-informed choices that are good for you and the planet.

 getting organized

HAVE A CLEAR OUT

Take a look at your bathroom cabinet and clear out everything but the essentials. If you've got more than one of any cosmetic product, pass it on and try not to buy duplicates in the future.

STICK TO THE SHELF-LIFE

Bear in mind that natural products won't contain the same levels of chemical preservatives as other brands, so their shelf life will be shorter. Always use products before their "best before" date and dispose of any after this time.

USE ESSENTIAL OILS

Choose products containing organic essential oils as many of them have the added benefit of acting as natural preservatives. Make sure you store them away from sunlight, preferably in dark glass bottles, and that way they will last longer.

 take care

WISE UP

Most people think that ingredients in personal care and cosmetic products are safety tested before they are sold but there is no such requirement under federal law in the US. Ingredients including mercury, lead and even placenta have found their way into cosmetics.

GO FOR PRODUCTS WITH PLANT-BASED INGREDIENTS

Natural, plant-based ingredients are the best option for any products that are likely to be absorbed into your skin. Pure essential oils have a therapeutic effect without stripping the skin of its natural oils. If you are pregnant, however, check with your doctor first about which oils are safe to use.

BE CAREFUL IF YOU'RE BREASTFEEDING

It pays to be extra cautious about the beauty products you use if you are breastfeeding. Studies have found that some chemicals, including a group of perfume chemicals still widely used in cosmetics, are stored in the mother's body fat and passed on to babies when they are breastfed.

NOT JUST SKIN DEEP

The outer layer of our skin can be penetrated quite well by some oils, which are often used in products to carry the active ingredients into the deeper layers of the skin. Therefore, it makes sense to give more consideration to the products that you apply and leave on the skin.

TOXINS IN BREAST MILK

A Swedish study revealed that triclosan, an ingredient found in products such as mouthwash, toothpaste and soap, has been found in high levels in 60% of human breast milk samples. Pregnant and nursing mothers should pay special attention to avoid using these products.

BEWARE THE COCKTAIL EFFECT

Research has found that the use of chemicals in cosmetics cannot be viewed in isolation. Because similar chemicals are found in a wide range of everyday items, as well as cosmetics, a cocktail effect is developing. The Women's Environmental Network says these chemicals are building up in, and damaging, the environment.

BE CHEMICALLY AWARE

The National Institute of Occupational Safety and Health in the US lists 884 chemicals in use by the cosmetic industry as toxic substances, including phthalates, acrylamide, formaldehyde and even some pesticides. Many of them have been linked to health scares including cancer and gender disruption. Reduce the number of products you use to avoid overexposure to the chemicals found in cosmetics.

CHOOSE NATURAL TO AVOID HARMFUL TOXINS

We absorb around 60% of what we put on our skin and the average woman comes into contact with as many as 175 different chemicals from the beauty products she uses every day. Choose natural products without synthetic or man-made ingredients to avoid the toxins.

SAY NO TO NANOPARTICLES

Nanoparticles are one of the latest buzzwords in the beauty world and they are already being used in a wide range of products, from lipsticks to foundations. Manufacturers don't have to list them in the ingredients, however, so they are hard to avoid but worth doing so because there are concerns that nanoparticles can end up in the bloodstream and cause inflammation.

DON'T MIX IT UP

Avoid combining different products together as this may encourage nitrosamines to form. Nitrosamines are contaminants accidentally formed in cosmetics either during manufacture or storage if certain ingredients are combined. There is no research to prove that they can cause cancer in humans but evidence exists that they are carcinogenic in animals.

SHOW YOUR SENSITIVE SIDE

Around 40% of the British population is now affected by allergies and, according to Allergy UK, over-exposure to chemicals can trigger a sensitivity that may lead to an allergy such as asthma, eczema or hay fever. Choosing natural products will reduce your exposure to chemicals.

AVOIDING SLS

Sodium lauryl sulphate (SLS) is a known irritant and a common ingredient in many beauty and bodycare products. Found in most shampoos, hair conditioners, body washes and bubble baths, SLS is a strong detergent and foaming agent. It can irritate eyes, skin and mucous membranes and has been linked to allergic reactions.

CHOOSE SLES RATHER THAN SLS
Sodium laurel sulphate (SLS) is a known irritant (see previous tip), but sodium lauryl ethyl sulphate (SLES) is a much milder foaming agent derived from coconut, which is thought to be gentler on the skin. If you are using commercial, non-organic products, choose one with SLES instead of SLS.

USE NATURAL HAIR DYES
Mainstream hair dyes use strong chemicals such as ammonia and have been linked to health problems including scalp irritation, facial swelling and even cancer. Choose natural dyes made with vegetable ingredients instead. These are still able to lighten hair by a couple of shades but without the potential side effects caused by harsher dyes and bleaches.

THINK BEFORE YOU DYE
Research studies have revealed that hair dyes pose an increased risk of cancer. One such study found that individuals who had worked for ten years or more as a hair stylist could have a risk of bladder cancer, which is five times greater than the general population.

AVOID PVC PACKAGING
Aside from the waste issue created by cosmetic packaging there are also health concerns. The manufacturing process of PVC is known to release cancer-causing dioxins into the environment. There are also concerns that chemicals, such as phthalates, may leach out of the plastic container into the product.

check the label

READ THE PACKAGING
Many cosmetic and skincare products contain ingredients classified as food items. In the UK look out for letters UKROFS followed by a number on the label, which shows that the product has been approved by the United Kingdom Register of Organic Food Standards.

LOOK AT THE LABEL

Many of us are used to scanning food labels to check out salt and fat content and it is worth doing the same with cosmetics and beauty products. Lack of regulation means that literally hundreds of chemicals can be included in just one ingredient name – such as "fragrance".

LOOK OUT FOR LABELS

Some labels such as "hypoallergenic" don't have to be substantiated. Other labels such as "unscented" or "fragrance-free" don't ensure that the product doesn't contain fragrance, just that they have been used simply to mask the odour of other chemicals.

READ THE LABEL

Don't take "natural" for granted – read labels and lists of ingredients to spot synthetics. In Europe and the USA, a product can call itself natural even if only 1% of its ingredients fall into that category. Make sure you're not being taken in by something claiming to be natural when it's not. Look for products that say they are phthalate-free and any seals that claim they are certified organic.

KNOW YOUR FOAMING AGENTS

Choose products containing plant-based foaming agents such as coconut oil and decyl glucoside, which is extracted from corn. These are preferable to sodium laurel sulphate (SLS), commonly used in bodycare products (see also page 286).

CHECK PRODUCTS FOR SODIUM BENZOATE

A common preservative in cosmetics and food is sodium benzoate, an antimicrobial preservative. However, it has been linked to health problems including gastric irritation, numbing of the mouth and nettle rash. It is widely used in products such as cosmetic wipes, where the chemicals are likely to remain on the skin, so avoid it, if possible.

FAIRTRADE LABELS

The Fairtrade Labelling Organization (FLO) is an international organization dedicated to ensuring that products are certified and labelled accurately (see www.fairtrade.net). FLO members, producer organizations, traders and external experts all participate in the initiatives.

BE GM-FREE

Some mass-produced cosmetics do contain genetically modified organisms (GMOs), usually in the form of either maize or soya. This is more common in the US than in Europe, where anti-GM feeling is stronger. Choosing certified organic products will ensure that they are GM-free.

READ BETWEEN THE LINES

Watch out for gender-bending chemicals known as phthalates, which are often hidden in the catch-all phrase of "fragrance" on beauty and bodycare products. They have been identified as hormone disrupters and studies have found they have reduced the male hormone action in rats.

AVOID PHTHALATES

Phthalates are a family of chemicals often used to soften plastics. They were banned from children's toys after it was discovered that kids were ingesting the chemical by sucking. Phthalates are still used in a number of products, such as hairspray, deodorants, body lotions, fragrances and nail polishes, usually to soften the formula or make it more flexible. However, the fact remains that they have been linked with birth defects and reproductive health problems.

BE CAREFUL WHAT YOU WASH DOWN YOUR SINK

Triclosan, a common ingredient in toothpaste, deodorant and soap, is known to be environmentally harmful. It can be converted to cancer-causing dioxin when exposed to sunlight in water and has been classified as toxic to aquatic organisms and the aquatic environment.

TRICLOSAN ALERT
This is also a common ingredient in many antibacterial products
such as hand and mouth washes, so look for it on the label.
Triclosan is a known irritant and its use has been linked with
an increase in bacteria that are resistant to antiseptics and
antibiotics. Recent research has also found that it acts as a
hormone disrupter.

DON'T PEG IT!
Propylene glycol is a wetting agent and solvent used in
shampoos, deodorants and aftershave, among others. It is
also one of the main ingredients in antifreeze and brake fluid.
Polyethylene glycol, which often appears as PEG, is used to
dissolve grease and is found in lots of facial cleansers as well
as oven cleaners.

PACK IN THE PETROLEUM PRODUCTS
Petroleum-based ingredients such as petrolatum, which is
also known as baby oil, strips the natural oils from the skin,
causing chapping and dryness, and even premature ageing.
The manufacture of petroleum-based ingredients also has a
major impact on the environment.

PARABENS ARE PRESERVATIVES
These chemicals are commonly used as preservatives in
cosmetics and as antibacterial agents in products such as
toothpaste. They have been found to have an oestrogenic
effect and have also been linked with cancer. The four main
parabens in use are methyl, ethyl, propyl and butyl parabens.

LOOK FOR THE LEAPING BUNNY
Products with the leaping bunny logo mean that the product
has been approved under the international Humane Cosmetics
Standard (www.eceae.org) and guarantees that the product
itself – or any of the ingredients it contains – have not been
tested on animals. The organization, a coalition of animal-
protection groups from the European Union and North America,
is the world's only international criteria for cosmetic or toiletry
products that are "Not Tested on Animals". See also www.
leapingbunny.org.

 # purchasing power

DON'T BUY LOTS OF DIFFERENT CREAMS
Why buy 20 different products when a few would do the job just as well? Start by asking yourself whether you really do need a separate hand, eye cream and moisturizer. Decide on a few key products such as a moisturizer, a sunscreen and a natural cleanser and stick to these.

SPEAK OUT
Why not take a stand by letting manufacturers and brands who consistently over-package their goods know that's the reason you've stopped supporting them? There's nothing like purchasing power to force changes.

ETHICAL BEAUTY
Manufacturers, by law, have to test their products and it is up to them how they do it, so use your purchasing power to send a message to cosmetics companies that testing on animals is unacceptable. The European Union has passed a ban on animal testing in cosmetics, starting in 2009 with a complete ban in 2013.

BUY RECYCLED PRODUCTS
Look out for cosmetics and skincare brands that only use recycled packaging for their products. REN, the skincare company, is one which also uses recycled cartons and filling material for delivering its products. It operates a take-back recycling scheme for its customers, where they will recycle empty bottles sent back to them.

DON'T BELIEVE THE HYPE
Avoid getting sucked into the advertising hype. Manufacturers employ marketing techniques to exploit women's insecurities about their body image, often using enhanced images of men and women to sell products. Studies in the US found that 70% of women say they feel worse about their own looks after reading women's magazines, so view advertisements and magazine pages with a degree of healthy cynicism.

CHECK IF YOUR BRAND IS CRUELTY-FREE
Several anti-vivisection websites feature search engines that allow you to see if your favourite brand has been approved under the Humane Cosmetics Standard. This includes European and North American manufacturers such as the American Anti-vivisection Society (www.aavs.org) and the British Union for the Abolition of Vivisection (www.buav.org).

DON'T BE FOOLED BY THE BAN
Despite the UK ban on cosmetic testing on animals, this doesn't necessarily mean that British cosmetics companies are cruelty-free. Many leading brands are still using products and ingredients that have been manufactured and tested overseas.

AVOID PALM-OIL PRODUCTS
Unethical sourcing of palm oil for cosmetics and a wide range of other products is having a devastating effect on the environment, endangered species and indigenous populations around the world according to the World Wildlife Fund (WWF). The Body Shop is the first global cosmetics company to introduce sustainable palm oil into its product lines.

BEWARE OF "NEW, IMPROVED" PRODUCTS
The average market life of a beauty product is between two and three years and so manufacturers have to be constantly coming up with new ways to market products. Be aware that these new formulations are often just a way to boost sales and sometimes the only new thing is the name.

CHOOSE ETHICAL BEAUTY
Following the international success of the fairtrade food market, ethical beauty and bodycare products are moving in the same direction. Knowing that the product has been made without harming the workers or the environment is becoming more important and some brands are using ethically sourced ingredients such as sustainably harvested herbs.

BUY FAIRTRADE COTTON WOOL

Make sure that your cotton wool isn't being produced at
the expense of the workers creating it by buying fairtrade-
certified cotton wool and cotton buds (swabs). Look for the
International Fairtrade Association FTO mark on products
(see www.ifat.org). In the UK fairtrade products must be
registered by the Fairtrade Foundation and carry the
fairtrade mark (see www.fairtrade.org.uk).

BUY FROM YOUR LOCAL HEALTH FOOD STORE

Visit your local health food or organic store when you are
buying beauty products and cosmetics. They will be more
knowledgeable than staff in supermarkets and larger stores,
and will be able to advise you on the right sort of product
for your skin.

DON'T BE FOOLED BY PRICE

Some of the more expensive products are not necessarily
better than cheaper versions. Products claiming added active
ingredients are often pricier than more basic products but
beware – the active ingredients may not transfer effectively
from the laboratory to the final product.

DON'T BUY INTO PACKAGING

Research has revealed that as much as 50% of the cost of
a bottle of perfume can be accounted for by packaging and
advertising. Some companies offer a refill service where you
can take in old bottles and get them refilled, cutting back on
waste and packaging.

BUY GLASS BOTTLES, NOT PLASTIC

Packaging will contribute a great deal to the environmental
impact of all beauty and bodycare products. Therefore, where
possible, buy products packaged in glass bottles rather than
plastic as these are easier to recycle. Good examples of this
include deodorants from Pitrok and Urtekram.

BUY IN BULK
It may not be the most glamorous option but try to buy products in the largest size available in order to cut back on packaging. You can then decant into a more convenient, smaller container at home. However, remember to check the shelf-life: you don't want to be left with products past the "best before" date.

 # natural style

CHOOSE PRODUCTS WITH FEWER INGREDIENTS
The more natural a product, the fewer ingredients it is likely to have. A good clue that a product is full of chemicals is the length of the ingredients list, so if in doubt avoid it. The more ingredients it contains, the more likely it is that you may react badly to one of them.

WHAT'S IN IT?
Don't be fooled by cosmetic products claiming to be natural. Check the ingredients for the Latin names of plants and for the word "fragrance", which is often code for chemical copies of natural products.

CHOOSE ORIGAMI-STYLE PAPER PACKAGING
A huge amount of the cost of a finished beauty product actually goes on the packaging but some companies are changing their ways. Pangea Organics' soap packaging is made from 100% post-consumer newspaper. It is moulded using origami techniques so it doesn't require glue and is infused with organic seeds.

TRAVEL LIGHT
Don't buy travel-sized versions of bodycare products when you are going on holiday. These containers are generally thrown away after use and end up on landfill. Instead, use your own small containers to decant your shampoo and shower gel, which can be rinsed out and re-used on your next trip.

RECYCLED COSMETIC BAGS

What better way to carry your cosmetics when travelling than in a recycled bag? Ranges of cosmetic and toiletry bags made from recycled juice packs – non-biodegradable foil and plastic packaging that would otherwise go into landfill sites or be incinerated – are made by Ragbag (www.ragbag.nl). The products are available in Australia, Germany, Japan, the Netherlands, Switzerland, the UK and the US.

GO ORGANIC

By using certified organic beauty products you will ensure you are not coming into contact with synthetic fragrances and colours. Different certifiers have different organic standards so it's worth checking who allows what ingredients. The Soil Association, for example, doesn't permit the use of the foaming agent sodium laurel sulphate (SLS), solvents or parabens.

SEEK OUT FREEZE-DRIED HERBAL INGREDIENTS

Parabens are often added to beauty products to preserve them but there are concerns about their safety. As an alternative, some manufacturers are moving toward using freeze-dried herbal ingredients, which don't need to be preserved.

HIGH IN HERBS

Herbs such as aloe vera and lavender have been traditionally used for their cleansing, moisturizing and soothing qualities. Products high in herbal content rather than synthetics are not only natural but also very effective. Look for organic or wild-crafted herbal products to ensure the environment is also being protected.

NATURAL PRODUCTS HAVE A SHORTER SHELF-LIFE

Be aware that many natural products have a shorter shelf-life than conventional products because they don't use as many preservatives. Don't use products beyond their "best before" date. If there isn't a date listed on the product it will have been formulated to have a minimum shelf-life of 30 months, so discard it after this period.

HEMP FOR BEAUTY

Hemp oil is an ideal ingredient for skin products because it is so rich in a unique balance of omega 3 and 6 oils. It is absorbed directly into the skin, nourishing and moisturizing it. Because it is a low-maintenance crop it doesn't require pesticides or fertilizers, making it an ideal crop for sustainable farming.

BEWARE OF EMPTY CLAIMS

The cosmetic industry loves to bandy around words such as "organic" and "natural" but without certification they are meaningless. This is because, legally, a product containing as little as 1% of natural ingredients can call itself a natural product.

WHAT IS A NATURAL INGREDIENT?

A natural substance is any plant or animal extract, or any rock or mineral obtained from the earth. It is possible to make exact copies of natural substances using raw materials from coal tar and petroleum and many manufacturers choose to synthesize ingredients rather than to extract them from natural sources.

USE PLANT RATHER THAN MINERAL OILS

Mineral oils are derived from petrochemicals and are therefore not sustainable. As well as being environmentally unsound, they have also been linked to allergic reactions when applied to the skin. Plant oils such as olive and almond oil contain essential fatty acids, vitamins and other nutrients which nourish the skin naturally.

KNOWING IT'S NATURAL

One way to be sure that a European product is as natural as it claims to be is if it has been certified by the BDIH in Germany. This means the ingredients have to be from a plant or mineral source; most petroleum based and synthetic ingredients are not permitted, and neither are GM ingredients.

perfectly perfumed

CHOOSE TO BE FRAGRANCE-FREE
Manufacturers are not legally required to list any of the potentially hundreds of chemicals in a single product's fragrance mixture. Fragrances can contain neurotoxins and are known allergens. Avoid them by choosing products fragranced only with pure essential oils.

SMELLS GOOD NATURALLY
Products containing natural fragrances are the most environmentally friendly choice. Fragrance from herbal infusions, floral waters and essential oils using organic herbs and spring water are the gentle way to smell good without the use of synthetic chemicals.

SAY NO TO SCENT
The majority of perfumes are made entirely from petrochemical products of which the manufacture is very damaging to the environment. They can contain phthalates, which have been shown to damage the lungs, liver and kidneys. Instead of buying petrochemical perfume, make your own with a few drops of essential oil in rosewater or carrier oil.

WHAT DO YOU REALLY SMELL OF?
Other unsavoury ingredients commonly found in perfumes and fragrances include castorium and ambergris. Castorium comes from beavers, which are reportedly trapped and killed before the secretion is obtained from the beavers' genital glands, and ambergris comes from the intestines of sperm whales. Many marine mammal protection laws ban trade in ambergris.

SMELL A RAT?
Don't spray yourself with a cloud of poison. Today 95% of chemicals used in fragrances are synthetic compounds, including some toxins capable of causing serious health problems. Limit perfumes to special occasions.

SNIFF AROUND

Although it does have to be listed in the ingredients, fragrance in a product can appear in a variety of different ways so it's good to familiarize yourself with the different terms. Perfume, parfum, aroma and fragrance are all common words used for perfume in a product.

COMMON SCENTS

Look out for the word "fragrance" on ingredients lists. Current legislation doesn't restrict the quantities or combinations of fragrance chemicals that can be used in everyday cosmetics. This means that it's not unusual for some products to contain as much as between 50 and 100 fragrances.

USE PERFUME SPARINGLY

To cut back on chemicals, cut back on perfume. If you can't live without your favourite scent, try to reduce the number of times you apply it. Instead of spraying it on day and night, keep it for special occasions and nights out. There are a growing number of natural and organic perfumes on the market so look out for these.

ORGANIC SCENTS

Avoid the synthetic fragrances that may contain hormone-disrupting chemicals such as phthalates and opt for organic fragrances instead. There are plenty of wonderful, certified organic scents to choose from and brands to look out for include: Organic Apoteke, Aveda and Parsème.

AVOID MUSK FOR DEERS' SAKE

Many upmarket perfumes contain substances such as musk and civet. Musk comes from the gland of a male musk deer which has been hunted to near extinction. Civet is a secretion from civet cats and there are reports that they are tormented to increase the secretions they produce. Avoid fragrances containing these ingredients.

allergy alert

MORE THAN A LITTLE SENSITIVE
Even natural and organic products can cause allergic reactions on people with particularly sensitive skin. Essential oils and natural ingredients can be extremely potent so if you are at all concerned, do a patch test on a small area of skin before slathering a new product all over your face or body.

AHAS MAY NOT PROVIDE THE RESULTS YOU WANT
The long term effects of alpha-hydroxy acids (AHAs), a common ingredient in cosmetics, are not yet known. One such chemical, salicylic acid, is banned in the EU from toiletries for use by children under the age of three, with the exception of shampoo.

BUY ORGANIC FOR SKIN ALLERGIES
People who suffer from sensitive skin and skin allergies sometimes find that using organic products is less likely to cause a reaction. Allergy sufferers can sometimes tolerate organic products better because they contain only tiny amounts of synthetic chemicals.

BE CAUTIOUS WITH OILS
Although essential oils are by far the greener choice over synthesized versions, it still pays to be cautious when using them as some may cause allergic reactions among very sensitive users. The key ones to be cautious with are tea tree, eucalyptus and citrus-based oils.

CHOOSE ESSENTIAL OILS, NOT SYNTHETIC FRAGRANCES
Manufacturers of synthetic fragrance oils do not have to disclose the ingredients used in their making, so you really have no idea what they contain although they are subject to safety guidelines. They are cheaper than essential oils though so are often used in beauty and bodycare products.

HAIR TO DYE FOR

Many people have allergic reactions to hair dye, ranging from tingling of the scalp and general discomfort to facial dermatitis and even facial swelling. Para-phenylenediamine (PPD), one of the ingredients that can trigger allergic reactions, is still found in the majority of mainstream hair dyes despite being banned in Germany, France and Sweden.

go greener

CUT BACK ON PACKAGING

A number of manufacturers are developing products that require little packaging, such as Lush's solid shampoo bar (see www.lush.com). Other ways to reduce waste from packaging include recycling schemes such as that offered by The Body Shop.

CHOOSE LOCAL AND HANDMADE

An increasing number of small manufacturers are making handmade beauty care products with natural and organic ingredients. The production methods are usually small scale so have minimal environmental impact and local production also cuts down on carbon emissions caused by transportation.

ORGANIC AWARENESS

A product carrying the Soil Association logo in the UK and the USDA Organic seal in the US must contain a minimum of 95% organic ingredients. However, a product that is labelled as "made with organic ingredients" must contain a minimum of 70% organic ingredients.

DON'T HAVE A SHOWER JUST TO WASH YOUR HAIR

Water is a precious resource and one way to save a considerable amount of it is not to have a bath or shower simply to wash your hair. Use a hand-held shower attachment instead and turn the water off while you apply the shampoo and conditioner.

GO BIODYNAMIC

There are an increasing number of biodynamic beautycare products on the market. These are products made using ingredients that have been produced using biodynamic methods. Biodynamic farming is sometimes seen as the next step up from organic farming. The ingredients are grown using holistic practices (such as homeopathic composts) that are in tune with the earth's natural rhythm. The resulting crops are believed to have more potency, too. Brands to look out for include Dr Hauschka, Weleda and Jurlique.

USE AN IONIC TOOTHBRUSH

The Soladay ionic toothbrush contains a metal rod made up of a patented semiconductor material. When this is activated by light it produces electrons that help to remove dental plaque without the need for toothpaste, although toothpaste can also be used, if you prefer the taste.

RECYCLE OLD TOOTHBRUSHES

When you've finished with your toothbrush, give it a new lease of life. Toothbrushes make great scrubbing brushes for hard-to-reach corners and holes in and around the bathroom. They also make useful nailbrush substitutes.

COLD-BLENDED IS BEST

Some manufacturers, such as Paul Penders, are developing cold-blended cosmetics. Many conventional products are manufactured using heat-processing, which can destroy the bioactive ingredients. Cold-blending protects the ingredients, thereby making the final product more effective.

GOOD ENOUGH TO EAT

A current trend in the beauty world is for making cosmetics using food-grade ingredients such as fruit, oats and vegetables that are designed to nourish your skin from the outside in. British cosmetic company NOe (Natural Organic edible) and US company Be Fine Food Skincare are good examples of this trend. Their products are natural and preservative-free.

LOOK OUT FOR ORGANIC
The global market for organic cosmetics is growing and in 2006, 1,600 organic products were launched worldwide. However, be cautious: manufacturers are not legally required to obtain organic certification to make organic claims. Make sure the products you buy carry the logos of either the Soil Association, Ecocert or USDA organic (United States Department of Agriculture). These products contain ingredients that are assessed to be safe to human health and guarantee that their manufacture and use causes minimum environmental impact.

BUY PRODUCTS WITH RECYCLED PACKAGING
Packaging is one of the things used to sell cosmetics and beauty products but it is unnecessary and adds to the growing global waste problem. Look for products that use recycled cardboard packaging such as those made by Living Nature and Lavera.

USE RECYCLED FACIAL TISSUES
Around 3.2% of the world's commercial timber production goes into the manufacture of tissue products and Greenpeace estimates that an area of ancient forest the size of a football pitch disappears every two seconds in order to feed the demand for paper production. Buying recycled products helps to reduce illegal logging.

beauty boosts

SUPPLEMENT YOUR REGIME
There is a wide range of vitamin and mineral supplements available specifically to boost hair, skin and nails. Combination formulas, such as Viridian's Beauty Complex, provide a one-stop shop for women wanting to boost their general appearance. Individual supplements can be taken for specific areas, such as silica for hair and nails and omega-3 fatty acids for skin.

CHANGE YOUR DIET

Following a diet high in antioxidants such as vitamins C and E will boost your looks and improve your immune system at the same time. Avoiding foods high in saturated fats and eating a diet based on fruit and vegetables are two of the best ways to preserve your looks and protect your skin from ageing and pollution.

A NATURAL BEAUTY FIX-IT

Making sure you have enough sleep – generally eight hours – will boost the appearance of your skin. This is because it gives your body the chance to repair and regenerate tissue. It is also important to get enough exercise, which helps to boost circulation and stimulate skin cleansing.

DRINK UP

One of the best beauty treatments ever is water, and plenty of it. Drinking around 1.5 litres (about 6 8-fl oz glasses) of water a day will help maintain your natural beauty, keeping skin hydrated and plump. You also need water to detoxify toxins in your body that can lead to problems such as blemishes.

EAT STRAWBERRIES

High in antioxidants, strawberries can be beneficial in the fight against premature ageing and wrinkles. They are particularly high in vitamin C, which is important for the formation of collagen – a key element that helps to keep skin firm. Strawberries also help to protect against broken capillaries beneath the skin's surface.

CHOOSE GOAT'S MILK

Goat's milk helps to seal moisture into the skin and maintain its natural pH level, making it an ideal ingredient for soap. In addition, goat's milk is higher in fat and richer than cow's milk, so is extremely moisturizing. It also naturally contains alpha-hydroxy acids which are known for their rejuvenating qualities.

BOOST YOUR BEAUTY WITH NATURAL YOGURT
Yogurt has many benefits for natural beauty, both internally
and externally. Live yogurt contains bacteria, which benefits
the digestive system and helps to keep skin clear. It is also an
ideal ingredient for a home-made face pack due to its natural
exfoliating properties.

DETOX TWICE A YEAR
One way to get clearer eyes and a radiant glow is to detoxify.
Natural health experts recommend detoxing twice a year
– around spring and autumn – to give your skin and overall
health a boost. Ridding your body of everyday toxins can help
to improve the texture and appearance of your skin and hair.
You should aim to eliminate all processed and refined foods as
well as caffeine, alcohol, sugar, salt, red meat, high-fat foods,
and food additives and preservatives. Most detox diets suggest
drinking lots of water and eating fresh organic fruit, vegetables
and herbs with only small amounts of whole grains and pulses.

DETOX THE HOPI WAY
Using Hopi ear candles, a traditional Native American therapy,
is an environmentally friendly way to detox. They are 100%
natural – being made from beeswax, honey and organic linen –
and many people report that they are beneficial for headaches
and earaches as well as general wellbeing.

EXERCISE YOUR FACE MUSCLES
Completing a regular session of face and neck muscles can
help improve the elasticity and appearance of the skin. Regular
stretching exercises help to boost circulation and tone up the
muscles around the eyes, necks and cheeks without the need
for any products.

DRINK GREEN TEA
Favoured by celebrities including Sophie Dahl and Victoria
Beckham, green tea has a number of beauty benefits. It is
naturally rich in antioxidants, which help to protect against free
radicals and premature ageing. The leaves can also be used as a
gentle exfoliant to give your skin a healthy glow.

LOOK TO THE EAST

For centuries Ayurvedic medicine has been using herbal remedies to treat skin complaints. Companies such as Pukka Herbs (www.pukkaherbs.com) have created Ayurvedic formulations designed to soothe irritated and inflamed skin, and to boost its general appearance. Pukka's Cleanse Tea is a blend of herbs designed to boost radiant skin.

STAY BEAUTIFUL WITH A DAILY DOSE OF YOGA

Daily yoga can help to improve your appearance naturally. Practised regularly, breathing and stretching exercises can reduce the appearance of wrinkles, dark circles under the eyes and bring colour to your cheeks. It will also improve your overall health and fitness.

 # treat yourself

SPEND TIME ON YOURSELF

Time and energy put into making your own home beauty treatments from natural ingredients should be considered part of a pampering programme, rather than another chore. Set aside time to make the beauty treatments yourself and enjoy the whole process. You will find it much more satisfying than spending lots of time and money shopping in a busy store.

TRY HOT STONE THERAPY

Avoid lots of pills and potions and try hot stone therapy instead. This therapy has been used by different cultures for centuries to ease symptoms such as aches and strains, arthritis and even insomnia. Warm stone expands the blood vessels, allowing blood to move faster round the body.

HAVE A MASSAGE

A relaxing massage has physical as well as psychological benefits. Massage helps to improve skin colour and tone by removing dead skin cells and boosting circulation. It aids detoxification and encourages more efficient waste removal, and can also encourage better lymph drainage and so reduce swelling.

A MARBLE MASSAGE
A great way to soothe sore feet is to give them a marble massage. Add a layer of marbles to a foot bath containing a few drops of essential oil and roll your feet around on them while you soak.

VISIT A HEALTH SPA
For an indulgent but natural treat, visit a spa. Treatments such as massages, facials and hot stone treatments all help the body to relax and detoxify naturally. Make sure the spa you visit uses organic or at least natural products during its therapies.

skin savers

BE A HONEY MONSTER
Manuka honey is one of the best ingredients to incorporate into your natural beauty regime. It has natural moisturizing, nourishing, healing and rejuvenating properties as well as being a natural humectant (a substance that attracts and preserves moisture). Manuka honey can be applied topically and appears in a wide range of beauty products.

NOURISH SKIN WITH AVOCADO
Avocado is arguably the most important food for well-nourished skin. It provides essential fats necessary to prevent wrinkles and dryness. Incorporate avocado into your diet on a regular basis and apply it, mixed with natural yogurt, once a week as a face pack to get the benefits, internally and externally.

YOGURT IS A NATURAL BEAUTY TREATMENT
Natural yogurt, ideally organic, can be used to reduce redness and irritation on skin. It can also be applied to the face like a face pack due to its cleansing and moisturizing properties. Natural yogurt is particularly beneficial for sunburn and acts as an effective aftersun.

SOLVE PROBLEM AREAS WITH LEMON

Dry and discoloured skin on knees and elbows can be dealt with by using a fresh lemon. Cut it in half and sprinkle with a teaspoon of sugar, then rub the lemon halves into elbows and knees for a few minutes.

CLEAR SKIN WITH STEAM

This is particularly good for oily and blemished skin. Bring a pot of water with fresh herbs such as parsley and peppermint to the boil, remove from the heat and stand for a few minutes. Put a towel over your head and lean over the infusion for 10 minutes.

LOOK FOR PURE FACE MASKS

If you do choose a commercial face mask, look for one that is hypo-allergenic and free from perfume, parabens or colours. If you make your own from all-natural ingredients, use distilled water instead of ordinary tap water, which can be high in minerals and may irritate sensitive skins.

GET A FACELIFT WITH EGG WHITE

Egg whites can be used to give an instant, natural facelift. Dab the whites directly onto lined areas and allow to dry before continuing your usual beauty routine. This gives skin an instant lift and helps to reduce the appearance of wrinkles. Egg whites can also be combined with honey and lemon juice for a reviving face pack.

A TASTE OF HONEY

Honey is well known for its antibacterial properties and ability to heal wounds, as well as its skin moisturizing and nourishing benefits. A natural humectant, it draws water to the skin. Mixed with olive oil and brown sugar, it makes an effective skin exfoliant. It can also be used as a face mask, or with olive oil as a hair mask.

BLAST SPOTS WITH TEA TREE OIL

For an overnight treatment to get rid of blemishes, mix a few drops of tea tree oil with half a teaspoon of cosmetic clay. Dab the mixture onto the spots and leave it on overnight to allow your skin time to heal.

ZAP SPOTS WITH HONEY

Honey contains phytochemicals that have powerful anti-inflammatory and antimicrobial properties. It is increasingly used to treat skin disorders because it speeds up healing and alleviates infection. These qualities also make it a great treatment for getting rid of blemishes. Dab some honey onto an affected area at bedtime and you'll soon see the difference.

IMPROVE YOUR SKIN WITH GARLIC

Garlic has many health-giving properties such as improving circulation and enhancing the flow of nutrients and oxygen around the body. It also boasts the antifungal chemical allicin and contains compounds that help the body to detoxify. This makes it ideal for people prone to spots.

HOMEOPATHY FOR HEALTHY SKIN

Homeopathy works by treating like with like. Tiny amounts of the remedies which are made from plant, animal or mineral extracts are used to treat symptoms and it is a very safe type of treatment. Homeopathy can be used to treat various skin problems including acne, eczema and allergic reactions.

CARE FOR SKIN NATURALLY

Your skin absorbs up to 60% of the products you put on it, and these products can build up over time, so choosing products that are as natural as possible is the sensible choice.

MOISTURIZER IS KEY

The vast majority of women, and an increasing number of men, think that moisturizer is one of the key beauty products in the fight against ageing and wrinkles, and around 92% of women use a moisturizer every day. Make sure yours is as natural as possible to reduce your exposure to chemicals.

BEAT CELLULITE WITH SAGE

Sage is also known for its cellulite-busting properties so try to incorporate plenty of the fresh herb into your diet. It works by improving the digestion and breaking down the fatty deposits in the body which cause cellulite.

COMBAT DRY SKIN WITH EFAS

Essential fatty acids (EFAs) are crucial for our overall health. They can also play a role in natural skincare. Some of the first signs of EFA deficiency are dry, flaky skin, dull hair and brittle nails. Make sure your diet is high in oily fish, nuts and seeds, and consider supplementing with EFA capsules.

MOISTURIZE WITH OLIVE OIL

For dry skin use olive oil, organic if possible. It has excellent moisturizing properties and has been traditionally used as an intensive conditioning and moisturizing treatment for areas prone to dry skin such as elbows, knees and feet. For great results, apply at night for smoother skin when you wake up. You can use it as a moisturizing hair mask without having to rely on chemical products with lots of packaging.

OTHER OILS TO TRY

Almond oil is a great favourite for sensitive areas, or use hemp or flax oil for hands. Jojoba oil is wonderful for a make-up remover, lip balm, hair conditioner and massage oil.

COFFEE GETS RID OF CELLULITE

Used coffee grounds can be applied as a body exfoliator to get rid of cellulite. Take the used grounds from your morning coffee and rub them onto problem areas such as thighs during your shower for a natural cellulite treat.

skin cleansing & bathing

DON'T FORGET YOUR BEDTIME RITUAL

It is important to remove all traces of make-up before you go to sleep, so never miss out on this step. Mascara left on the eyes can flake into the eyes and scratch the corneas, or cause irritation or infection. Leaving make-up such as foundation on overnight will clog pores and dehydrate the skin.

WATER IS THE BEST TONER
Avoid expensive, chemical-based toners by rinsing your face water with cold tap water. Some toners contain unnecessarily harsh and astringent chemicals that strip your skin of its natural oils. Cold water will do the same thing toner is designed to do – close up pores and freshen skin after cleansing.

NATURALLY ROUGH
Use an organic cotton muslin face cloth as part of your skin-care regime. As well as having less environmental impact than conventional cotton, organic muslins will also be better for your skin. They act as a very gentle natural exfoliant to remove dead skin cells without causing irritation.

BICARBONATE OF SODA FOR HOMEMADE BEAUTY
Bicarbonate of soda (baking soda) is an incredibly versatile natural ingredient. As well as being good for household cleaning, it can also be used for a number of different beauty treatments. Try mixing a small amount with your normal face-cleansing lotion for a homemade exfoliator. Using homemade treatments cuts down on the manufacture, packaging and expense of products, and so reduces your carbon footprint.

EXFOLIATE WITH CAUTION
Exfoliants, such as AHAs, are chemicals that soften or dissolve the outer layer of dead skin cells. They may well improve the appearance of fine lines but they have also been known to cause skin damage and some people are extremely sensitive to them.

DON'T SOAK IN A CHEMICAL BATH
Having a long soak in a bath containing foaming bath oils or bubble bath formulations is a common source of skin and urinary tract irritation. Many bath products also contain UV absorbents such as benzophenone, which is a known irritant, to prevent colour fading.

BABIES DON'T NEED BUBBLES

It may seem inviting to bathe your little ones in water full of soapy suds but in reality you are simply exposing them to an unnecessary chemical soup. All that's needed to keep infants clean is warm, clean water so avoid the millions of so-called baby-friendly products on the market and keep it simple.

RELAX AND RENEW WITH BATH SALTS

Change your bath routine to one using restorative bath salts such as Epsom salts rather than foamy bubbles with synthetic fragrances and colours. Epsom salts not only relax the muscles and draw out toxins but also sedate the nervous system, reduce swelling and they are a natural emollient and exfoliator.

MIX YOUR OWN SMELLS

Many bath oils that claim to be natural products actually contain chemical compounds that have been designed to mimic the smell of herbs and fragrances. Instead of wasting your money on artificial smells, why not mix your own with essential oils?

GET DARK GLASSES

If you're storing essential oils for use around your home (such as to create your own bathtime fragrance), make sure you keep them in a cool, dark place and in dark glass bottles (rather than plastic containers). The dark glass protects the oil from sunlight and so helps preserve its natural properties.

BODY BEAUTIFUL

When you're choosing products to use in the bath or shower, go for plant-based rather than petroleum-based products because they are more natural and require a lot less manufacture.

SALT OF THE EARTH

Instead of foaming bath oils and bubble bath that can contain chemicals like sodium laureth sulphate, choose bath salts to help you relax and unwind when you lie back in the tub.

MAKE YOUR OWN BATH SALTS

Avoid fragrances and preservatives found in conventional bubble baths and create your own natural bath salts. A good recipe for a tension-relieving bath is to mix Epsom salts with baking soda and a few drops of lavender and marjoram essential oils.

MAKE YOUR OWN BATH LOTIONS

Dried thyme and some raw oats make a relaxing and soothing all-natural herbal bath. Place them in a muslin (cheesecloth) square and tie it under the tap (faucet) as the water is running or place it directly in the bath. The oatmeal will soften the water.

CHOOSE SOAP INSTEAD OF DETERGENT

Shampoos, shower gels and bubble baths all rely on detergents, very often the same ones used in heavy industry and cleaning products. Choose soap instead – it's a natural product made using a fairly low-intensity manufacturing process.

HAVE A SHOWER RATHER THAN A BATH

A bath uses around 170 litres (45 gallons) of water compared with 80 litres (21 gallons) for a five-minute shower. Therefore, switching from your daily bath to a shower can save over 32,000 litres (8,450 gallons) of water a year. Also, a shower uses only 40% of the hot water necessary for a bath.

CUT OUT THE CHLORINE

Chlorine, which is routinely used to purify water, can also cause skin to appear dry and flaky. If you are concerned about this you can remove the chlorine from the water in your shower by fitting a dechlorinating shower filter. Or you could remove it from all the water in your house by installing a whole-house water purifier.

BUY VEGETABLE OIL SOAPS

Look for vegetable soaps made using the traditional cold-processing method which involves low energy, hand-crafted techniques. These soaps tend to be more suitable for people with sensitive skins and also allergy sufferers as they contain no additives. Caurnie soaps from Scotland also use a double saponification process to produce extra-gentle cleaning products.

MAKE YOUR OWN SOAPS

It is not that difficult to create your own homemade soaps and they will be gentler for skin than industrial versions. You will also know exactly what ingredients went into the product. Soap-making kits, widely available from craft stores and online shops, can easily be created in the average kitchen. The main ingredients are vegetable oils, caustic soda and essential oils for fragrance.

RELAX IN A BATH LIT BY PETROCHEMICAL-FREE CANDLES

Vegetable-based or beeswax candles are better for the environment and better for your health. When lit, normal paraffin candles emit trace amounts of toxins including formaldehyde and petroleum soot. Choose vegetable-based candles such as soy candles perfumed with pure essential oils for a greener alternative.

DON'T BUY ANTIBACTERIAL SOAP

We are inundated with advertising telling us the best way to get rid of germs from our homes and promoting the use of antibacterial soap in the bathroom. Some studies have found that antibacterial soaps actually contribute to the increase in "superbugs", and can cause dry skin and hand eczema.

LOOK OUT FOR HANDMADE VEGETABLE SOAPS

Vegetable oil and glycerine soaps work as well as any shower gel and come without the cocktail of chemicals in many products. Choose soaps made from coconut, hemp and olive oils – organic, if possible. Handmade soaps are even better as they further reduce the product's environmental impact.

GO NUTS FOR SOAP

If you want a totally natural and biodegradable alternative to soap, grind up some soap-nuts and use the powder as a general-purpose soap.

LIQUID ASSETS

Plastic soap dispensers are a great choice when it comes to hygiene but bad in terms of packaging. Make your own liquid soap by putting a bar of soap in boiling water and use the liquid to top up your existing applicators.

MAKE YOUR OWN SOAP

For a green alternative to chemical-ridden multi-surface cleaner, mix 125 ml (½ cup) pure soap with 4 litres (1 gallon) hot water and 60 ml (¼ cup) lemon juice. For a stronger cleaner, double the amount of soap and lemon juice.

BUY ORGANIC COTTON WOOL

Cotton production has a huge environmental impact due to the amount of chemicals used. A recent report found that cotton is responsible for the release of 15% of global insecticides, more than any other single crop. Buy certified organic cotton balls instead.

USE ECO CLEANSING PADS

Even better than organic and fairtrade cotton wool pads or balls are washable cleansing pads. Designed to be used with cleanser instead of cotton wool to remove make-up, they come complete with a wash bag, which can be placed in the washing machine and used over and over again.

WIPE AWAY WITH WASHABLE WIPES

Instead of relying on disposable baby wipes, some of which contain ingredients such as parabens, which have been linked to cancer, use washable wipes for baby's bottom. As well as avoiding exposure to chemicals, you will also reduce the amount of waste you create.

GO ORGANIC WITH BABY WIPES

Lots of the mainstream brands of baby wipes contain parabens and propylene glycol, a common ingredient in anti-freeze, so look for certified organic, hypoallergenic and flushable varieties. Alternatively, avoid altogether: a damp cloth or cotton wool dipped in water will do the job just as well.

USE A NATURAL SPONGE

Sea sponges are a non-endangered species and make a much greener alternative to synthetic sponges. Natural sea sponges also absorb a greater amount of water and clean more easily than synthetic varieties, resisting bacteria, mould and mildew. They are also longer-lasting and more durable than manmade versions.

LOVE YOUR LOOFAH

Instead of lathering up with a manmade sponge, use a natural loofah, but make sure it has been grown organically and is unbleached. A loofah is a dried plant related to the squash family. Gentle enough to be used every day, it will boost your circulatory system, cleanse and exfoliate your skin, and help prevent cellulite build-up.

SOURCE YOUR SPONGES SUSTAINABLY

Natural sea sponges are a greener alternative to synthetic versions, which are generally derived from petrochemicals. However, they are only acceptable if they are sustainably harvested – in the past natural seabed habitats have been disturbed by unsustainable harvesting.

CHOOSE WOODEN BRUSHES

Avoid plastic brushes and choose wooden body brushes with natural-fibre bristles to clean nails and backs instead. Make sure that the wood comes from a sustainable source, and ideally is Forest Stewardship Council (FSC) certified. This also applies for toilet brushes.

MAKE YOUR BATHROOM PLASTIC-FREE

Swap plastic soap dishes for wooden alternatives and make your bathroom a plastic-free haven. Plastic is derived from petrochemicals and has a major environmental impact during its manufacture and disposal. Stainless steel, which can be recycled, is also a greener option.

DISPOSE OF COTTON BUDS WISELY

Cotton buds (swabs) are one of the worst polluters of our seas, mainly because they are non-biodegradable and yet lots of people flush them down the toilet rather than throwing them out as waste. Research by the Marine Conservation Society in the UK found that cotton buds are the second most common polluter of beaches and seas.

bodycare

KEEP THE POWDER ON YOUR NOSE
Research has found that women who regularly use talcum powder in their underwear have a 17% higher risk of ovarian cancer than those who did not. Previous studies have suggested that the use of talcum powder might increase the risk of ovarian cancer by as much as 33% over a lifetime.

MAKE YOUR OWN TALC
Since talcum powder has been linked to an increased risk of ovarian cancer, it's better to make your own, natural version. A simple body powder can be made by mixing one cup of cornflour (cornstarch) with 10 to 30 drops of essential oil of your choice, such as lavender or ylang-ylang.

DITCH THE AEROSOL FOR A ROLL-ON
Research has found that women who use aerosol deodorant are more likely to have health problems such as headaches and depression than those who don't. The evidence also revealed that using aerosols around young children could adversely affect their health, causing diarrhoea and other symptoms.

DON'T SWEAT IT
A natural crystal deodorant will stop bacteria from multiplying and provide protection from sweating while reducing your exposure to chemicals such as parabens, found in many standard deodorant products. Parabens have been linked with breast cancer and hormone disruption, with scientists finding traces of parabens in tissue taken from women with breast cancer.

CHOOSE NATURAL DEODORANTS
Deodorants often contain antibacterial ingredients and fragrance to minimize the odour-producing bacteria created by sweat. However, these often include triclosan, a known irritant, and parabens. Choose deodorants containing essential oils for fragrance, with natural antibacterial properties instead.

DO SWEAT IT

Much has been written about aluminium's potential to adversely affect our health. Aluminium salts are widely used in antiperspirants because they are very effective at preventing sweating; this in itself is not a great idea because perspiring is an essential way to naturally eliminate toxins from the body. More worrying is the fact that aluminium in antiperspirants has been linked to cancer and found in the breast tissue of women suffering from breast cancer. Use a natural mineral salt or plant extract-based deodorant instead.

RAZOR YOUR RUBBISH

Instead of buying disposable razors and throwing them away after one or two uses, get a metal razor with refillable blades to cut down on the volume of waste leaving your bathroom door.

STAY AT HOME

Instead of travelling to the salon to get your legs waxed, use one of the natural home-waxing kits available. Look for one that doesn't require heating – therefore no extra energy – and that is made of natural ingredients. Nad's (www.nads.com) makes a version with molasses, honey and lemon.

DITCH YOUR DISPOSABLE RAZORS

Men and women should avoid using disposable razors that are simply destined for the garbage bin. There's no need to purchase a product that has to be thrown away after a couple of uses – the emissions caused by its production and the waste created is completely avoidable. Invest in a decent razor and simply replace the blades when necessary.

GET A CLOSE SHAVE WITH RECYCLED RAZORS

The award-winning Preserve recycled razor is an environmentally friendly alternative to the disposable razor. Made from recycled yogurt pots, the razors have a twin-blade head that can be easily replaced. The handle is made from 100% recycled plastics, 65% of which is recycled yogurt pots. For more information on Preserve-branded products, see Recycline at www.recycline.com.

DON'T BE A SQUIRT

Don't squirt out the shaving foam every time you want to de-fuzz – aerosol canisters are environmentally unfriendly. Choose soap instead, or, if you find soap too drying, small amounts of moisturizer do a great job as well.

UNSCENTED IS BEST

If you're using so-called "unscented" products, make sure they don't contain a whole array of products to mask scents instead of actually having had nothing added. Check the ingredients to be sure.

GO MINIMAL FOR INGREDIENTS

When it comes to products for your body, how green they are is often directly linked to the number of ingredients. In general, those with fewer ingredients are the better choice, unless it's a long list of essential oils or natural products.

SOLAR SHAVING

Invest in a solar-powered shaver for the ultimate in green shaving. The Sol-Shaver, a solar-powered shaver, has an integrated solar panel and needs to be left out in the sun to charge first. Ideal for travel and camping trips as well as everyday, energy-free shaving, you can charge it on a windowsill, outside in the sun – or even on the dashboard of your car.

PUMP UP THE ACTION

Wherever you can, choose pump-action sprays for beauty products like hair spray and leave-in conditioner rather than aerosol cans. Most products come in alternative packaging nowadays so there's really no excuse to buy an aerosol.

♂ male matters

TURN ON YOUR MAN
Take advantage of the growing number of natural and organic brands specifically targeting male grooming. The number of paraben-free and SLS (sodium lauryl sulphate)-free shaving foams and gels is rapidly growing so even the greenest men have a wide choice of products. Scoop of Nature is a men-only range of organic skincare (see www.scoopofnature.com).

TRY SHAVING SOAP RATHER THAN FOAM
Using a soap to prepare hair for shaving rather than shaving foam will mean less exposure to the solvents and propellants in shaving foam, all of which can cause allergic reactions. Even better, use a vegetable-based shaving oil, which will help to moisturize the skin naturally at the same time.

ALOE, ALOE
Aloe vera gel is a great alternative to shaving foams and gels. This is because it has natural anti-inflammatory and skin-softening properties without any added chemicals. You can buy pure aloe gel from most health food stores but why not get your own aloe vera plant?

CALM SKIN WITH ALOE VERA
Rather than buy an after-shave lotion containing chemicals that may actually irritate newly-shaved skin, use 100% aloe vera gel instead. This is available from health food stores and will soothe and calm the skin without causing any adverse skin reactions.

# tanning & suncare

GUARD AGAINST SUN DAMAGE

Despite an increase in the amount of sunscreen we are using, the rates of skin cancer continue to increase, which is not surprising as we are battling with greater pollution, ozone depletion, unregulated tanning salons and longer lifespans. One theory, though not proven, is that damage is enhanced by exposure to some of the ingredients used in sunscreens. In particular, avoid: parabens (butyl-, ethyl-, methyl- and propyl-), PABAs (para-aminobenzoic acid), padimate-O or parsol 1789, and benzophenone, homosalate or octy-methoxycinnamate (octinoxate).

CHOOSE YOUR SUNSCREEN CAREFULLY

A report by the Environmental Working Group (EWG) in the US revealed that 84% of 831 name-brand sunscreens offered inadequate protection from the sun or contain ingredients with significant safety concerns. Only 16% were considered safe and effective.

BEAUTY MINEFIELD

Titanium oxide, a common ingredient in many sunscreens, and talc have been linked to environmental damage during the mining process and manufacture. Talc has also been associated with health problems such as ovarian cancer.

WATCH OUT FOR SUN SENSITIVITY

We are all much more aware of the need to protect ourselves from the UV rays of the sun, but some of the beauty products available actually increase sun sensitivity in certain people. This is true of products containing vitamin A, also known as retinol.

AVOID USING A HIGH SPF WHEN YOU DON'T NEED IT

Remember you don't need a moisturizer with an added Sun Protection Factor overnight. Check that the products you are using don't have any added extra ingredients that you don't need in order to reduce your exposure to an unnecessary number of chemicals.

CHOOSE A BIODEGRADABLE "BLOCK" SUNSCREEN

Sunscreens reduce the risk of skin cancer but they don't protect you from the sun's rays. Many contain chemicals that are not biodegradable but can wash off into the water supply, too. Most sunscreens offer a combination of both chemical and physical-barrier ingredients to protect you from the sun. Zinc oxide is the best physical-barrier screen as it has no harmful side-effects, no extra ingredients and is a mineral, so it is not absorbed into the bloodstream. Traditionally available in the thick white formula, there are now transparent versions.

ALOE SOOTHES SUNBURN

Aloe vera gel is naturally soothing and calming, and the perfect antidote to skin that has been overexposed to the sun. Look for natural skincare and after-sun products with a high aloe vera content or, even better, 100% aloe vera gel. It will help to reduce redness and ease irritation.

GIVE SUNBEDS A WIDE BERTH

Some experts have said that the risk of developing skin cancer from using sunbeds has trebled in the last decade, mostly due to the development of super-powerful tanning beds. Cancer research organizations always advise against the use of sunbeds, especially by young women.

ALL IN THE PREPARATION

Before applying fake tanning products, exfoliate and moisturize the skin so the coverage is even and streak-free. For a natural exfoliating body scrub, mix 2 cups of sea salt with 4 cups of almond oil and add a couple of drops of your favourite essential oil. If you have sensitive skin, choose a commercial product that uses rounded abrasive particles as the salt may be too harsh.

CHOOSE SELF-TAN RATHER THAN A SUNTAN

The sun's rays are one of the main reasons for premature ageing and they also increase the risk of developing skin cancer. The same is true for sunbeds. Research has found that people using sunbeds in their teens and twenties have a 75% increased risk of developing skin cancer. Manufacturers Lavera and Green People both do a natural self-tanning lotion.

SAY NO TO TANNING PILLS

Tanning pills usually contain the pigment canthaxanthin, which is highly dangerous. Although approved for use in food in minimal amounts, in tanning pills it is ingested in high doses and works by changing not only the skin to an orange-brown colour, but also the internal organs. Canthaxanthin has been linked to hepatitis and canthaxanthin retinopathy (yellow deposits in the retina of the eye).

anti-ageing advice

STAY OUT OF THE SUN

One of the most ageing things you can do to your skin is expose it to the sun, but if you have to be out in strong sunlight for prolonged periods, sunscreens are essential. There are an increasing number of natural sunscreens available but the best alternative is to wear a hat with a brim and stay out of the sun altogether, particularly in the middle of the day.

BLINDED BY SCIENCE

Products claiming to get rid of wrinkles overnight with the latest skin-boosting technology may sound impressive but probably won't live up to the hype. A simple, chemical-free beauty regime and healthy lifestyle may be just as effective.

KNOW YOUR AHAS

Alpha-hydroxy acids (AHAs) are used in products such as moisturizers and exfoliants. They effectively remove the outer layer of skin and are known for their anti-ageing effects. However, research has revealed concerns that they could cause increased sun-sensitivity and the risk of sun-related skin cancers.

GET RID OF PUFFINESS NATURALLY

Propping your head up with an extra pillow 15 minutes before you get out of bed in the morning will reduce the eye puffiness that makes you look older than your years. Gravity helps to drain fluid so it doesn't pool around your eyes.

GET YOUR ANTIOXIDANTS NATURALLY

Antioxidants are one of the key weapons in the battle against wrinkles and ageing skin. These days, many mainstream products market themselves as high in antioxidants but it may be that a diet rich in fruit such as strawberries, which are an extremely good source of vitamin C, is a more effective way of boosting your antioxidant intake.

BE SCEPTICAL OF PRODUCTS WITH VITAMIN A

Studies have shown that vitamin A, or retinol, can help to reduce the appearance of wrinkles. However, the type of vitamin A found in beauty products is a very diluted form which is likely to be far less effective. This is because at high concentrations it can cause side effects such as peeling and stinging.

DO PEPTIDES REALLY PEP UP YOUR SKIN?

Peptides have recently been a buzzword in the beauty industry. They are thought to promote production of collagen, thereby, improving the elasticity and appearance of skin, making it look younger and healthier. However, boosting your diet with vitamin C-rich foods, which is crucial for the formation of collagen, is a more natural alternative.

BETTER OFF WITHOUT BOTOX?

Botox is now seen as a mainstream beauty treatment, but is it safe? Common side effects include mild bruising and sometimes drooping of the eyebrow or eyelid. In high doses it can be toxic and cause serious health problems. Perhaps the best option is to avoid the sun and accept wrinkles as an inevitable part of growing old gracefully.

THE NEW "COSMECEUTICALS"

The term "cosmeceutical" is used to describe cosmetic products that act like drugs in the way that they function on the skin. Although the market is growing rapidly, research has revealed there isn't much difference between these and more basic products. Products typically labelled as cosmeceuticals include anti-ageing creams.

BE SUSPICIOUS OF ANTI-AGEING PRODUCTS

Like it or not, no product can prevent ageing, something worth remembering the next time you are tempted to shell out for the latest age-defying cream. Instead, make sure you drink lots of water, have enough essential fatty acids and a diet rich in fruit and vegetables.

ROSEHIP OIL FOR MATURE SKINS

Although no beauty product can ward off the signs of ageing, mature skin benefits from rose-hip oil. This plant oil contains nutrients to keep skin soft and supple. It is also extremely beneficial for people with scars or stretchmarks and will help to reduce their appearance. However, make sure it has been ethically sourced.

eyes that sparkle

CHILL OUT

Cooling your eyelids can also help to eliminate puffiness naturally. Apply a cold tea bag and a slice of cucumber or potato to each eye, straight from the fridge, for 10 minutes to give your eyes a refreshing boost and deflate under-eye bags. Alternatively, keep an organic under-eye gel in the fridge and apply when needed for a tightening effect. Excess sodium or alcohol in the diet can also be factors in eye puffiness, so increase your water intake and eliminate toxins from your diet to help reduce puffy eyes.

SWAP CONTACT LENSES FOR GLASSES

Contact lenses have a much greater impact on the environment than spectacles due to their disposable nature and the energy that goes into their manufacture. If you can bear it, swap your lenses for a pair of glasses that you will enjoy wearing, or at least wear your glasses more often to reduce your reliance on contact lenses.

AVOID HARSH EYE-WASHES

Eye-wash solutions often contain harsh chemicals. Brighten eyes naturally by using a cold-water wash instead. Then place a hot flannel over closed eyelids and press gently with your fingertips. Alternate this process several times and finish by placing a slice of chilled cucumber over each eye.

OPEN YOUR EYES TO NATURAL MASCARA

Many people react badly to mascara and this is usually due to the chemicals and preservatives, including parabens, used in manufacture. The chemicals employed as drying agents can cause itchy, watery eyes, redness and swelling. Invest in a natural or organic mascara that is free from petrochemicals and alcohol.

brow bar

GET THREADING

If you regularly get your eyebrows waxed, try threading for a natural alternative. A traditional Middle Eastern and Asian technique for hair-removal, the specially-trained therapist uses a thin cotton strand, which is twisted and pulled along the skin surface, to lift the hair directly from the follicle. The only material used is the cotton thread and you avoid exposure to the chemicals used during waxing. As it is completely natural, it is suitable for all skin types, and won't result in any irritation or rashes.

SOOTHE EYEBROWS WITH HONEY

After plucking your eyebrows apply an astringent such as witch hazel with some cotton wool. Then smooth on a thin layer of honey using your fingers. Leave for a few minutes before rinsing off with warm water. The natural antibacterial properties of honey will soothe and cleanse your brows.

LOOK AFTER YOUR LASHES

Never use permanent hair dyes to colour eyebrows or eyelashes. The chemicals found in these products can cause an allergic reaction or even blindness. Avoid home-tinting kits completely and go to a salon if you really can't bear to go "au naturel".

 teeth & mouth care

CHOOSE YOUR TOOTHPASTE CAREFULLY
Toothpaste is one of the worst culprits when it comes to
excessive packaging, with most relying on plastic tubes
surrounded by cardboard containers. Look out for brands
that use tubes made from biodegradable cellulose, such as
Kingfisher, which has a range of natural toothpastes containing
ingredients such as lemon, fennel and peppermint.

AVOID PUMP-ACTION DISPENSERS
When buying toothpaste avoid the pump-action dispensers.
These are really unnecessary and use even more plastic than
regular tubes. They cannot be recycled easily and therefore end
up on landfill sites where they won't decompose.

BRUSH UP WITH BICARBONATE OF SODA
Avoid additive-laden toothpastes by mixing your own using
bicarbonate of soda (baking soda), an ingredient which most
early toothpastes were based on. It can be mixed with lemon
juice to form a toothpaste-like consistency and used in the
same way.

AVOID ARTIFICIAL COLOURS IN YOUR TOOTHPASTE
Look out for natural, SLS (sodium lauryl sulfate)-free toothpaste
without added colours. There's no need for multicoloured stripes
when you're brushing your teeth. Look for brands using natural
ingredients such as fennel and peppermint, which have natural
breath-freshening and antiseptic properties.

FORGET FLUORIDE
There is enough fluoride in the average-sized tube of family
toothpaste to endanger the life of a small child if ingested,
and in some countries, including the US and Sweden, fluoride
toothpastes carry a health warning. In the US this includes the
instruction to contact a poison-control centre if more than the
amount used for brushing teeth is swallowed. Fluoride has also
been linked to allergic-type reactions, diabetes, bone problems
and mental impairment.

JUST BRUSH, DON'T WHITEN

A report by the Trading Standards Institute in the UK recently reported that 18 out of 20 teeth-whitening products that it tested contained illegal levels of the bleach hydrogen peroxide. High levels of hydrogen peroxide are thought to cause health problems such as chemical burns to the mouth, as well as exacerbating gum disease and heightened sensitivity in teeth.

REPLACE YOUR HEAD

Reduce plastic waste and landfill impact by using a toothbrush with a replaceable head. Monte Blanco and Smile Brite brands do ranges of replaceable head toothbrushes in various firmnesses for adults and children that are no more expensive than standard brushes and work out cheaper in the long run.

TAKE CARE WITH TITANIUM DIOXIDE

Research has shown that many currently fashionable teeth-whitening toothpastes and agents contain titanium dioxide. A suspected carcinogen which can be absorbed into the skin, it is also harmful to the environment and has been found to acidify rivers and seas. It is used both as a pigment and a thickener in many other cosmetic and skincare products.

NATURAL TOOTHBRUSHES

The root of the araak tree (*Salvadora persica*) has traditionally been used to clean teeth for centuries in the Middle East. Natural araak toothbrushes, also known as sewak or siwak brushes, resemble twigs and contain a number of nutrients that are ideal for maintaining healthy teeth, including vitamin C and minerals. They also have the advantage of not needing toothpaste.

USE SAGE FOR HEALTHY TEETH

Traditionally the herb sage has been used for dental care. It is thought to whiten the enamel of the teeth as well as strengthen the gums. The herb is often included in natural toothpastes and mouthwashes but you can make your own handmade products by mixing sage, fennel and cinnamon essential oils with water.

KEEP IT PLAIN WHEN FLOSSING

There are concerns that some varieties of dental floss may be contaminated with mercury-containing antiseptics, as well as being coated with ingredients derived from petrochemicals. Choose varieties without colourings or flavourings, as these additives are likely to include harsh chemicals.

WASH YOUR MOUTH OUT

There are concerns that conventional mouthwashes may cause an increased risk of throat and mouth cancers. This is because they often contain alcohol, which is drying and changes the acidity of the mouth. Make your own instead by adding a few drops of peppermint oil to water.

FRESHEN UP WITH FENNEL

Chew on fennel seeds between meals instead of using conventional mouthwashes or toothpastes. The seeds have an anise-like flavour and act as an instant, natural breath freshener. If you choose organic seeds you will ensure that you're not coming into contact with any pesticide residues.

BANISH BAD BREATH WITH A TONGUE SCRAPER

Tongue scrapers have been used in dental hygiene for centuries. They are particularly effective for eliminating bad breath because they dislodge bacteria at the back of the tongue that can be the underlying cause. Using a tongue scraper to freshen breath is a much more natural and environmentally friendly alternative to harsh mouthwashes.

natural nails

GO BARE

Instead of using nail polish, protect your nails by rubbing organic almond oil into the nails and cuticles to strengthen them. Clean discoloured nails by scrubbing them with a slice of lemon, which will get rid of stains, and gently buff for all-natural shine.

STRENGTHEN NAILS NATURALLY

Conventional nail-strengthening products often contain formaldehyde, which many people are allergic to and which is also a known carcinogen. Strengthen nails naturally by taking supplements with essential fatty acids and biotin (one of the B vitamins), and by eating enough protein (your nails are made of the natural protein keratin). Keep your nails from drying out and splitting by moisturizing daily.

CHOOSE NATURAL NAIL POLISH

Conventional nail varnishes and removers are cocktails of toxic chemicals, such as toluene and colour lakes (colour bases that don't break down in nature), acetone, formaldehyde and phthalates. Look for the BDIH label: this is a respected German association for certified natural cosmetics that guarantees a product based on plant oils and herbal and floral extracts from managed cultivation. The products it endorses do not include any organic-synthetic dyes, synthetic fragrances or mineral oil derivatives. Sante Natural nail polishes are certified by the BDIH.

BE AWARE OF DBP

Dibutyl phthalate (DBP) is a chemical used in nail polishes to keep the colour from chipping. However, it has been connected to cancer in lab rats and linked to long-term fertility problems in newborn boys. Although products containing DBP have now been banned in Europe under the EU Cosmetics Directive, they are still allowed in many other countries, so look out for imports or those you are buying when abroad. Sometimes DBP is not listed in a product's ingredients but is concealed in the term "fragrance".

PAINT JOB

Because nail colours can contain powerful chemicals such as formaldehyde, solvents and allergens that may irritate the skin, protect your cuticles with a vegetable oil before you paint your nails. Dab on plain organic olive or almond oil around the nail bed, or alternatively look for a natural cuticle cream containing such ingredients as shea butter, seabuckthorn berry extract and essential oils.

FORGET THE FALSE NAILS
Artificial nails that are not stuck down properly can lead to bacterial or fungal infections, which can in turn cause the loss of a fingernail. Removing artificial nails is also problematic because solvents for artificial nail glue can be extremely toxic – some have been banned in the EU. A report by the University of Toronto revealed that children whose mothers worked in nail salons during pregnancy performed poorly in tests for concentration and language.

 # let's make-up

BE ANIMAL-FRIENDLY
Vegetarians and vegans should be aware that make-up often contains a number of different animal ingredients. These include stearic acid and glycerin, sorbitan or octyl stearate, cochineal/carmine and silk. Vegans should also look out for beeswax, honey and lanolin. Animal-friendly brands include Dr Hauschka and The Body Shop.

SUPPORT COMPACT FOR SAFE COSMETICS
Choose cosmetics brands where the manufacturers have signed up to the Compact for Safe Cosmetics campaign, which is run by the US-based Environmental Working Group. Each company pledges not to use chemicals that may cause cancer or birth defects in their products and to replace any hazardous materials with safer alternatives. For more information on the companies who partake in the campaign, visit www.safecosmetics.org/companies.

MAKE-UP WITH MINERALS
Mineral make-up, based on titanium and zinc oxide, has virtually no allergy risk, acts as an anti-inflammatory for sensitive skin, doesn't contain any fillers and contains natural sunscreens. It is particularly good for people with sensitive skin or those suffering from acne, rosacea or post-surgery. Good brands are Lily Lolo, Jane Iredale and Purity Cosmetics.

CREATE YOUR OWN MAKE-UP REMOVER

Avoid chemical-based products and create your own make-up remover using milk. Dip an (organic) cotton wool ball into cold milk and use immediately. An alternative for oil-based make-up remover is sweet almond oil – look out for an organic variety, if possible.

BARE-FACED CHEEK

Try going make-up free for one or two days a week to give your skin a chance to recover and breathe, especially if you are a regular wearer of pore-blocking cosmetics like foundation. Being bare-faced will also help reduce your exposure to chemicals.

REMOVE MAKE-UP WITH A COMBINED CLEANSER

Instead of buying two different products, one for make-up removal and one for skin-cleansing, pick a product that is formulated to do both jobs. Choose a gentle, plant-based product that won't irritate your eyes when taking off mascara, but which will moisturize your skin as well as cleanse it.

CHOOSE LESS VIVID COLOURS FOR YOUR MAKE-UP

They are pretty but at what cost? A general rule of thumb when it comes to cosmetics is that the brighter the colour of a particular cosmetic, the more toxic it is likely to be. By choosing more neutral shades you will be helping to reduce demand for the most environmentally unfriendly pigments.

WAX OR WANE?

Look for natural waxes in mascaras and foundation, like beeswax and carnauba, rather than their manufactured counterparts. These will be easier on your face as well as on the environment.

REFILL YOUR PALETTE

When buying make-up, choose refillable palettes – particularly for lip and eye colours or powders. With refillable palettes you'll have less packaging, less wastage and it will be less expensive in the long run.

THE NATURAL LOOK

Instead of wearing cosmetic products every day, go for a more
expensive but greener organic brand and wear less of it. You'll
be doing your skin as well as the natural world a favour.

KEEP AN EYE ON INGREDIENTS

Many mainstream eyeshadows contain coal tar, albeit in tiny
amounts. Lipstick is another product that sometimes holds high
levels of artificial colourings made from coal-tar derivatives.
Coal tar has been linked to cancer and has been found to cause
allergic reactions in some people.

get lippy

LOOK CLOSELY AT YOUR LIPSTICK

The average woman will consume 1 kg (2 lb) of lipstick in her
lifetime. Not a pleasant thought when you consider that most
lipsticks contain synthetic dyes and fragrances, petroleum
derivatives, preservatives such as butylated hydroxyanisole
(BHT) and even lead. Choose lipsticks and glosses made using
natural products such as beeswax and plant oils; you won't
then ingest toxins.

CRANBERRY DIY LIPSTICK

Avoid the petrochemicals and other ingredients found in lipsticks
such as castor oil and even lead by making your own. Mix almond
oil with 10 fresh cranberries and a teaspoon of honey. Heat in a
microwave for a couple of minutes. Mash the berries and then
strain through a fine sieve before allowing it to cool.

LOVE YOUR LIPSTICK

You may want your lipstick to last all day but did you know
that a conventional lipstick is made up of synthetic oils and
petroleum-based waxes? It is also likely to contain plastics,
nylon and silicones that help to make the colour last even
longer. Natural versions use such ingredients as shea butter
and vegetable wax to lock the colour onto your lips.

LOOK OUT FOR LEAD IN LIPSTICK

Recent research by the Campaign for Safe Cosmetics revealed that lipstick manufactured in the US contains surprisingly high levels of lead. Around 61% of lipsticks tested contained detectable levels of lead but none of them listed it as an ingredient. Lead is a known toxin that can affect learning abilities and cause behavioural problems.

GET ORGANICALLY LIPPY

The first certified organic lipstick in the UK was launched by Green People in 2006, following organic lipsticks by Nvey Eco and Hemp Organics in the US and Australia. Organic lippy is made using plant-based oils such as coconut and jojoba rather than petroleum-based ingredients. Green People's version contains fairly traded cupuaçu butter from the Brazilian Amazonian basin. See www.greenpeople.co.uk and www.econveybeauty.com for product information.

 # crowning glory

MISS A WASH (OR TWO)

If you usually shampoo your hair every day, try leaving it for two or three days instead. Over-washing hair with chemical-based shampoos and conditioners can strip it of its natural oils. Once you have got used to the new regime you will probably find that your hair looks better and can go even longer between washes. You may find you only really need to wash your hair twice a week.

EMBRACE GREASY HAIR

Give dry hair a natural conditioning treatment with olive oil. The oil helps repair split ends and improves the texture and appearance of parched hair. Heat the oil first in a cup placed in a pan of hot water. Then massage it into your hair and scalp and cover with a shower or swimming cap. Leave for 30 minutes before washing out with a gentle shampoo. Try this treatment once a week to give hair a natural boost or to remedy a dry, itchy scalp.

KEY CHEMICALS FOR ASTHMA SUFFERERS TO AVOID

There is increasing evidence that the following ingredients, often found in haircare products, have been linked to asthma in hairdressers. They are: ammonium persulfate, potassium persulfate and sodium persulfate. Asthma sufferers should try to avoid them.

DON'T PUT EXTRA PRESSURE ON YOUR HAIR

Hair extensions can put too much stress on the scalp and cause problems such as traumatic alopecia. This is where bald patches form as a result of hair being pulled for prolonged periods. Boost your own hair with a diet rich in green, leafy vegetables and protein-rich foods.

BEAT DANDRUFF NATURALLY

Dandruff is an embarrassing problem that sufferers would like to get rid of quickly. Although conventional anti-dandruff shampoos are often effective, they also contain chemicals such as coal tar, which has been linked to cancer. Use a natural shampoo and supplement with essential fatty acids (EFAs) to boost your skin internally instead.

DON'T EXPECT TO LATHER UP

Natural shampoos don't generate lots of suds in the same way as more conventional products. However, this won't make them any less effective at cleaning because lather doesn't assist the cleaning process. Most shampoos rely on an ingredient called sodium laurel sulphate (SLS) to create the foam and this is a known irritant.

HOLD THE HAIRSPRAY

Conventional hairsprays coat the hair with a plastic film to hold it in place. Many hairsprays contain phthalates, hormone-disrupting chemicals which have been linked with a number of health scares including birth defects. Instead choose hairspray made with natural ingredients in pump action rather than aerosol dispensers.

AVOID COAL TAR DYES IF YOU HAVE ASTHMA
Coal tar dyes appear in many products including hair dyes
and cosmetics. Some people are sensitive to them, especially
asthmatics, eczema sufferers and those sensitive to aspirin. They
can also cause hyperactivity in children and severe headaches.

GET GREEN
Go green in more ways than one by washing your hair in green
tea, thought to have natural antibacterial properties that will
help reduce scalp sensitivity and cut down on dandruff.

GIVE YOUR HAIR A DRINK
Lacklustre hair can be given a real boost with a slug of beer. Mix
up one part beer to three parts water and pour over your hair
for the final rinse. The natural sugars contained in the beer will
leave your hair smooth and shiny.

NATURAL WAYS TO COMBAT HAIR LOSS
Increasing the amount of protein-rich foods such as eggs, fish
and tofu is one way to combat hair loss. Another is to take
regular exercise, which will help boost circulation and increase
blood flow to the scalp. Massaging your scalp also encourages
the blood supply to stimulate hair growth.

WASH THOSE CHEMICALS OUT OF YOUR HAIR
Conventional shampoos use the same detergents found in
everything from cleaning products to shower gels. One of the
health concerns about shampoo is that some of the common
ingredients can break down into formaldehyde during storage.
Formaldehyde is a known irritant that has been linked to cancer.

LOOK FOR SHAMPOOS WITH THE FEWEST INGREDIENTS
Detergents in shampoo can be problematic because they
may break down into formaldehyde during storage. When
formaldehyde-forming agents mix with other ingredients they can
form nitrosamines, which are linked to cancer. Avoid this cocktail
effect by choosing formulas containing minimal ingredients.

HALVE YOUR AMOUNTS
Most people use far more shampoo and conditioner than they need. Why not halve your shampoo and conditioner for a week and see if you can tell the difference – chances are that your hair will be just as shiny.

NATURAL HAIRBRUSHES
Made from wood and animal hair, natural hairbrushes are kinder to your hair. They also have less of an impact on the environment during production and are naturally biodegradable. A wide range is available, usually made with beech wood for the base and goat or pig's hair for the bristles.

BE CAUTIOUS OF ADDED INGREDIENTS
Hair conditioner may be effective in many ways but it cannot magically repair damaged hair. Neither can it make hair more healthy by adding proteins, vitamins, amino acids or other ingredients. Give your hair a boost with a homemade mixture of fresh rosemary and mint with cider vinegar.

VEGGIE ROOTS
Next time you get your roots touched up at the hairdresser, ask for vegetable-based dye rather than chemical alternatives. Not only is it kinder to the environment, it's also better for your health as you won't absorb potential toxins.

UNPLUG THE STRAIGHTENERS
Repeated use of hair straighteners can actually damage your hair, especially if it is fine. From an environmental perspective there is also the consideration of the energy used in their manufacture and during their use. Try to eliminate or reduce your reliance on hair straighteners, tongs, blowdryers and other electric devices to reduce your carbon footprint and save the health of your hair.

eco fashion choices

A RAYON OF LIGHT
Rayon is a great choice for clothes because it's made from trees and plants and therefore involves less of an intensive manufacturing process than some man-made materials.

IRON OUT THE KINKS
Many crease- or iron-resistant fabrics have been treated with formaldehyde, poisonous to many a living thing. Avoid buying non-iron items all together.

SOLE SISTER
Choose shoes with wooden soles rather than plastic, which is harder to manufacture. Wooden soles will last longer so you won't need to replace them so often.

DON'T TREAT YOURSELF
If you're buying leather bags and shoes, go for untreated leather or those dyed using vegetable dyes rather than chemicals. Sometimes leather treatment agents can be toxic to natural life.

QUALITY OVER QUANTITY
Instead of buying cheap, mass-produced clothes that will have to be thrown away at the end of the season, try to invest in as many high-quality pieces as you can. You'll need fewer of them and they will last longer.

GO VEGGIE
Look for vegetable rather than chemical dyes in fabric. Vegetable dyes are squeezed from vegetable sources, making them a more natural, non-polluting choice, and at the same time completely sustainable.

BE A WOOLLY JUMPER
If you're buying organic wool, make sure it comes from a farm that hasn't used organophosphates. These are environmental hazards and can cause allergies.

BE A COTTON TOP

Despite being a natural product, cotton is not actually that environmentally friendly because the plants are treated with so many pesticides and fertilizers. Make sure you always go for organic cotton.

BAG A FRESH DRAWER

Instead of fabric conditioner, which contains a host of unwanted chemicals, use aromatherapy bags in drawers to freshen clothes up and make them smell sweet and fresh. If you find that lavender is too strong, try dried sage, thyme or marjoram instead.

WHITE AS A SHEET

Always try to buy unbleached cotton, which is a much better environmental choice than the pure white varieties. If you can't find unbleached, choose those bleached with hydrogen peroxide – they are marginally greener than chlorine bleaches.

HEMP IT UNDER

Hemp is a great natural alternative to cotton, especially for underwear, but you can also get hemp outerwear, fitness clothes, footwear, homewares and linens. The plants are fast-growing and hardy, so don't need pesticides or fertilizers. It's also ideal for sustainable organic farm systems. Be wary of Chinese hemp, which is often processed with chemical acid.

SILKY SMOOTH

Choose your silk carefully as many chemicals are used during its manufacture. Make sure you purchase your silk from ethical and responsible suppliers who can vouch for the production process.

PURITAN POWER

When choosing wool products, the best label to go for is 100% pure new wool, so you can be sure it is a totally natural product. Try to find those dyed with natural dyes to keep chemicals used to an absolute minimum.

FAIRTRADE FASHION

It's not just coffee and chocolate that can be Fairtrade. Look for the Fairtrade mark on cotton clothing. This ensures that the cotton is made to Fairtrade standards, which means the farmers were paid fairly and had safe working conditions.

BE A TECHNOPHILE

Get creative with materials when you go clothes-shopping. Be on the lookout for the latest techno fabrics, such as PCR (post consumer recycled) or eco-fleece, which is made from recycled plastic bottles.

THINK ABOUT FABRIC

Where possible, avoid clothes made with nylon and polyester. Not only are they non-biodegradable, making them difficult to dispose of, but both are made from petrochemicals that pollute the environment and add to the problem of global warming.

OLD-STYLE GLAMOUR

Vintage clothing has become increasingly fashionable in recent years, allowing you to invest in one-off classic pieces while helping the environment at the same time. Many towns now have vintage shops – or look out for markets in your area.

DYE DISASTERS

Try to avoid patent leather and the colour turquoise – both are very pollutant in terms of the chemicals they create during production. Copper in real turquoise dyes gets released into the environment through waste water.

LEAVE LEATHER BEHIND

Follow in the footsteps of the rich and famous and buy a pair of vegan shoes or a vegan handbag. Actress Natalie Portman is a fan of elegant and stylish vegan shoes, while designer Stella McCartney is famous for only ever sending shoes made entirely without animal ingredients down the catwalk. Check the Peta website (www.peta.org) for vegan companies.

CHARITY CHIC
Green, cheap and ethical, charity shops are often the ideal place to pick up a bargain. By buying (and taking) your clothes to charity stores, not only are you helping the environment but you are also giving to those in need.

HIGH-STREET ETHICS
Many of the big high-street chains are waking up to the demand for eco-friendly products and have launched their own organic ranges. Many now stock clothes made from organic cotton for only a fraction more than the price of their ordinary ranges.

FAKE IT
Fact: faux is in. There's no need for small, furry creatures to suffer for your style. In the last 10 years, pretend fur has come a long way and is now used to adorn anything from boots to coats and hats – it's as beautiful and luxurious as the real thing, too.

EARTH-FRIENDLY ACCESSORIES
More and more designers are making handbags and belts from recycled or sustainable materials. Check out bags made of recycled tyres and the latest handbag shapes in environmentally friendly natural fibres such as cotton, hemp and canvas.

GREEN PEACE OF MIND
Everybody likes a bargain but at what cost? Sometimes there are reasons why clothes are so cheap and often it's because they have been shipped over from China or India, where costs of labour are a tiny amount of the price paid. Check out the policies of your favourite stores – sometimes it's worth paying a little more for peace of mind.

LEADER OF THE PACK
Hand-reared Alpaca hair is a greener alternative to more conventional sheep's wool as it's spun locally and so keeps transport to a minimum. Look for sweaters made from this yarn on the internet.

reuse & recycle fashion

GO RECYCLABLE
Hard-wearing outdoor clothing often doesn't break down
naturally when disposed of. Choose Ecolog – a range of 100%
recyclable polyester clothing, or pick water-based coatings rather
than plastics. Made by a German outdoor gear company, vauDe,
the clothing is widely available. Everything, including the zips and
buttons, is made of 100% recycled polyester. Retailers take back
worn clothing to recycle and make more items. In addition to
outerwear, the company makes tents and backpacks.

PATCH IT UP
Instead of throwing patterned textiles away, collect them until
you have enough to make a patchwork quilt to cover sofas or
armchairs, to be used as a floor throw or to keep you warm in bed.

YOU CAN BANK ON IT
The average rubbish bin contains 10% of unwanted household
textiles. Textile banks make the best use of your unwanted
textiles by recycling them and turning them into other fabrics,
often insulating fabrics.

GET IT ALTERED
If you have a lot of clothes that don't fit you, don't throw them
away. Take them to a clothes alteration service or alter them
yourself, if you can. This is especially true for clothing that is too
large, which can almost always be easily made smaller.

GET A SHOESHINE
Don't throw away your shoes. If they're still
in good condition you can give them to
charity shops so they can be reused. If
they're not wearable, try separating
the different materials like fabric,
leather or wood.

ADD A RIBBON

Collect ribbons from giftboxes, boutique shopping bags and haberdashery stores or markets, and use them to give your existing clothes a new lease of life. Use the ribbons – or lace remnants or fringing – to replace shoulder straps on dresses and camisoles. Add wide ribbon as a border to the hem of dresses and skirts, or use it to edge a jacket. Simple sewing skills are all you'll need.

SWAP YOUR CLOTHES

Don't throw old clothes away. Instead, organize clothes' swapping parties with a few friends. Items wanted by no one can be taken to a charity (thrift) shop. There are often good designer pieces available from second-hand shops.

MAKE DO AND MEND

Put your grandmother's words into practice and do some simple alterations and repairs. The rise in cheap clothing has led to some people simply throwing away clothes that could easily be made as good as new with a little cutting and sewing. It's estimated that 500,000 tonnes of unwanted clothes end up on landfill sites every year. If you're not handy with the needle, find a tailor you trust and you'll be helping out local business at the same time.

DARN IT

Instead of leaving holes in socks until they are big and difficult to mend, make a point of repairing them as soon as the tiniest one appears. That way, you're less likely to have to throw the sock away and it will take less material (and effort) to mend it.

SEW IT UP

Many women's magazines carry free patterns so you'll only need to pay for materials, which you can buy from markets and discount material stores. Find a pattern that suits you and use it for several different items.

EMBROIDER AND EMBELLISH

If you are handy with needlework, you can lift an old fashion item, handbag or accessory with a little decorative embroidery. This is especially useful to hide stains or faults in the garment.

DYE IT, PRINT IT AND PAINT IT

Old T-shirts can be tie-dyed, painted with fabric paints or stamp-printed with motifs to create new clothes for almost no cost. Fabric marker pens may be used to outline fine details. These techniques work best on 100 per cent, tight-weave cotton.

BELT UP

Think imaginatively about ways to make belts from all kinds of fabrics and haberdashery items. Use a man's necktie, a scarf, or a woven or braided ribbon sewn to a D-ring or diamanté buckle. You may also like to attach rhinestones or studs to a cheap, simple mesh belt.

PURSES AND TOTES

Look in thrift stores and charity shops for old placemats or table runners that can be used to make durable handbags and totes. Sew two squares together or fold one rectangle over and stitch up the sides. Turn the top under and stitch it all the way around, leaving an opening to thread a drawstring through. Alternatively, sew on bought handles.

SAVE THEM

If you have clothes that are damaged, or so old you can't donate them to a charity (thrift) store, keep them instead of throwing them away. They are great to use for packing up delicate items when you move house or if you are simply packing them up to store away.

COTTON HANDS

Make a pair of cotton hand mitts from an old shirt or T-shirt and wear them when you put on your tights (pantyhose) or stockings to avoid snagging or causing a ladder (run). By doing this, your hosiery will last longer and you'll save money on having to buy replacements.

SAVE YOUR BUTTONS

Never throw away a garment before removing and saving the buttons. They can be used for decorating or as replacements on other clothes, to augment charity- (thrift-) store bargains or even sold on to people who will use them.

Shopping Advice

FROM UNDERSTANDING FAIRTRADE regulations to identifying items that reduce your carbon footprint, your choices as an eco-consumer can make a huge impact on the environment. Whether you are buying food at your local supermarket or considering big purchases like a new car or house, this chapter will help you make informed and responsible decisions that enable you to live in a more sustainable way.

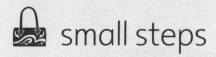# small steps

DO LESS SHOPPING
One of the most beneficial things you can do for the
environment is shop less. Just 20% of the world's population
is consuming more than 80% of the earth's natural resources
due to our insatiable demand for products, be it cheap fashion,
new foods or groovy gadgets. Start by observing "Buy Nothing
Day", an annual event celebrated in more than 40 countries
worldwide. For more information, see www.adbusters.org
(for North America) or www.buynothingday.co.uk (UK).

BUY LOCAL AND SMALL
Independent local shops and street markets are probably
the greenest grocers. A recent study has shown that big
supermarkets emit on average three times as much CO_2
per square foot than the average independent grocer,
while a separate study has found that a higher proportion
of packaging from street markets was recyclable than that
found in the big supermarket chains.

WRITE A LIST
It's incredibly simple – but it works! To avoid too many impulse
purchases, pin a shopping list up in your kitchen and you can
update it as you run out of things. Then take it to the store
and stick to it. If you still find it hard to fight temptation, then
consider buying goods online where you can be systematic
about your shopping.

ARMCHAIR SHOPPING
The internet offers the chance to reduce the impact of your
shopping by buying secondhand goods (through online
charities or eBay, for example) or by sourcing goods from ethical
and fairtrade sources. One such site is www.onevillage.com,
which supports artisans' cooperatives and sells handmade,
sustainable products from partner enterprises that strive to
build up communities' quality of life.

GO ORGANIC

By buying certified-organic products you will be supporting
a farming system that is better for wildlife, uses less harmful
pesticides and produces less CO_2.

LOOK FOR FAIRTRADE

Look out for products that have been certified by FLO-CERT,
which will carry the fairtrade mark. The organization guarantees
that disadvantaged producers in the developing world are
getting a better deal by receiving a minimum price that covers
the cost of sustainable production, as well as an extra premium
that is invested in social or economic development projects.

GO BIG

If you have to buy water in plastic bottles, remember that
small bottles are heavier on packaging than large ones. Jumbo
bottles are the best option of all.

BRING YOUR OWN BAGS

We use over 1.2 trillion plastic bags a year – an average of about
300 bags for each adult on the planet – but only for an average
of 12 minutes before throwing them away. The damage goes
beyond visual pollution – plastic bags in landfill sites take up to
500 years to decompose, while those that end up in our oceans
kill at least 100,000 birds, whales, seals and turtles every year.

TAKE YOUR OWN

Instead of reaching for the roll of plastic bags when you're
shopping for fruit and veg, take your own brown paper bags or
reuse plastic bags so you don't contribute to more plastic waste
than you need to.

DON'T BUY CIGARETTES

You know it makes sense to quit for your health, but did you
know it will help more than the air around you? It could also
help the environment – each year, 200,000 hectares (50,000
acres) of woodland are destroyed in order to clear the way for
tobacco plantations.

CHOOSE A STURDY SHOPPER
Rather than using the plastic or paper bags supplied by your supermarket, invest in a few shopping bags made from renewable materials such as jute, linen, hemp and cotton. Make sure they are sturdy so they last for years, and keep them handy by the door or in your car so you never forget them when you go shopping.

BAG A GREEN DEAL
If you want to invest in a reusable shopping bag to cut down your reliance on disposable plastic bags, choose a sturdy version made from hemp or jute. This will last a lifetime and is more energy-efficient to produce than plastic versions.

responsible shopping

LIMIT "MADE IN CHINA" ITEMS
The "made in China" logo can be seen just about everywhere, but demand from western countries plays a large part in the expansion of the Chinese economy, which is a big user of fossil-fuel intensive energy and is highly polluting.

WATCH OUT FOR LUXURY ITEMS
Celebrity-endorsed luxury brands haven't scored well in a World Wildlife Fund UK investigation into their eco-friendliness. Its report, "Deeper Luxury", claims luxury brands have been slow to recognize their responsibilities to the environment and the charity is now launching a Star Charter for celebrities to adopt, which commits them to considering the environmental and social performance of the brands they endorse.

BE WARY OF ECO "JUNK"
Being green is about saving the planet, not your status. Don't fall into the trap of buying goods that are labelled as "eco" or "fairtrade" just because they are "worthy". Whereas many of these products are perfectly legitimate, you may not actually need them and the best thing you can do for the planet is not to buy things you don't need in the first place. Find ways of reusing what you do have or trading with someone else instead.

SELECT SUSTAINABLE

Get to know the certification schemes for sustainable production, such as Forest Stewardship Council (FSC) certification for wood from sustainable forests, and Marine Stewardship Council (MSC) for fish from fisheries that are well managed and sustainable. The Rainforest Alliance also certifies sustainable agriculture, tourism and forestry (www.rainforest-alliance.org).

AVOID PETRO-CHEMICALS

From mineral oil in beauty products, to solvents in paints and detergents in washing powder, petro-chemicals are present in many of the things we buy. But the clue is in the name – they are derived from petroleum, which is itself derived from fossil fuels. Read the label before you buy and try to avoid these products.

BE LABEL-WISE

You can't be a truly green shopper until you've mastered the art of labelling. Products that claim to be "natural" and "pure" could be no more so than any other – these terms do not have to be proven. Many ingredients do not have to be listed – the ingredient "parfum" (fragrance), for example, can be used to describe up to 100 different chemicals. Arm yourself with as much information as you can and always read the label!

GET SYMBOL SAVVY

There are few internationally recognized "green" symbols such as the EU's Ecolabel flower or the star logo for US Energy Star. But new ones are cropping up all the time – such as the new Future Friendly logo, which is an initiative of multinational giant Proctor & Gamble. Many of these symbol schemes have not been independently verified as being truly green so check with trusted sources such as the Ethical Consumer Research Association.

SINGLE-USE IS A WASTE

Energy is used to make and distribute single-use products such as disposable cameras and barbecues. You use them just the once and then energy is used to transport them to a landfill, where they could take hundreds of years to decompose, leaching toxins as they do so.

THE BEST YOU CAN AFFORD
The better quality an item is, the longer it is likely to last. If you are a "buy cheap, buy twice" kind of person, you are likely to be throwing things away far more than is good for the planet – and your wallet.

HOW WAS IT MADE?
The average manufacturing wage in China is 64 US cents an hour, according to the US Bureau of Labor Statistics, and wages in Mexico and Indonesia are similarly low. Avoid buying products from manufacturers known to use sweatshops and write to these companies telling them you won't give them your business because of their labour record.

PLAGUED BY PLASTIC
The world's annual consumption of plastic materials has increased from around 5 million tonnes in the 1950s to nearly 100 million tonnes today. Plastics may be cheap, but they cause pollution at all stages of their production and use, with some forms of plastics, such as vinyl, constantly giving off harmful gases. If you must buy plastic, make sure you do what you can to recycle it.

REMEMBER THE FOUR RS
Few products seem to be built to last and many of us don't know how to carry out basic repairs, but before buying you should check whether a product is rechargeable, repairable, refillable or reusable. Make it your policy not to buy an item – or throw one away – unless it can do one of these four.

KEEP THEM IN THE KNOW
Make choices about the food and other goods you buy based on packaging and content, and let your retailer know you're doing so. There's nothing like the prospect of losing money to effect change!

A GREEN WASH?

Retailers and manufacturers have realized that having good green credentials will help their sales, but make sure there is substance to their claims. There is an international standard for environmental labelling – ISO 14021 – so if you suspect a product is not as green as a company claims, ask the company if its wording complies with ISO 14021.

OPT FOR LESS PACKAGING

We all wade through mountains of packaging to get to the things we actually want and it's getting worse – in the UK packaging increased by 12% between 1999 and 2005, and the US generates around 135 kg (290 lb) of packaging waste per person each year. Choose the least-packaged items possible; you are also entitled to leave any unnecessary packaging with a retailer so that they get the message.

CHAIN OF COMMAND

It is often impossible to track the history of your product because there can be as many as nine different subcontractors involved in one clothing item, from fibre to packaging, with unfair labour practices employed anywhere down the line. But the more questions you ask, the more companies will acknowledge the need for them to be accountable. Ask where the materials are sourced and where the manufacturing takes place and under what labour conditions.

TREAT CLAIMS WITH CARE

A new generation of degradable, biodegradable and compostable packaging is hitting the store shelves but they may not be the answer to all our packaging woes. Compostable packaging will often only break down at temperatures higher than the average home compost. If they are not disposed of correctly they could end up in landfills, where they will increase the amounts of methane gases generated.

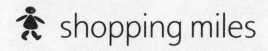

shopping miles

KEEP IT LOCAL
Buying products flown in or transported halfway around the country via distribution centres will do nothing to help you reduce your carbon footprint. Ideally, buy directly from local producers. In the UK, some food retailers are labelling products that have been imported by air with a small aeroplane symbol and the words "air freighted".

SHIPPING DOWNSIDE
You may think buying a product that has arrived on your shores by boat is a green option, but think again. According to Friends of the Earth, diesel-powered ocean-going ships burn some of the dirtiest fuel on the planet today and research has shown that the number of people dying from heart and lung disease as a result of under-regulated shipping emissions is estimated to grow by 40% by 2012.

IT'S NOT ALWAYS SIMPLE
Many shopping decisions are complicated. For example, research has shown that the emissions produced by growing flowers in Kenya and flying them to the UK can be less than a fifth of the emissions that come from flowers grown in Dutch greenhouses. Plus, what can be good from a green perspective could be bad from an ethical one. British shoppers spend over £1 million a day on imported fruit and vegetables from Africa, and the livelihoods of more than a million farmers and their families depend on this trade. Do as much research as you can.

A ROAD LESS TRAVELLED
Walk or cycle to the shops – driving 10.5 km (6½ miles) to buy your shopping emits more carbon than flying a pack of Kenyan green beans to London. If you absolutely have to drive, make sure you make fewer trips by buying in bulk when you get there and look into sharing your shopping trips and car with neighbours or friends.

IMPORT MADNESS

Globalization has led to some bizarre figures for international trade. According to the 2007 New Economics Foundation report "Chinadependence", the UK sent 21 tonnes of mineral water all the way to Australia and brought 20 tonnes back in 2006; and the amount of beer the UK sold in Spain is almost the same as the amount Spain sold in the UK. The environmental cost of these import/exports is very high, so avoid buying imports.

hazardous materials

CHEMICAL COCKTAILS

More than 300 man-made chemicals have been found in human bodies; unsurprising perhaps given they are everywhere – in our food, beauty products, sofas, carpets and washing powders. There is growing evidence that links some of these chemicals to birth defects, cancer and other diseases. Minimize your exposure by buying chemical-light products.

PROBLEMS WITH PALM OIL

Palm oil is found in one in ten supermarket products including chocolate, bread, detergents and lipsticks. But palm oil plantations are the most significant cause of rainforest loss in Malaysia and Indonesia – palm oil plantations were responsible for 87% of deforestation in Malaysia between 1985 and 2000 and the industry could drive the orangutan to extinction. Check whether palm oil is present – it could be lurking under the generic label "vegetable oil".

PVC – THE HARD FACTS

It can be found in wallpaper, shower curtains and other plastics around the home, but polyvinyl chloride (PVC) contains chemicals including phthalates that have been linked to cancer and reproductive health problems. Also, when produced or burned PVC plastic releases dioxins, which can cause cancer and harm the immune and reproductive systems.

TOXIC FIRE RETARDANTS

Polybrominated diphenyl ethers (PBDEs) are used as a flame retardant in many everyday products, including furniture, mattresses, computers, TV sets and cars – and they are now found in people, animals and the environment. The levels of PBDEs in women's breast milk have been doubling every five years, with the exception of Sweden where PBDEs have been banned since the 1990s. The EU has banned the most toxic forms of PBDEs, but in the US only a few states have gone ahead with bans.

LOOK AT THE LABEL

Read labels carefully and avoid anything containing triclosan or other antimicrobial agents – from soaps, toothpaste, cosmetics and sponges, to carpets, plastic kitchenware and even toys.

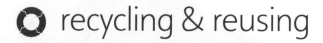

recycling & reusing

REUSE AND RECYCLE WHAT YOU DO BUY

Make sure you get the most out of your money and the resources used to make a product by doing your utmost to reuse or recycle it. From using yogurt pots for planting seeds to joining an online recycling service like Freecycle or eFreeko, there's more to this than a weekly trip to the bottle bank.

PLASTIC TEXTILES

Look out for items made from recycled plastic bottles. The company Patagonia, which has used recycled soda bottles to create fleeces for many years through their Common Threads programme, claims it has now kept 86 million soda bottles out of landfills. They also give you background on their products – where the materials were sourced and the manufacturing processes involved.

TRY FIXING IT FIRST
Before you throw something away because it is old, stained or broken, try to repair it. Old furniture can be reupholstered or revarnished, while clothing may be taken to a tailor's and repaired. After a couple of months, you'll find it becomes a habit to fix rather than discard.

BUY RECYCLED
Buying products made from recycled materials instead of products made from new materials saves natural resources and reduces greenhouse gases. This doesn't just mean recycling your own goods – make sure you buy recycled products as well.

GET RECYCLED PAPER
Whether it's toilet paper or office paper, recycling one tonne of paper saves 15 average-sized trees and 28–70% less energy is used to produce recycled rather than virgin paper. On top of this, the paper would otherwise end up on landfill sites where it biodegrades to produce methane gas – a potent greenhouse gas and contributor to global warming.

CAN YOU RECYCLE IT?
Whenever you buy something, you are taking responsibility for its impact on the planet from then on. Make sure it can be recycled – look out for a recycling logo and find local recycling services. For electrical items such as fridges and freezers, check with the manufacturer who made it or the retailer who sold it – they have a responsibility to provide assistance with recycling.

NO NEED FOR NEW
Vintage clothes, second-hand books and videos ... charity (thrift) stores, fleamarkets, car boot (garage) sales and the church jumble sale are still great places for green shoppers. Many charities have also branched out into offering online shopping options, too.

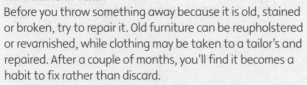

# home & property

SUSTAINABLE PROPERTY
Look for a property that already has good green credentials – well insulated and double-glazed for starters. In the UK, there is a voluntary standard for new housing – the Code for Sustainable Homes. The government expects all new homes to be carbon neutral by 2016 but at present only 2% of new private homes meet minimum standards. In the US, the Leadership in Energy and Environmental Design (LEED) is the nationally accepted benchmark for the design, construction and operation of green buildings.

A SUSTAINABLE LOCATION
When shopping for your next home, take a look at the sustainability of the town or city in which it's located. Some have become plastic-bag free, for example, or might have ambitious plans for cycle networks or green spaces. Or you could be a pioneer and take up residence in one of the world's eco-towns or cities – ten are planned for the UK, while others are to be built in China and Abu Dhabi.

BE A GREEN BORROWER
Make sure your home loan benefits the environment by getting a green mortgage. The lender will either plant a certain number of trees per loan to offset its carbon footprint or will donate cash to environmental projects on your behalf. Some green mortgage providers will only lend on properties that provide "an ecological payback", such as new homes built with recycled or sustainable materials, or homes that will be made as energy efficient as possible.

BUY DOUBLE-GLAZING
Stop your heat flying out the window by installing double-glazing, ideally using low emissivity (Low-E) glass. Double-glazing cuts heat loss through windows by 50%. If this is too costly, then at least invest in some plastic insulating film and stick a layer over each pane – it will achieve a similar effect for a fraction of the price and if applied correctly won't show.

CONDENSING BOILER IS BEST

If the 4 million old, inefficient boilers in UK homes were replaced it would save 2.5 million tonnes of CO_2 each year by 2010. Choose a high-efficiency condensing boiler – it's the most efficient and should reduce your heating bill by around 30%. In the US there is a tax rebate for the installation of condensing boilers. Remember to buy an insulating jacket for your boiler and insulate pipes at the same time to lessen heat loss.

SEAL THE GAPS

If there's one thing you should buy for your home, it's insulation. Draught excluders for doors and windows, loft insulation, cavity wall insulation, under-floor insulation – there are plenty of areas you need to consider. Around half of the heat lost in a typical home disappears through the walls and loft so they should be first on the list. Choose sustainable materials such as sheep's wool or cellulose fibre made from recycled fire-proofed newsprint.

MEASURE YOUR ENERGY

An energy-saving meter will help you monitor the amount of electricity you are using around the home and should ultimately make it easier for you to cut back. A sensor and transmitter is attached to your meter and updates a remote monitor every six seconds. You can install it and can see how much power you're using, when you switch on the television, for example. Some meters can also give data on the price of electricity throughout the day, enabling you to know when power is cheapest.

RESIST THE AIR CONDITIONER

With hotter summers predicted the demand for air conditioners is also likely to rise – already around two-thirds of all homes in the US have them – but they can double the electricity consumption of a house. In the US, air conditioning accounts for 16% of the average household's electricity consumption – the same as all lighting, music systems, televisons, video and DVD players, desktop computers and printers combined. There are other ways to cool your home, such as drawing curtains, improving ventilation, installing loft insulation or even building a green roof on your home.

TAKE A WIND CHECK

Putting a turbine on your roof may not be the best renewable energy option for your home. It is unlikely to get sufficiently strong and consistent winds at roof height, especially as most houses are built in sheltered areas, and the vibrations might actually damage your home. Check with an experienced advisor before going ahead.

THE POWER OF GREEN

Rather than use non-renewable sources of power – coal, oil and natural gas – go for green power instead. Many electricity companies now offer power from renewable sources such as solar, hydro or wind. It might cost more but it will cost the planet less.

BUY FROM A GREEN AGENT

To help narrow down your search for a carbon-light home, consider using specialist real estate agents. Examples include GreenMoves, an "eco property for sale" website for the UK market, and the GreenHomesForSale site for properties in the US.

SUN-WARMING WATER

A solar water-heating system uses heat from the sun to work alongside your conventional water heater. It can provide about a third of a home's hot water needs and will reduce CO_2 by around 350 kg (770 lb) per year. Check first, though, that it will suit your property and it is positioned to get maximum sun.

LET THE SUN SHINE IN

In areas where there is plenty of daylight, it may be worth installing solar photovoltaic panels on your roof to convert light energy into electric energy. They are unlikely to meet all your power needs but you should be able to cut your power use and costs. Check for any government grants that might make it less expensive and find out about options for selling the energy generated back to your energy supplier.

COOKING WITH WOOD

As long as the wood used comes from a sustainable source, using wood as a fuel will not cause a net increase of CO_2 in the atmosphere. It also produces less acid rain chemicals than any fossil fuel and, if burned efficiently, will release minimal amounts of soot, hydrocarbons or other pollutants. Choices include: a wood stove, which will usually heat one room but could have a back boiler to heat water, a central heating wood boiler, wood pellet stoves and boilers that use wood industry waste, and wood-chip boilers for larger houses.

BUY A LOGMAKER

For free fuel, make your own logs from old newspapers using a logmaker. Just soak the paper and place in the mould, squeeze and after drying the log will burn as well as wood for up to an hour in a woodburning stove.

INVEST IN A HEAT PUMP

Heat pumps transfer heat from the ground (geo-thermal), air or water into a building to provide heating and, in some cases, to pre-heat hot water. They can also be reversed to cool a house in the summer. A geo-thermal heat pump will save 2–8 tonnes of CO_2 per year, depending on the type of fuel being replaced.

THE POWER OF WATER

If you're lucky enough to have a stream or river running through your garden, consider buying a hydropower system. The output will depend on the flow rate of the waterway, but the energy generated will avoid the use of fossil fuels, help cut CO_2 emissions and save on your electricity bills. Start small with a battery-charging micro-hydro system, which costs about the same as a good-quality washing machine.

green interiors

BUY A GOOD-QUALITY DOORMAT

A typical household carpet will be harbouring a selection of particularly nasty chemicals carried into a house on the soles of shoes. A US Environmental Protection Agency study has found that domestic pesticide levels are increased up to 400-fold by contamination trodden in on the feet of people and pets. By using a good-quality doormat, and taking shoes off at the door, you should be able to reduce the toxicity of your carpets.

CHOOSE HEAVY CURTAINS

When you next consider buying new curtains, choose thick ones, which can be as effective at keeping in warmth as an extra layer of glazing – particularly if they have thick thermal linings. Unlined curtains cut heat loss through windows by a third; insulated curtains reduce it by half.

PICK ECO-FRIENDLY WALLPAPER

Look out for greener wallpapers – they should use chlorine-free paper sourced from sustainably managed forests, be printed using water-based inks, which have less impact on the environment and contain no hazardous solvents. Check also whether the manufacturer recycles its waste from edge trimmings and look out for paste made from natural materials and free from fungicides, preservatives and synthetic resins.

OPT FOR CFLS OR LEDS

A house has on average 23 light bulbs, which could all be replaced by energy-saving compact fluorescent light bulbs (CFLs). These use only a fifth to a quarter of the electricity of ordinary bulbs and last up to ten times longer. Even better, opt for light emitting diodes (LEDs), which use even less energy than CFLs and can last up to ten times longer (and 130 times longer than conventional incandescent bulbs).

THE FLIGHT OF THE FLOWER

Avoid buying cut flowers unless you are certain of their origin. Flowers bought in supermarkets have often been airfreighted and refrigerated. There is also the issue of pesticides used in commercial flower production, which have an impact on the environment as well as the welfare of workers. UK consumers spend around £1.9 billion on cut flowers every year. The US is the second-largest importer worldwide – in 2006, cut flower imports totalled $768 million.

LOW VOC PAINTS

Decorators have a 40% increased risk of developing lung cancer due to the toxic effect of chemicals in paints, such as volatile organic compounds (VOCs), biocides, fungicides and solvents. Make sure the paints you use are as natural as possible and contain none of these chemical hazards.

LOOK INTO SPECIALITY ECO PAINTS

Some natural paint manufacturers have developed paints that absorb pollutants such as formaldehyde, solvents and VOCs given off by synthetic furnishings. Wall-insulating paints are also available which help to regulate the temperature inside throughout the year.

TRY WATER-BASED PAINT STRIPPERS

Conventional paint strippers contain solvents that carry health risks, such as dichloromethane – a highly toxic carcinogen. Instead, buy a water-based stripper that is solvent-free and will biodegrade. It does not dry out quickly, enabling you to strip a large area in one go, and will wash off with water.

NATURAL WALL COVERS

Rather than painting your walls, consider lining them with natural materials from renewable sources such as bamboo, jute, sisal, seagrass and even recycled paper. They help to absorb more noise than uncovered walls and also act as extra insulation.

LINO INSTEAD OF VINYL

Vinyl flooring is made from PVC combined with fungicides, pigments and plasticizers. Opt for lino as an alternative. It is a natural floor covering made from linseed oil and other natural and renewable ingredients such as cork and wood flour. Lino is one of the most sustainable flooring materials available; it has a lifespan of 30–40 years, is naturally antibacterial and will biodegrade at the end of its life.

PUT A CORK IN IT

With its many environmental and social benefits, cork is a renewable and sustainable resource. But check that the cork tiles you pick have not been sealed with PVC or polyurethane, neither of which are desirable chemicals to have in the home. Instead, source unsealed cork flooring and seal it yourself with low-VOC varnish.

FEEL THE WOOD BENEATH YOUR FEET

A hardwood floor from reclaimed sources not only looks great but it also can be a good environmental choice. If you can't get reclaimed wood, the next best thing is wood that has come from sustainable sources and is Forest Stewardship Council (FSC) certified.

TREAT WOOD NATURALLY

Invest in some natural finishes for your wooden floors (and other woods in your home). These include jojoba oil, linseed oil and tung oil from the nut of the tung tree that grows naturally in regions of China. But be sure to get 100% pure oil —many modern linseed and tung products are cut with solvents and other chemicals.

BUY RECLAIMED

You will not only feel virtuous for doing your bit to support the recycling of products, but will also have a unique and often amazing piece of furniture. Go to salvage yards or buy from companies that specialize in selling reclaimed items or re-using them to make new products. Items to look out for are those from schools, libraries, hospitals or churches such as seats, doors, worktops, tiles, bricks, sinks, free-standing baths and fireplaces.

CARE WITH CARPETS

Avoid synthetic carpets made from nylon and polyester – they are less durable, often use dyes derived from petrochemicals and may be pre-treated with fire retardants. Opt for natural carpets made from wool, linen or cotton but be aware that wool can sometimes be contaminated with pesticides or treated with stain-proofing chemicals. The backing material should also be natural – hessian, hemp, cotton or jute rather than polyurethane or latex foam, or PVC underlays, which can emit VOCs.

furniture options

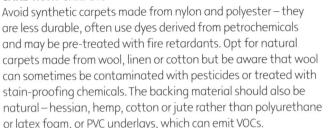

CHECK IT'S CERTIFIED

If you are buying wooden furniture make sure it comes from a sustainable source – and the easiest way to be sure is to check if it carries the Forest Stewardship Council (FSC) logo or is certified by the umbrella organization, the Rainforest Alliance.

AWAY FROM THE NORM

There are plenty of recycled furniture options out there, including tables and seating made from washing machine drums, recycled cardboard and recycled plastic, or even reclaimed cinema chairs. Be different and buy something unexpected and possibly unique.

SUPPORT CRAFTSMEN

Just like your food, furniture can be shipped miles to reach you. Cut down on your carbon footprint and support your local community by buying furniture from a local craftsman or employing a carpenter to make bespoke furniture for you. It doesn't always cost much more than mass-produced items.

BE GREEN WITH GREENGUARD

Many furniture manufacturers such as Herman Miller, Haworth, Paoli and Knoll offer Greenguard certified furniture that is low-toxicity. The Greenguard programme provides certification of products based on their low-emissions.

WELL UPHOLSTERED

Avoid upholstery that uses synthetic foams, foam rubber, latex or plastic coverings, because these emit VOCs (volatile organic compounds). Cotton is one of the most pesticide-ridden crops and leather uses hazardous chemicals in its processing, so look for the most natural coverings possible – such as those made from organic cotton, hemp and linen.

SECOND-CYCLE FURNITURE

Many furniture designers are now using existing wood rather than new wood. Some comes from flawed wood or factory scraps while others are sourced from remnants from the logging industry. Artek, the manufacturer of Alvar Aalto chairs, has worked with British designer Tom Dixon to create a "2nd Cycle" line which rescues historic pieces, such as the Aalto Model No.60 chair, and resells them with information about that particular item's history (seewww.artek.fi).

BUY CRADLE-TO-CRADLE

The cradle-to-cradle idea is that a product is endlessly recyclable – it never reaches a "grave" or landfill at the end of it's useful life. Examples include office chairs from Herman Miller and Steelcase, but look for the C2C certification logo (see www.mbdc.com). Choose furniture that can easily be taken apart as this means the pieces can be recycled in other ways.

BE AWARE OF OFFGASSING

New non-metallic products that contain VOCs will "offgas" for years, which means they will release chemicals into the surrounding air by evaporation (this is what you can identify as the "new car smell") in your home or office. The effects are even more toxic in a well-insulated building. Buying second-hand furniture means that it has done most of its offgassing already.

VINTAGE IS GOOD VALUE

Pre-owned furniture can be the greenest option of all, and many vintage pieces have a charm and value that new items just don't have. Mid-century modern vintage, such as Eames chairs or Robin and Lucienne Day pieces, are also good investments as they have a high re-sale value. You can bid for them on eBay.

 beds & linens

BED DOWN ON AN ORGANIC MATTRESS

Certified organic mattresses made from natural fibres like cotton, wool and hemp provide comfort and reduce carbon emissions and pollution created during the manufacturing process. Also you won't be exposed to the chemical residues that can cause allergies. Look out, too, for other natural mattresses made with latex, coir, horsehair and camel hair.

SLEEP ON A FUTON

Save on the wood or metal needed to make a bed frame by sleeping on a futon mattress, which is designed to be placed directly on the floor or on a woven rush mat. Look for futons made with organic and unbleached cotton and wool.

NATURAL BEDLINEN

There is evidence that the fire retardants, moth repellents, easy care and anti-pilling finishes which are routinely applied to bed linen may contribute to childhood asthma, eczema and even cot death. Explore natural alternatives such as hemp and organic unbleached cotton – virtually all polycotton, all "easy-care", "crease-resistant", and "permanent-press" cottons are treated with formaldehyde.

FIGHT THE MITES

Neem oil is a natural insecticide and spraying it on to your mattress and bedding could help prevent dust mite colonization. It is derived from the seed of the Neem tree and is an entirely natural product. Either dilute some neem oil with water and use a spray dispenser or buy a ready-made neem oil spray.

REST YOUR HEAD ON BUCKWHEAT

Try using a buckwheat pillow that has been filled with certified organic, unfumigated buckwheat hulls and then covered with organic cotton. They contour to your head or body, regulate temperature by allowing air circulation between the hulls, and you can remove or add hulls to adjust the pillow to suit you. Buckwheat is a natural, inexpensive and renewable resource.

BUY BAMBOO TOWELS
You can buy towels that are made from 70% bamboo fibre and 30% cotton. Bamboo grows extremely quickly and doesn't need any pesticides. Bamboo towels are three times as absorbent as cotton, and should be laundered on a delicate wash before first using them as they have not been subjected to any wet processes such as scouring, bleaching or dyeing after weaving.

 # bath & beauty products

PICK YOUR PAPER WISELY
The average British person uses over 100 rolls of toilet paper per year. Look out for products marked as 100% recycled and unbleached. Products carrying the FSC Recycled logo are guaranteed to contain only post-consumer waste material. The next best choice is toilet roll with a high-recycled content or products carrying the FSC Mixed Sources label, which guarantees that the product is a mixture of fibres from an FSC-certified forest or a controlled source, or post-consumer reclaimed material.

SMILE GREEN
Just think how many plastic toothbrushes you'll get through in a lifetime and you'll see the point in buying 100% recycled and recyclable plastic toothbrushes. Find them online and buy some natural toothpaste at the same time – these use natural herbs, oils and minerals rather than detergents, sodium lauryl sulphate, saccharine, artificial colours or chemical whiteners.

GO SKIN DEEPER
You can find safety information on specific products online by checking the Skin Deep database of nearly 25,000 bodycare products (www.cosmeticsdatabase.com). It will also tell you if a company has signed the Compact for Safe Cosmetics, whereby they pledge not to use chemicals linked to cancer, birth defects or mutation and to replace them with safer alternatives within three years.

NATURAL OR NOT?

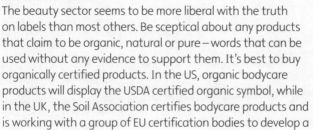

The beauty sector seems to be more liberal with the truth on labels than most others. Be sceptical about any products that claim to be organic, natural or pure – words that can be used without any evidence to support them. It's best to buy organically certified products. In the US, organic bodycare products will display the USDA certified organic symbol, while in the UK, the Soil Association certifies bodycare products and is working with a group of EU certification bodies to develop a common European organic beauty and cosmetic standard.

BEAUTY CHEMICAL-FREE

According to the Environmental Working Group, nearly 90% of ingredients in US personal care products have not been assessed for safety by anyone and nearly 400 products sold in the US contain chemicals that are not allowed in other countries. Although in Europe the situation is slightly better due to new laws which will ban certain chemicals, it is still best to buy the least chemical-laden beauty products you can.

NATURAL NAILS

Nail varnishes, glues and other nail products can contain a cocktail of chemicals such as formaldehyde and toluene – known carcinogens. A study has shown that 89% of the 10,000 chemicals used in nail-care products in the US have not been safety tested by an independent agency. Look out for natural nail products that do not contain phthalates, toxins, formaldehyde, toluene or colour lakes.

 # accessories & jewellery

ECO HANDBAGS AND ACCESSORIES

There are now many retailers that use recycled or discarded goods for handbags, totes and other fashion items. Ecoist (www.ecoist.com) uses discontinued or defectively printed snack wrappers to create stylish clutches, coin purses, bags and totes, while other companies such as Passchal (www.passchal.com) use tyre rubber to construct new items.

SECOND-HAND DIAMONDS

If you're in the market for a diamond, buy an antique stone rather than support the diamond industry, which has a poor environmental and human rights record. Conflict diamonds (also known as blood diamonds) are diamonds mined and traded illegally to help fund wars in Africa. Although a certification scheme – the Kimberley Process – has been set up, they are still being smuggled.

BUY RECYCLED JEWELLERY

Forget about conventional gold and diamonds and buy jewellery made from recycled materials. The choice is huge, with bracelets, rings and necklaces created from recycled plastic bags and old shampoo bottles, recycled glass, old buttons, cutlery and more.

CLEAN UP YOUR ACT

If you're buying gold jewellery, make sure your gold isn't "dirty". The No Dirty Gold campaign makes sure the jewellery you buy hasn't been produced at the expense of communities, workers or the environment.

ALL THAT GLITTERS

The gold produced for a single 18-karat gold ring leaves in its wake 18 tons of mine waste. Every year the smelting industry adds more than 140 million tons of sulphur dioxide to the atmosphere, representing 13% of global emissions. Think carefully before you buy.

GO FOR VINTAGE

Instead of choosing new gold for your necklace or wedding ring, buy recycled or vintage gold. About one-third of the gold in use or storage today comes from scrap or recycled sources.

GREEN GEMS

Choose a gem supplier who has strict environmental and labour standards, such as making sure that labourers are fairly treated and that a mine site is restored to its original condition once mining has been completed.

GOLD ETHICS

In the UK alone, nearly 20 million hallmarked gold articles are sold each year – equivalent to around a third of the population – but for every gold ring made, 18 tonnes of waste is produced, including cyanide and arsenic, and a large gold mine will draw around 830 litres (220 gallons) of water per minute. It is also estimated that between 1995 and 2015, roughly half the world's gold will have come from indigenous people's lands – much of it without those communities' consent. Look instead for ethically sourced gold.

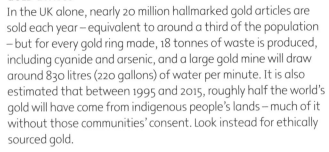

 # clothes shopping

CHOOSE REPUTABLE GREEN BRANDS

Fashion retailers such as People Tree (www.peopletree.co.uk), Edun (www.edunonline.com) and Loomstate (www.loomstate. org) are established as having good green credentials but are also able to keep up with every current trend. Their clothing has been spotted on celebrities and the catwalk.

BUY ORGANIC COTTON

If you are keen to "green" your wardrobe, start with organic cotton items. Cotton farming uses one-quarter of the world's pesticides and 20,000 deaths occur in developing countries each year from pesticide poisoning. According to the World Health Organization, many of these can be attributed to cotton production.

LOOK FOR LOCAL MANUFACTURERS AND DESIGNERS

Socially responsible fashion retailers such as American Apparel have made good use of keeping all the processes close to home – in this case, materials, design and manufacturing are based in Los Angeles. Obviously, the green idea gets diluted the further afield the brand sells, so take matters into your own hands and find a local solution. Something as simple as employing a neighbour to make beautiful knitwear for you can help the cause.

CHECK YOUR LABEL

If the garment you are buying has a label naming a country or organization that you suspect employs unfair labour, find out more before you buy. Any developing country should automatically be considered of potential concern.

BUY ORGANIC COTTON

If buying cotton soft furnishings, bedding, towels or clothing, always buy organic. Cotton farming uses one quarter of the world's pesticides and the number of cotton farmers suffering acute pesticide poisoning each year is between 25 and 77 million worldwide, according to a report by the Environmental Justice Foundation (EJF) and the Pesticide Action Network.

A WIDER CHOICE OF FRIENDLY FABRICS

Eco-fashion has moved on from organic cotton and hemp. Check out the many other fabrics being used, including ingeo, which is derived from corn sugar, and fabrics made from bamboo, soybean oil and a Japanese leaf called sasawashi (which has excellent water-absorbing qualities and is naturally antibacterial and odour resistant).

THE WHOLE PROCESS

Eco-friendly clothing doesn't just rest on the type of fabric used. There are now entire clothing and accessory lines devoted to sustainable production practices – using wind power to provide the necessary energy for manufacture, using only organic fibres, and donating profits back to earth-friendly causes. For example, Prana, which designs and distributes yoga and climbing gear, supports wind farms and now supplies wind power to 400 retailers worldwide.

REMADE CLOTHES

Check out companies that take discarded clothes, give them a refurb and sell them on. TRAID (Textile Recycling for Aid and International Development) in the UK, for example, operates textile recycling banks, then repairs and customizes items before selling them. In this way they raise funds for overseas development and environmental projects.

SHAWL WARNING

Never buy Shahtoosh shawls – they are woven from the hair of the Tibetan antelope, which is killed in the process. Due to poaching, the Tibetan antelope is an endangered species. Look out for alternatives including nettle shawls (yes, woven from the plant), hemp shawls or a wool pashmina.

DON'T DRY-CLEAN

Despite its name, dry-cleaning is not totally dry. It involves the use of solvents that remove most stains, and most drycleaners use perchloroethylene, or PERC, as their main solvent. In high levels, PERC has been shown to cause cancer and its release into the air, ground and water is an environmental concern. There are greener alternatives offered by some cleaners but the best solution is to buy clothes that you can wash at home.

THE GREENEST CLOTHING...

... is already owned – by you! Look at mending and repairing existing clothes, having a tailor take them in or let them out, or otherwise re-structure them so you can get more mileage without further outlay of cost or manufacturing. If your clothing is completely beyond repair, cut it up to use in a patchwork quilt or as household rags. Get into the habit of reusing items until they can't be reused any longer.

WASH CLOTHING LESS

Even the most eco-friendly garment, such as an organic cotton T-shirt, can be costly in green terms due to the frequency it needs to be washed. Try to get several uses out of a garment before washing it, and sponge off small stains and marks rather than washing the entire garment.

BUY QUALITY CLOTHES

Don't be tempted by bargain-basement clothing stores and the idea of wearing today and throwing away tomorrow – this is ecologically unsound. Instead, buy better-quality items that may cost more but last many years. They will be made from good fibres so can be recycled and reused, and will be closer to natural sources than cheaper manmade alternatives.

FRIENDLY FOOTWEAR

There are a growing number of eco-friendly shoe options out there, such as those from clothing company Patagonia, who use leather uppers from tanneries that comply with ISO 14001 (a strict set of environmental standards), outsoles made from up to 30% recycled scrap rubber and latex outsoles or midsoles made from the milk of the hevea tree.

REUSE A SHOE

Support companies which offer recycling options such as Nike's Reuse-A-Shoe programme, which collects old trainers (sneakers) and turns them into "Nike grind" – a material used to make playgrounds and sports' surfaces.

RECYCLED AND FAIRTRADE SPORTSWEAR

When shopping for trainers (sneakers), consider those with ethics in mind. Several companies are manufacturing styles that are totally green but also have street-cool good looks, such as Worn Again (www.wornagain.co.uk), Green Toe by Simple (www.simpleshoes.com/greentoe) and Ethletic (www.ethletic.com).

LEATHER-FREE SHOES

If you are concerned about animal rights and the use of leather in your shoes, choose leather-free and animal-derivative-free alternatives. You don't need to sacrifice style for ethics. Fashionistas can do no better than buying Stella McCartney styles, but Beyond Skin (www.beyondskin.co.uk) and Moo Shoes (www. mooshoes.com) are also good alternatives.

 # household appliances

SEEK OUT ENERGY-EFFICIENT PRODUCTS

Many electrical products now come with an energy rating – the EnergyGuide (www.energyguide.com) and Energy Star (www.energystar.gov) labels in the US, for example. Energy Star has more than 60 product categories to choose from. Check any product you are about to purchase and make sure it has the highest possible rating.

AN EFFICIENT MODEL

After central heating, fridges and freezers are the biggest domestic users of energy, because they're on all the time. Choose the most energy-efficient models – in the UK they will display the Energy Saving Recommended logo, in the EU buy only those that have achieved A+ or A++ on the EU Energy Label and in the US, look for the Energy Star symbol.

PUTTING ON THE PRESSURE

Microwave ovens use 75% less energy than conventional ovens and don't produce surplus heat, while a pressure cooker can cook three or four times quicker than a conventional cooker, so both are good choices.

THE RIGHT REFRIGERANT

You should insist on a fridge or freezer that uses a hydrocarbon (R600a) refrigerant and which is labelled "CFC and HFC free". Chlorofluorocarbons (CFCs) and hydrochlorofluorocarbons (HCFCs) are powerful greenhouse gases which are being phased out, while the hydrofluorocarbons (HFCs) that replaced them are also greenhouse gases – at least 1,200 times more powerful than CO_2 – so should be avoided. Greenpeace says that at expected rates of usage, by 2050 HFCs will contribute as much to global warming as all the private cars on the planet.

A QUICKER, MORE EFFICIENT COOK

Induction hobs are more expensive than traditional hobs but consume half as much electricity as electric hobs and are more efficient in heat transfer. Manufacturers estimate that power savings of 40–70% are achievable in comparison to conventional hobs.

CHOOSE A CHEST FREEZER

Freezers consume the most energy of all refrigeration products so opt for a chest freezer, rather than upright one, as they tend to be more energy efficient. Avoid frost-free freezers, which use on average 45% more energy than manually defrosted models. Look out too for "dual control" fridge-freezers that allow you to turn the fridge off and leave the freezer on when you go away for longer.

BUY A DECENT DISHWASHER

Research has found that dishwashers use only half the energy, one-sixth of the water and less soap than handwashing your dishes (provided they are used when full). Buy the most energy-efficient model possible as they can use up to 40% less energy than an inefficient appliance.

 # electronic goods

AN ELECTRONIC TAKE OVER

By 2010, the consumer electronics sector will be the biggest single user of domestic electricity, overtaking kitchen appliances and lighting, and by 2020, entertainment, computers and gadgets will account for 45% of electricity used in our homes. In the UK alone, it will take the equivalent of 14 average-sized power stations just to run them! So choose and use your electronics carefully.

E-WASTE DANGERS

Greenpeace is campaigning against the dangerous growth of electronic scrap (e-waste) containing toxic chemicals and heavy metals that cannot be disposed of or recycled safely and that often end up being illegally dumped in developing countries. Check its Green Electronics Guide, which rates the major electronics makers.

SAY GOODBYE TO STANDBY

The average household has up to 12 gadgets left on standby or charging at any one time, with the television left on standby for up to 17.5 hours a day. Look out for products without a standby function or those which have been designed to use less power on standby. There are also products available that connect all your appliances and let you turn them all off at the socket with one click, including one which turns off PC peripherals (printers, monitors and so on) when you turn off your computer.

BUY UPGRADABLE COMPUTERS

Avoid operating systems and software that cannot be upgraded electronically – such as cheap factory sealed computers that are designed to be thrown away once no longer needed. Two million working Pentium PCs end up in landfill sites in the UK every year and only 20% of all discarded UK computers are recycled. When buying a new computer ask for readily upgradable hardware, make sure spare parts and service will be available, and check to see that memory is easily expandable.

WOOD WORK

Have a break from plastic and opt for a more natural look – a Swedish company (www.swedx.se) now sells computer monitors and keyboards in wooden cases and even a mouse made of ash, which can be recycled. Online, you can also buy bamboo casings for your computer screen, keyboard and mouse.

LOW-ENERGY LAPTOPS

Laptops consume one-eighth of the power of desktop computers because mobile processors are designed for long battery life, which means they are state-of-the-art in terms of power management. Laptops also use the bare minimum of components in order to keep their size and weight down, so there will be less waste when they are no longer needed.

RETURN TO MAKER

Try to buy from a manufacturer who is prepared to take your old computer back for disposal, whether it is their brand or not. You will be supporting a more responsible approach to e-waste.

GO DIGITAL

Save on film and processing chemicals by investing in a digital camera. By picking the shots you like, you'll reduce the waste that comes from printing an entire roll of film. Just be sure to print on the most eco-friendly paper you can find. And, while you're at it, invest in an MP3 player and give up your CD habit – they're bad for the environment.

HOLD ONTO YOUR MOBILE

There are more than 7 billion mobile (cell) phones in the world
and only 1.3 billion users. On top of that, the average user
replaces their handset every 18 months and over 100 million
mobiles are thrown away each year. Mobiles that end up in
landfill leak several contaminants such as lead, brominated
flame retardants and cadmium. Instead of upgrading every
year, hold onto your phone for as long as possible and recycle it
when you no longer want it – there are many charities that offer
this service. Look out too for phones with biodegradable covers
that are already available in Japan.

A NEW NETWORK CAN WORK

Not all mobile (cell phone) service providers are equal in green
terms. Look for the greenest possible, such as Green Mobile
in the UK (www.greenmobile.co.uk), which asks its customers
to hold on to their existing handset for one more year and in
return gives a rebate and donation to the one of its two partner
charities: the Woodland Trust or Friends of the Earth.

RECHARGE YOUR BATTERIES

Conventional batteries contain cadmium and mercury, and
must be treated as hazardous waste. The UK generates
20,000–30,000 tonnes of waste general-purpose batteries
every year, with less than 1,000 tonnes being recycled. Three
billion household dry cell batteries are sold and discarded in the
United States each year, producing more than 125,000 tonnes
of waste. Rechargeable batteries last longer, cost less to use
and help keep toxins out of the waste stream.

GO BACK TO AN INKJET PRINTER

Inkjet printers use up to 90% less energy than a laser printer.
To save on power and paper, check also that your printer can
shrink your document to fit two, four or more pages on a single
sheet and that it can handle double-sided printing.

SMALL-SCREEN ENTERTAINMENT

There are real concerns that the new wave of hi-tech televisions will increase CO_2 emissions because flat-screen televisions that are larger than 60 cm (24 in) use over three times the electricity of their conventional counterparts. Liquid crystal display (LCD) screens consume the least electricity and also contain less lead than the cathode ray tubes (CRTs) used in electronic televisions, but you should choose the smallest screen you can.

THE POWER OF WATER

You can now buy digital alarm clocks and calculators that run on water-powered batteries. To keep the battery going, refill it as the water evaporates, typically every two to three months. The battery will last a minimum of two years and all the components of the H_2O battery are recyclable.

INVEST IN A SOLAR CHARGER

You can buy solar chargers that let you recharge your iPod, phone, camera or other mobile device virtually anywhere if you position the solar panels in direct sunlight. A full charger delivers enough charge to extend your play time up to 9 hours, or fully charge your iPod with enough power left over to top up your mobile phone.

GO DIGITAL

Instead of listening to the radio through your TV, invest in a digital radio. You consume 10 to 20 times more power using your TV to listen to your tunes rather than through a digital radio.

CLOCKWORK MUSIC

Buy a wind-up radio to save energy. They come in several different styles, including ones with solar panels to help charge the batteries. There's even a digital multiband solar/wind-up radio complete with built-in clock/alarm.

 office supplies
& services

RECYCLE PRINT CARTRIDGES
Over 700 million ink cartridges were thrown away worldwide
in 2003 – and they are all non-biodegradable. Cut your
environmental impact by buying remanufactured cartridges
and recycling old ones.

SWITCH SERVICE PROVIDERS
A growing number of internet service providers are now operating
energy-saving business practices such as encouraging staff to
use public transport. Some use solar-power in their offices while
others offset their carbon emissions, so check them out.

PAPER FOR PRINTING
Buy recycled paper for your printer and be sure to recycle it after
use. Did you know that recycling 1 tonne of printing or copier
paper saves more than 2 tonnes of wood? But do remember to
avoid printing in the first place – 115 billion sheets of paper are
used annually for personal computers and the average daily
web user prints 28 pages daily. Given that an estimated 95% of
business information is still stored on paper, there is still a long
way to go.

 media & books

POST-CONSUMER READING
Buy only books or magazines that have been printed on recycled
paper. Paper production accounts for about 43% of harvested
wood and recycling of newsprint saves about 1 tonne of wood.
It is also estimated that recycling one tonne of newspaper
saves about 4,000 kWh of electricity – enough electricity
to power a three-bedroom European house for a year, or to
heat and air-condition the average North American home for
almost six months.

SWAP A MAG

Instead of buying several magazines every month, make a deal with your friends to buy one title each and then swap to take a stand against paper waste. This is a way to save yourself some money as well as paper. Or alternate the magazines you buy, limiting yourself to one a month.

buying gifts

BUY LESS AT CHRISTMAS

This is the one time of the year when even the most eco-friendly among us seem to be lured into a consumer frenzy, but it is incredibly wasteful. In the UK alone, people get through 83 sq km (32 sq miles) of wrapping paper, a billion Christmas cards, plus 125,000 tonnes of plastic packaging, and nearly 3,000 tonnes of aluminium foil from the turkey. Buy less of everything at Christmas and you can feel virtuous as well as festive!

LESS OF THE TWINKLE

Each Christmas sees increasing numbers of homes decked with hundreds of twinkling lights. It has been estimated that decorating your whole house with lights indoors and out could use up 1,000 kWh of electricity – almost a third of the annual electricity used by an average home. If you must, choose LED – they are 90% more energy-efficient than incandescent lights.

BE GREEN WITH GIFTS

From adopting an endangered animal (through the World Wildlife Fund) to a solar-powered toy car, the scope for green gifts is enormous. There are hundreds of eco gift stores online so there's no excuse for that pile of plastic under your tree on Christmas morning.

GET PLANTED

If possible, buy plants instead of cut flowers to give to your family and friends. Plants continue growing and can be replanted outdoors, whereas flowers will be thrown away and wasted after just a few days or weeks.

DECK THE HALLS WITH BOUGHS OF GREEN

In 2006, the UK imported 60,000 tonnes of Christmas decorations from China, most of which was discarded at the end of the festive season. There are so many greener ways of decorating your home – collect and paint some pine cones or fallen branches, make gingerbread tree decorations instead of using plastic baubles, get the children to make paper chains, etc. Failing that, several websites now offer eco-friendly decorations that should last and last.

WRAP WITH CARE

Don't forget to wrap your green gifts carefully – choose 100% post-consumer recycled paper or pick a hand-made and hand-printed, fairly traded gift wrap. Instead of using sticky tape, use either ribbons, string or wool – they can be re-used and make the paper easier to reuse. Avoid bubble wrap or polystyrene packing material for delicate items and instead use old newspaper to cushion fragile items.

LOOK INTO LEDS

For lighting up your tree this Christmas, consider using LED (light emitting diodes) lighting. They use a fraction of the energy of a conventional bulb (estimates say around 10% of the power used by conventional fairly lights). LED lights are expensive but remember "less is more" when it comes to Christmas decor.

GIFT A TREE

Next time you have to fork out for a birthday present (or want to celebrate the birth of a child or an anniversary), why not buy a tree instead of the latest toiletries? If the recipient doesn't have space for a tree, there are several global organizations who will organize tree planting in endangered rainforests. In the UK the Woodland Trust (www.woodlandtrustshop.com) allows you to dedicate a tree to a loved one.

GET ADOPTIVE

If you're thinking of buying a present for an animal-loving friend, don't forget you can adopt an animal for them in many of the world's endangered habitats. Popular choices include tigers, pandas and orangutans.

PAY BY CARD
If you're looking to buy birthday, Christmas or other greeting cards, do so at a charity shop. Their recycled cards will make money for the charity without you spending any extra cash.

TAKE CARE WITH GREETINGS CARDS
When shopping for greetings cards look for 100% post-consumer waste content and processed chlorine-free (PCF) paper products, where no additional chlorine or chlorine derivatives were used to bleach the final recycled-fibre product. Better still, make your own. Remember also to recycle your cards.

SEND AN E-CARD
Send an e-card instead of buying cards made from paper and then relying on road or air transport for them to be delivered. It's cheaper, easier and much better for the environment.

THE GIFT OF ADVENTURE
Instead of giving clothing or electronic goods, consider buying a green alternative for your friends and family for birthdays, anniversaries or Christmas presents. The gift of an "experience" such as a day at a spa or a lesson in rock-climbing is more eco-friendly and potentially more life-affirming than a costly handbag or electronic gift.

BUY RIGHT
If you're buying gifts for new or expecting parents, expose them to the wide array of alternatives, including sleepers made from organic cotton, toys made from non-dyed wood and baby soaps made without synthetic ingredients.

CHARITY-GIVING GIFT
Consider a gift of charity for a present – this is usually something people want to do but don't get around to, so do it for them! Whether it's giving money for a specific environmental cause (see www.oneclickatatime.org), buying laptops for children (One Laptop Per Child, www.laptopgiving.org) or a product from any number of charity websites, such as the WWF or Oxfam, it makes a thoughtful gift. You could help provide school supplies, water or health services worldwide.

shopping for children

KIT OUT YOUR KID FOR SCHOOL
Give your children an eco-friendly school starter kit and look
online for the following: lunchboxes made from recycled juice
packs, fairtrade and organic cotton uniforms, school bags made
from recycled plastic bottles, pens made from recycled car parts,
pencil cases made from recycled car tyres and pencils made from
CD cases and plastic cups. Top it all off with a water-powered
calculator.

THE NAPPY (DIAPER) MOUNTAIN
Disposable nappy (diaper) waste is the third largest source of
solid waste in the US, where some 18 billion nappies are thrown
away annually, while in the UK nearly 3 billion are binned
each year – 90% of which end up in landfill and take years to
decompose. Avoid adding to the waste mountain by buying real
nappies, ideally made from organic cotton and hemp and worn
with organic wool waterproof overpants.

WOODEN TOYS
Say no to plastic battery-operated toys and instead look for
toys made from sustainably sourced wood. It is estimated
that up to 80% of toys in US stores have been made in China,
but wouldn't it be great if more of us bought our toys from
local manufacturers to avoid the energy and emission costs
of transportation?

LUNCHBOX CHOICES
Food manufacturers are coming up with increasing numbers
of lunchbox products that are usually among the worst
offenders in terms of wasteful packaging. Avoid the
separately packaged biscuits (crackers), cheeses and yogurts,
and instead buy in bulk and use reusable pots to provide
snack-size portions.

GIVE A GREEN PARTY

Ditch the plastic party bags with cheap plastic toys that are thrown away after each party. Instead buy brown paper bags, which your children can decorate, and include a slice of cake along with some useful non-plastic items such as paint brushes, crayons or books. Or use an eco-friendly and ethical party bag supplier that offers recycled or reusable bags filled with fairtrade chocolate and recycled gifts.

KEEP YOUR KIDS CHEMICAL-FREE

Avoid conventional, processed food if you want to have a calm family life. A recent study by the UK's Food Standards Agency has found that children behaved impulsively and lost concentration after consuming a drink containing additives and certain mixtures of artificial-food colours, along with sodium benzoate (E211) – a preservative used in ice cream and confectionery. Most of the 290 additives allowed are prohibited in organic foods, including all artificial colours or flavourings.

BUY RECYCLED LITTER

The litter from America's 90 million pet cats results in around 2 million tonnes of cat litter being sent to landfills each year. To reduce the environmental impact, avoid the clay-based varieties of pet litters, which don't biodegrade and are often dusted with silica, a known carcinogen that can cause respiratory disease. Choose a litter made from recycled material, such as sawmill scrap or waste from wheat or corn.

BABY BOTTLE WARNING

A recent US study has found a toxic chemical called bisphenol A, which is linked to developmental, neural and reproductive problems, leaches into liquids and foods from commonly used clear plastic baby bottles. The US Center for Disease Control and Prevention found bisphenol A in the urine of over 95% of people they tested. It's best to either buy glass bottles or check with the manufacturer whether the bottle contains the chemical.

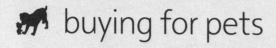 # buying for pets

POOP DISPOSAL
Removing your pets' faeces from public areas is an environmental must – America's 73 million dogs produce around 10 million tonnes of dog poop per year – but be sure it goes in a biodegradable bag so all of it breaks down once disposed of.

TREAT PETS NATURALLY
Flea powders and worm tablets are just some of the chemical nasties we buy for our pets, but they are dangerous to have in the home and could end up polluting the environment when disposed of. There are plenty of natural alternatives, such as homeopathic remedies, that are worth a try.

DITCH THE PACKAGING
Pet food should be bought in bulk to avoid throwing away huge amounts of packaging. Especially avoid food that is sold in individual sachets for each meal and look out for compostable or biodegradable packaging.

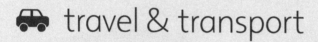 # travel & transport

INVEST IN A GREENER CAR
Those featured at the top of the Environmental Transport Association list are the Honda Civic 1.4 IMA Executive, a petrol/electric hybrid, and the Toyota Prius 1.5 Hybrid – the most efficient mass-produced car on the market with the lowest CO_2 emissions of all cars.

GET GOOD TYRES
There are over three billion discarded car tyres in the US, with over 200 million more added each year. They pollute landfills, present a fire hazard and waste oil. When you shop for tyres, look for the longest-wearing tyres you can find and keep them properly inflated to reduce wear and save fuel. Retreading saves about 1.5 billion litres (400 million gallons) of oil each year.

GREEN CYCLE STORAGE

If storing your bike is a problem, then Cycloc could be the answer. Made from 100% recycled plastic, Cycloc fixes to the wall and allows you to store your bike above the floor, which means you can win back your hallway, or make space in your garage.

ELECTRIC MOTORING

Consider buying an electric car. With absolutely no emissions, these are a great solution to our society's reliance on petrol (gas). Although hampered by low speeds, they are excellent alternatives for city-users and small commutes. Battery-cell versions simply plug into an electric outlet. Alternatively, choose a hybrid vehicle, which uses a combination of battery and petrol – the battery is used for slower speeds with petrol only kicking in for the higher mph.

BEWARE BIOFUELS

Biofuels, particularly ethanol and diesel made from plants such as corn, sugarcane and rapeseed, may not be the easy answer. Although they offer a way of reducing greenhouse gas emissions, they are also a real threat to biodiversity. To keep up with demand, huge areas of land could be planted with these crops, which would involve the loss of wildlife-rich landscapes. There is also a chance that switching to such crops could lead to food shortages.

DON'T BUY A CAR, USE A CAB

If you are an urban dweller, think carefully about buying a car. Taxis, which are already on the road, are a service that's used by others when they're not being used by you. Look out for hybrid vehicles or pedi-cabs and cycle rickshaws.

ON TWO WHEELS

In the UK, 6.6 million people travel less than 8 km (5 m) to work, so if they all travelled there by bike it would save 44 million tonnes of CO_2 – equivalent to the emissions from heating more than 16,000 homes for a year. In the US only 0.4% of commuters use a bicycle, while in the Netherlands 50% of commuters bicycle to work and in China 77% commute by bike.

HAIL A GREEN CAB

They are on the road night and day, so imagine the benefits if cabs were to go green. Well, some taxi operators are now offering "greener" services by using greener cars. In London, there are already several services to choose from, most of which use Toyota Prius cars, which they claim emit 60% less CO_2 than standard taxis.

SHARE IN A CAR RENTAL SCHEME

There are now car-sharing schemes operating in many major cities. These allow you to book a car online, pick it up around the corner and drop it back into a designated bay on a pay-per-hour basis. This has all the benefits of owning a car but without any of the hassle.

THE ENV MOTORBIKE

Motorbikes emit 16 times the amount of hydrocarbons, including greenhouse gases, compared to cars, but innovation is on the way with the Emissions Neutral Vehicle (ENV) fuel-cell motorbike by Seymour Powell. It has a top speed of 80 kmh (50 mph) and can run for four hours before the fuel cell needs to be recharged.

SAVE FARES AND TIME

Learn to love public transport by searching out cheap weekly or off-peak tickets, which will encourage you to use the service. In addition, buses, trains, light rail and ferries have dedicated travel routes that are usually much faster than car travel.

REDUCE AIR TRAVEL

A single flight across country in the US produces about 10% as much carbon as the total of everything else that the average American does in a year. If you can replace a jet trip with a train ride, it will reduce carbon dioxide emissions by 85–96%.

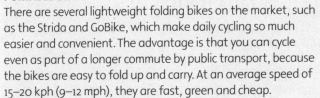

PORTABLE BIKES

There are several lightweight folding bikes on the market, such as the Strida and GoBike, which make daily cycling so much easier and convenient. The advantage is that you can cycle even as part of a longer commute by public transport, because the bikes are easy to fold up and carry. At an average speed of 15–20 kph (9–12 mph), they are fast, green and cheap.

NO NEED FOR FOUR-WHEEL DRIVE

One of the biggest green "crimes" is buying a larger version of a product than you actually need, and this really applies to four-wheel drives (SUVs). Most people who drive them never take them off the highway. Not only are they petrol- (gas-) guzzling polluters, but they aren't even being used for their purpose. Environmental issues aside, before buying one consider whether you will actually use this car for the purpose for which it's intended.

OFFSET YOUR MILES

Carbon offsetting is a way of neutralizing the carbon emissions you emit when you drive or fly. You subscribe to an offsetting organization and donate money every time you travel – these funds then go toward planting trees and installing solar panels and wind turbines. Some airlines are now routinely asking for offsetting donations when people book their trips.

STOP FLYING ENTIRELY

Aviation accounts for just over 3.5% of total CO_2 emissions worldwide and the Intergovernmental Panel on Climate Change estimates that by 2050 emissions from aircraft could be responsible for up to 15% of total global warming produced by human activities. Aviation emissions are estimated to have between two and four times the climate change impact of carbon emissions alone.

trips & holidays

ECO-FRIENDLY BREAKS

Holidays don't have to mean a highly polluting flight to a resort in a hot and usually water-stressed part of the world. Choose from a huge variety of eco-friendly holidays, preferably close to home, such as a boating holiday on a UK canal, with a percentage of the booking cost donated to the Waterways Trust Green Fund.

STAY IN AN ECO-LODGE

Why not get into the green spirit on your holiday by staying in one of the many eco-lodges dotted around the globe. These are purpose-built to blend in with the environment and use as little external resources as possible.

LOOK BEFORE YOU BOOK

Before you book your holiday hotel, get in contact and check what attempts the hotel makes to save energy. If you can, choose one with energy-saving devices such as timers or sensors on light switches – this means that lights wouldn't have to be left on all night in public areas.

SAVE IT FOR THE SHORT HAUL

Instead of taking exotic long-haul journeys abroad, look closer to home for your holidays and breaks to cut down on air miles. If you can't go by train or bus, even a short flight is more eco-friendly than one that takes you halfway around the world for a change of scenery you can get in a two-hour flight.

SUSTAINABLE SOUVENIRS

The campaign group Common Ground is campaigning for producers and those working in tourism to provide locally distinctive souvenirs that are made nearby, from local renewable materials, demonstrating sustainable production and that are ethically derived, fairly traded and offering fair value (www.commonground.org.uk).

DODGE ENDANGERED

Many tourist spots have local markets that can be fun to browse, but beware of animal products unless you can be sure they are not sourced from endangered species, particularly in the case of jewellery and carved products. If in doubt, don't buy.

THREATENED SPECIES

What seems like a good souvenir purchase at the time could be costing the planet dear and land you in prison. Products to watch out for are those made with ivory, coral and turtle-shell products – six of the seven species of marine turtles are endangered or critically endangered and all international trade in marine turtle products is banned. Find out if you need a CITES (the Convention on International Trade in Endangered Species of Wild Fauna and Flora) permit to bring it home from your travels.

MAKE YOUR TRIP COUNT

Check out volunteering breaks so that during part or all of your vacation you can contribute to bettering the local environment, whether it's cleaning beaches or planting crops.

LINGER LONGER

Instead of heading off on a holiday a couple times a year, try to take all your annual leave in one go to minimize the time you spend travelling by air. Or limit yourself to two shorter breaks – one in winter and one in summer.

CLEAN A REEF

Why not do some good on your next holiday by volunteering to clean up a coral reef? You'll spend an afternoon, day or even a week enjoying the beauty of one of the world's most amazing treasures while helping to preserve it for future generations.

SIDESTEPPING THE SNOW

Cross-country skiing is a greener choice for your next winter break than downhill skiing or snowboarding because it requires very little extra equipment or machinery, which means a smaller environmental impact.

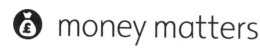 money matters

ETHICAL INVESTMENTS

You may not see your financial agreements as part of your weekly shop, but they are and they could be green. Your bank or investment fund may put your money into the oil or GM-food business. Move your money to a bank, or insurance company that supports environmentally and ethically sound businesses. Choose one with humanist, animal welfare and environmental credentials to ensure you're helping all round.

INSURANCE WEATHER WATCH

The increase in extreme weather conditions around the world has prompted some insurance companies to look at the causes and effects of climate change in order to re-evaluate calculations which were traditionally based on past findings. Ask your insurer how climate change effects, such as increased risk of flooding and storms, will affect your cover.

ECO-FRIENDLY CREDIT

There's even a green store card for you card junkies out there. CarbonCred lets shoppers earn green points at high-street stores and the virtual card is accepted at 1,000 online stores. The reward points you notch up can then be spent on carbon-busting products and services (www.CarbonCred.co.uk). Many credit card companies in the US now offer eco-friendly choices for its reward-card holders – for such options as donating to a renewable-energy cause.

planning for the future

GREEN COFFIN OPTIONS
This may be one shopping trip you won't be on, but you can
specify in advance what your choice would be! Consider asking
for a green coffin. They can be made of bamboo, wicker, willow
or cardboard and are biodegradable and made from sustainable
sources – some even carry a fairtrade mark.

LEAVE A LEGACY
You can leave money to environmental causes in your will,
to help preserve the earth and wildlife habitats for future
generations. These charity donations can sometimes be
tax-free as well.

GO THE GREEN WAY
Make your last action on earth a green one by choosing an
eco-burial. Many localities now have forest burial sites, where
a tree is planted on each plot.

resources

This section is an invaluable resource for green companies, manufacturers, campaigning and information groups. You will find suppliers of many of the products mentioned throughout the book in the following pages, along with further information on how to get more involved in a green lifestyle if you choose.

Green consumerism is a great way to flex your consumer spending power but it is not always the most environmentally friendly option. Before you buy something new make sure you can't mend, upgrade, update the thing you are replacing.

Organizations like Freecycle are brilliant for circulating unwanted items and preventing waste ending up in landfill sites. Remember – the item you are getting rid of may be exactly what someone else is looking for, so make good use of these networks.

Big Green Switch
Tips on switching to a greener lifestyle.
www.biggreenswitch.co.uk

BTCV
Supports volunteering opportunities in the countryside and outdoors. www.btcv.org

Building For Health Materials Center
A central supplier for healthy, environmentally sound building materials, appliances and home comforts.
www.buildingforhealth.com

Campaign for Safe Cosmetics
A coalition that campaigns for the health and beauty industry to phase out the use of chemicals linked to cancer, birth defects and other health problems and replace them with safer alternatives.
www.safecosmetics.org

Campaign to Protect Rural England
Campaigns on light pollution and landscape issues.
www.cpre.org.uk

Community Composting Network
Supports community composting projects.
www.communitycompost.org

The Composting Association
Promotes composting.
www.compost.org.uk

Cornish Organic Wool
For a range of organic wools and knitting kits. www.cornishorganicwool.co.uk

Ecocentric
A green interiors website hosted by environmentally aware designer, Oliver Heath. It sells everything from eco friendly wallpaper and paints to LED lighting. www.ecocentric.co.uk

Ecos Paints
For a range of anti formaldehyde and ELR-neutralizing paint, as well as wall insulating paint. www.ecospaints.com

Ecotricity
Green energy supplier in the UK. www.ecotricity.co.uk

Energy Saving Trust
A non-profit organization funded by the UK government and the private sector to address the issues of climate change. www.energysavingtrust.org.uk

Energy Star
A joint programme of the US Environmental Protection Agency and the US Department of Energy to provide energy-efficient products and practices. www.energystar.gov

Environment Agency
Provides information on your local environment and guides on rainwater harvesting and sustainable urban drainage. www.environment-agency.gov.uk

Environmental Working Group
An organization that works to protect public health and the environment. www.ewg.org

Farrow & Ball
For environmentally friendly paints made without the use of ammonia or formaldehyde. www.farrow-ball.com

Food Commission
Campaigning for safer healthier food in the UK. www.foodcomm.org.uk

Gene Watch
Monitors developments in genetic technologies from public interest, environmental protection and animal welfare perspectives. www.genewatch.org

The Green Roof Centre
An independent research and demonstration hub on green roofs. www.thegreenroofcentre.co.uk

**Green Roofs
for Healthy Cities**
Promotes green roofs in North
America. www.greenroofs.com

Green Space
A registered charity which
works to improve parks ands
green spaces, providing advice
and a directory of community
and friends groups.
www.green-space.org.uk

Good Energy
Supplier of renewable electricity
to homes and business.
www.good-energy.co.uk

Green Building Store
For products that promote
energy efficient, sustainable
and healthy buildings.
www.greenbuildingstore.co.uk

Green Fibres
For a wide range of
certified organic bed
linen and mattresses.
www.greenfibres.co.uk

Green Glass
Website selling a range of
recycled glass products such as
drinking glasses and jewellery.
www.greenglass.co.uk

Green Home
A store for green
home products.
www.greenhome.com

**Guide to Less
Toxic Products**
Provides information about
potential health risks of
commonly used products.
www.lesstoxicguide.ca

ISP Services
For green ISP services.
www.greenisp.net
www.phonecoop.coop
www.gn.apc.org

It's Your Space
A website containing advice
for people wanting to transform
a local green space.
www.itsyourspace.org.uk

Learning through Landscapes
A national school grounds
charity able to provide advice
on school gardens in the UK.
www.ltl.org.uk

Living Roofs
For independent advice
on green roofs.
www.livingroofs.org

Marine Conservation Society
A UK charity that campaigns
for clean seas and beaches,
sustainable fisheries and
protection for all marine life.
www.mcsuk.org

Marine Stewardship Council
Certifies sustainable fisheries.
www.msc.org

**National Association
of Diaper Services**
The international professional
trade association for the nappy
(diaper) service industry.
www.diapernet.org

**National Coalition for
Pesticide-Free Lawns**
Provides the public with useful
information on pesticides and
alternatives to their use.
www.beyondpesticides.org

National Grid
Green energy options for
US consumers.
www.nationalgrid.com

**The National Society
of Allotment and
Leisure Gardeners**
An organization for all
allotment holders and
vegetable growers in the UK.
www.nsalg.demon.co.uk

The Natural Collection
For a range of recycled office
equipment including pens and
pencils, mouse mats made from
recycled tyres and recycled
printing paper and notebooks.
www.naturalcollection.com

Natural England
Provides information on
wildlife gardening.
www.naturalengland.org.uk

The Natural Store
For a range of silk-filled duvets
and other home supplies.
www.thenaturalstore.co.uk

Nigel's Eco Store
Sells a range of LED lighting ideal
for home office environments.
www.nigelsecostore.com

Onya Bags
These very lightweight, reusable
bags fold up into a pouch which
can be clipped on to a key ring
or bag. www.onyabags.co.uk

Oxfam International
International charity which
recycles mobile phones and ink
cartridges. www.oxfam.org

Patagonia
Produces fleece made from
recycled plastic bottles.
www.patagonia.co.uk

**Pesticide Action
Network North America**
Works to reduce the use of
hazardous pesticides worldwide.
www.panna.org

Project for Public Spaces
A nonprofit organization
dedicated to helping people
create and sustain public
places that build communities,
including local green spaces.
www.pps.org

Raft
A range of beds and other furniture made from reclaimed hardwood. www.raftltd.co.uk

Recycle Now
UK site with general information about recycling a broad range of materials. www.recyclenow.com

Recycle Your Jeans
Turn your old denim jeans into brand new sandals. www.recycleyourjeans.com.

Renewable Energy Association
Renewable energy trade association in the UK. www.r-p-a.org.uk

Roundtable on Sustainable Palm Oil
Promotes a sustainable palm oil industry. www.rspo.org

Royal Horticultural Society
For advice on green gardening. www.rhs.org.uk

Royal Society for the Protection of Birds
Provides advice on gardening for birds and other wildlife. www.rspb.org.uk

Seasalt
For organically certified organic clothing. www.seasaltcornwall.co.uk

Scottish Allotments and Gardens Society
An allotment body for Scotland. www.sags.org.uk

Shoppers Guide to Pesticides in Produce
A guide to the pesticides in your food. www.foodnews.org

Skin Deep
A cosmetic safety database. www.cosmeticsdatabase.com

Slow Food
A movement to promote locally grown food. www.slowfood.com

The Solar Cooking Archive
For information on solar cooking. www.solarcooking.org

There Must be a Better Way
For natural nail varnishes and acetate-free removers, as well as certified organic cuticle oil products from Sante and Zebra Prescot brands. www.theremustbeabetterway.co.uk

Think cans
Information about cash for cans and drink can recycling facts. www.thinkcans.com

Timber-framed double glazing
For more information on timber-framed windows visit www.greenbuildingstore.co.uk

or the British Woodworking Federation at www.bwf.org.uk.

TRAID - Textile Recycling for Aid and International Development
Operates textile recycling banks across the UK. It diverts clothing from ending up on landfill by repairing and customizing items before selling them, raising funds for overseas development and environmental projects. www.traid.org.uk

UK Craft Fairs
Learn how to make your own vegetable dyes. www.ukcraftfairs.com

Urbaneliving
For a range of natural, handmade wall coverings and wallpapers, as well as fungicide free wallpaper paste. www.urbaneliving.co.uk

US Department of Energy Efficiency and Renewable Energy
Gives advice on energy saving. www.eere.energy.gov

Warren Evans
For handmade organic mattresses and beds traditionally made from natural materials. www.warrenevans.com.

Waste Online
An online document library. www.wasteonline.org.uk

The Water Guide
Provides water-saving tips. www.water-guide.org.uk

The Wildlife Trusts
For advice on gardening for wildlife. www.wildlifetrusts.org

Women's Environmental Network
Educates and informs on environmental and health issues, and runs the Real Nappy Project. www.wen.org.uk

Woodland Trust
For advice on trees and community woodlands. www.woodland-trust.org.uk

World Wildlife Fund
For a guide to toxic chemicals. www.panda.org/about_wwf/ what_we_do/policy/toxics/ index.cfmWWF chemicals

index